COETHNICITY

COETHNICITY

DIVERSITY AND THE DILEMMAS OF COLLECTIVE ACTION

JAMES HABYARIMANA, MACARTAN HUMPHREYS,
DANIEL N. POSNER, AND JEREMY M. WEINSTEIN

A VOLUME IN THE RUSSELL SAGE FOUNDATION SERIES ON TRUST

Russell Sage Foundation • New York

The Russell Sage Foundation

The Russell Sage Foundation, one of the oldest of America's general purpose foundations, was established in 1907 by Mrs. Margaret Olivia Sage for "the improvement of social and living conditions in the United States." The Foundation seeks to fulfill this mandate by fostering the development and dissemination of knowledge about the country's political, social, and economic problems. While the Foundation endeavors to assure the accuracy and objectivity of each book it publishes, the conclusions and interpretations in Russell Sage Foundation publications are those of the authors and not of the Foundation, its Trustees, or its staff. Publication by Russell Sage, therefore, does not imply Foundation endorsement.

Library of Congress Cataloging-in-Publication Data
Coethnicity : diversity and the dilemmas of collective action / James
  Habyarimana . . . [et al.].
    p. cm. — (Russell Sage Foundation series on trust)
  Includes bibliographical references and index.
  ISBN 978-0-87154-420-9 (alk. paper)
  1. Multiculturalism.   2. Ethnicity.   3. Collective behavior.   4. Social
action.   5. Cooperation.   I. Habyarimana, James P.
  HM1271.C634 2009
  307.1'4160890091724—dc22
      2009008102

Text design by Suzanne Nichols.

RUSSELL SAGE FOUNDATION
112 East 64th Street, New York, New York 10065
10 9 8 7 6 5 4 3 2 1

The Russell Sage Foundation
Series on Trust

The Russell Sage Foundation Series on Trust examines the conceptual structure and the empirical basis of claims concerning the role of trust and trustworthiness in establishing and maintaining cooperative behavior in a wide variety of social, economic, and political contexts. The focus is on concepts, methods, and findings that will enrich social science and inform public policy.

The books in the series raise questions about how trust can be distinguished from other means of promoting cooperation and explore those analytic and empirical issues that advance our comprehension of the roles and limits of trust in social, political, and economic life. Because trust is at the core of understandings of social order from varied disciplinary perspectives, the series offers the best work of scholars from diverse backgrounds and, through the edited volumes, encourages engagement across disciplines and orientations. The goal of the series is to improve the current state of trust research by providing a clear theoretical account of the causal role of trust within given institutional, organizational, and interpersonal situations, developing sound measures of trust to test theoretical claims within relevant settings, and establishing some common ground among concerned scholars and policymakers.

Karen S. Cook
Russell Hardin
Margaret Levi

SERIES EDITORS

Previous Volumes in the Series

Contents

Acknowledgments

MUCH OF this book was drafted around the dining room table of a country house on Pender Island in British Columbia. Although we faced many challenges in analyzing data and melding our four distinct voices into one, one of the greatest hurdles we confronted involved conserving water from the well that fed our writing retreat. A long shower, too many loads of laundry, a tap left running—such actions by a colleague would be enough to endanger our water supply and potentially leave our well dry for days on end.

As it turns out, the management of water resources on Pender is a critical issue in town politics more generally. While the house in which we stayed generates water from a well, most households on the island draw from a rain-fed reservoir. During the month we spent on Pender—in the middle of the summer—the demand for water far outstripped the supply. Households were exhorted to conserve, but as with any common pool resource, it was difficult to control people's choices. Any household's water usage was a private matter, and residents made decisions based on what they needed or wanted, not taking into account the consequences of their actions for the overall availability of water for others. Figuring out how to provide incentives for people to conserve was a critical town priority.

One day, as we were driving around the island taking a break from our writing, we stumbled across the town's solution to the problem. On a big billboard we found a list of residents' names with a number indicating how much water each household had used in the previous week. This number was easily compared to the target usage per household posted at the top of the billboard. Here on Pender Island, facing a situation in which households had every incentive to overuse a common pool resource, town members sought explicitly to change people's calculus. By making information about water usage publicly available, it was hoped that the threat of social sanctions might lead people to conserve.

Pender Island is thousands of miles away from the poor, urban neighborhoods of Kampala, Uganda, which are the focus of this book, but the challenge of organizing a community to act collectively to solve its problems is a universal one. On Pender Island, town residents needed to prevent individual households from using too much water. In the poorest communities across the developing world, local leaders seek to mobilize people to police the streets, maintain public infrastructure, dispose of garbage in an organized fashion, and contribute limited funds to under-resourced schools and clinics. In both contexts, the challenge is almost identical: individual incentives to shirk (for example, by overusing water or not contributing to the production of a public good) have the potential to undermine collective well-being.

This challenge appears to be particularly severe in the presence of high levels of ethnic diversity. A decade's worth of scholarship has demonstrated—from the villages of East Africa to the mountains of Pakistan to the cities of the United States—that diverse communities experience lower levels of public goods provision. In this book, we seek to figure out why. Our goal is to understand how diversity so often impedes the ability of communities to act collectively. At the same time, we seek to uncover what it is about shared ethnicity that often facilitates cooperation.

The example provided by the residents of Pender Island is powerful: institutional innovations that rely on the power of social sanctioning can help communities maintain their common pool resources. Just because residents have an incentive to overuse a resource or to avoid contributing to a public good does not mean they will. Communities have tools at their disposal that can alter the decisions that individuals make. But whether this sort of institutional fix can work in Kampala or more broadly in diverse communities depends on what it is about diversity that gets in the way of social cooperation. Finding an answer to this question is a task that has consumed us for nearly a decade.

Our intellectual journey began when all four of us were graduate students at Harvard University. We shared a common tutor, Robert Bates, who patiently shared with us his accumulated wisdom about the politics of ethnicity in Africa; who gently prodded us to explore new theoretical approaches and empirical methodologies; and who, by his example and through his encouragement, gave us the confidence to undertake an ambitious program of data collection in the field. His influence as a scholar and a mentor is reflected on every page of this book.

As we conceptualized this project, it became increasingly clear that experimental approaches—in particular, those drawn from behavioral economics—offered great promise as tools for identifying the ways in which ethnic identities condition behavior. But none of us had any academic background in behavioral economics or experimental methods.

For not calling us crazy when we initially outlined our plans, we are grateful to David Laitin. His excitement about the potential of the project gave us the courage to move forward, and his willingness to talk through the experimental protocols we proposed (and to offer up more creative designs of his own) shaped the games described in this book.

We benefited also from the extraordinary counsel of a group of experimentalists who were willing to run (in effect) a graduate seminar on experimental design for a group of excited but naive recent PhDs. Rick Wilson read drafts of every experimental protocol we wrote; he joined us for two days of intensive consultation in New York before we embarked on our fieldwork in Uganda; and he provided detailed feedback on every paper and chapter we have written. Jean Ensminger and Abigail Barr took great interest in our project, offering us thoughtful advice on our research design and introducing us to many of their colleagues who had pioneered the use of behavioral games in field settings. Karen S. Cook, Russell Hardin, and Margaret Levi, through their leadership of the Trust Initiative at the Russell Sage Foundation, took an enormous risk in supporting this project but provided us with the feedback and intellectual network we needed to make it a success. Sam Bowles, Rob Boyd, and Herb Gintis made us feel welcome in the MacArthur Network on Norms and Preferences and offered invaluable feedback on a draft of the manuscript.

Even with a perfect research design, this book would not have been possible without the residents of Mulago-Kyebando. When we set up shop in a building on the main road, we were not at all confident that people would be open and willing to participate in what, from their perspective, must surely have been off-the-wall experimental games. What we found, however, was that community members welcomed us with open arms. Our subjects worked diligently to get the rules right for each game and came back week after week (on time and ready to play!) to fulfill their role in the experiments. Local council leaders and residents entertained our probing questions, guided our research assistants through the community, and provided us with crucial insight into the politics of public goods provision. They have our most sincere thanks.

The project described in this book required far more energy than could be found even in four young professors. We joked sometimes that we might as well have registered as a nongovernmental organization: at one point in the project, four directors, five graduate students, one undergraduate, and over thirty Ugandan staff were working full-time on the experimental games. We appreciate the leadership of Sylvester Mubiru, who identified, hired, trained, and managed a truly outstanding field team: Deo Byabagambi, Kenneth Ekode, Alex Kunobwa, Douglas Musunga, Winfred Nabulo, Ruth Nagawa, Susan Najjuuko, Brenda Nakkazi, Harriet Nambi, Winfred Naziwa, Livingstone Ntensibe, Alex

Odwong, Geoff Sentongo, Elizabeth Suubi, Alex Tindyebwa, and Sheila Watuwa. The students who accompanied us on this adventure—Claire Adida, Bernd Beber, Elizabeth Carlson, Nathan Falck, Alexandra Scacco, and Daniel Young—worked many more late nights than they could have possibly imagined; we are grateful for their energy, insights, and good humor throughout. Claire and Alex played an especially important role in piloting many of the protocols employed in the games, and Nathan's wizardry with computer interfaces constantly amazed us. Pepine Bulambo made us aficionados of Congolese Belgian fusion cuisine, and Simon Semakula ensured that our drive from Bunga to Mulago was uneventful, even in the worst weather. And our colleagues at the Economic Policy Research Centre (EPRC) at Makerere University, especially John Okidi, provided an intellectual home for our research.

In our pilot work at the University of California–Los Angeles (UCLA) and the University of Southern California (USC), we also benefited from the talents and energy of the staff at the California Social Science Experimental Laboratory (CASSEL) and a wide range of individuals: Chris Crabbe, Donna Horowitz, Kevin Thelen, Daniel Young, and Walter Yuan. We are grateful to the subjects at UCLA and USC, whose participation helped us to further develop and refine our experimental protocols.

The project came to life in the context of two intellectually vibrant research communities: the Laboratory in Comparative Ethnic Processes (LiCEP) and the Working Group in African Political Economy (WGAPE). We are grateful to members of both research networks for critical feedback and support, especially Kanchan Chandra, James Fearon, Michael Hechter, David Laitin, Ted Miguel, Steven Wilkinson, and Elisabeth Wood. Kanchan Chandra in particular gave generous feedback at multiple stages of the project and shared written responses on the entire manuscript. We also benefited from the feedback of seminar participants at the University of Michigan, UCLA, UC–Berkeley, UC–San Diego, UC–Davis, Massachusetts Institute of Technology (MIT), New York University (NYU), Wharton, Northwestern, Oxford, Stanford, California Institute of Technology, UC–Santa Barbara, University of Cape Town, the World Bank, Loyola Marymount, and the EPRC (Kampala). Ken Scheve invited us to present the full manuscript for a daylong session as part of the Leitner Series in Political Economy at Yale; we sincerely appreciate his invitation and learned a great deal from the feedback provided by both our formal discussants—Susan Stokes, Donald Green, Dean Karlan, and Thad Dunning—and the many other active participants in the workshop, including Sam Bowles, Eric Dickson, Alan Gerber, Susan Hyde, Ken Scheve, Elisabeth Wood, and a set of outstanding graduate students. The final book manuscript also reflects the excellent critiques provided by other colleagues, including Diego Gambetta, Andrew Gelman, Alan Jacobs, Rebecca Morton, and Paul Richards, and anonymous reviewers at the *American Political Science Review* and the Russell Sage Foundation. Our thanks are due as well to Jonathan Kastellec and Eduardo Leoni, whose graphs (and the code to generate them) inspired many of the figures used in the book.

Funds for various stages of this research were generously provided by the Harvard Academy for International and Area Studies, the Harry Frank Guggenheim Foundation, and the Russell Sage Foundation. Our respective universities—Georgetown, Columbia, UCLA, and Stanford— each have offered an exciting intellectual environment in which to develop our ideas and test out our conclusions. Thank you also to Harvey and Rhona Weinstein for making a writing retreat available to us on Pender Island.

Nearly ten years have passed since we first began thinking about this project as graduate students. While our lives have been enriched in innumerable ways by this academic collaboration, we would never have made it through without the love, encouragement, and unbelievable patience of our partners: Charity, Jacobia, Rebecca, and Rachel. They put up with endless conference calls, a summer spent in Uganda, a month-long writing retreat in British Columbia, and hectic races to finish the book. All this as the time we had available to us gradually disappeared, with each of us welcoming a first child into the world. To this next generation—Benja, Aoife, Jacob, and Jonah—this book is for you.

About the Authors

James Habyarimana is assistant professor of public policy at the Georgetown Public Policy Institute.

Macartan Humphreys is associate professor of political science at Columbia University.

Daniel N. Posner is associate professor of political science at the University of California–Los Angeles.

Jeremy M. Weinstein is associate professor of political science at Stanford University and an affiliated faculty member at the Center for Democracy, Development, and the Rule of Law and the Center for International Security and Cooperation.

Chapter 1

Diversity and Collective Action

JUST OFF the main road that cuts through the slum area behind Kampala's main hospital lies the local council zone (LC1) of East Nsooba.[1] An ethnically mixed neighborhood, it is set at the base of a steep hillside with small, closely spaced houses stretching down the incline and across the swampy valley floor. The houses are simple, with concrete floors and walls and zinc roofs. Few have windows or electricity. None has indoor plumbing. But the biggest hardship for the area's residents comes not from the plainness of their houses or the absence of amenities like electric lights and indoor toilets, but from rainy season flooding, which transforms the neighborhood's unpaved streets into rivers of mud, submerges houses in filth, and leaves putrid standing water that breeds cholera, malaria, and other diseases. Drainage channels designed to carry away the excess rainwater snake throughout the area, but the government has not maintained them for years, and they are too choked with garbage and debris to be of any use. So when the rains come, the floodwaters rise.

To the north of East Nsooba lies Kisalosalo, an area less prone to flooding but more troubled by crime. Break-ins occur almost every night, and some thefts are accompanied by violence. People feel insecure. The Ugandan government used to sponsor and equip local defense units (LDUs) to patrol neighborhoods like Kisalosalo. But government support for the LDUs ceased in 2002 when they were incorporated into the formal police system; since then, Kampala's slum areas have been overtaken by crime and violence.

Fredrick Ssalongo has been the chairman of East Nsooba's local council since 1987, when Uganda's system of decentralized administration was initiated. Geoffrey Kashaija has served in the same capacity in Kisalosalo since 1991.[2] Both men describe their deep frustration at the unwillingness of the central and local governments to provide basic ser-

1

vices in their areas. They also describe their disappointment at the inability of members of their communities to work together to help solve some of their areas' problems. A few years back, for example, the Kampala City Council had arranged for a private company to pick up trash in poor neighborhoods, but the trucks stopped coming to East Nsooba because only a handful of the people there were willing to pay the fees. Even without regular garbage collection, the area's flooding problems might be reduced if residents heeded Chairman Ssalongo's calls to clean the channels of debris periodically and to refrain from throwing their trash in the drains. But these efforts, too, have failed. In Kisalosalo, Chairman Kasaijja's attempts to set up community patrols to deal with the area's crime problem have been similarly unsuccessful. Although everyone in the neighborhood agrees that crime is a critical issue, only a relative handful of residents have been willing to participate in the nightly patrols, and most have been reluctant to contribute funds to remunerate those who have.

The hardships faced by the residents of East Nsooba and Kisalosalo are like those confronted by many people living in impoverished urban areas and villages around the world. Largely abandoned by their governments, these local communities are left to fend for themselves to provide basic public services like sanitation, flood protection, and security. Often they fail. This is because the services in question are what economists call "public goods" that can be consumed and enjoyed by everyone in the community irrespective of whether they contribute to their provision. As Chairmen Ssalongo and Kashaija have learned, this feature of public goods creates strong incentives for people to attempt to "free-ride" on the contributions of others.[3] Residents of East Nsooba calculate that if they lie low while others do the dirty work of extracting the foul-smelling trash from the drainage channels or pay the fees for the private haulage company, they can reap the benefits of less flooding while avoiding unpleasant work and keeping their money. Residents of Kisalosalo similarly figure that they can enjoy the benefits of reduced crime without contributing to providing it. The problem, of course, is that if everyone makes the same calculation, then the garbage collection, drainage channel maintenance, and public safety will never be provided. The powerful individual incentives to shirk undermine the collective action necessary for providing these goods and thus reduce everybody's well-being.[4]

Given the enormous social costs of such collective action failures, why is it so difficult for communities to find ways to work together to provide critical public services? It turns out that while most cannot find ways to engage in effective collective action, some can. How do we explain this variation? In situations where the government has abdicated responsibility for providing public goods, why are some communities able to work together to generate public goods themselves while others are not?

Wealth is obviously a factor: prosperous communities can afford to hire security patrols, build clinics, pay teachers, and install water and sewerage systems. But wealth provides, at best, only a partial answer, for we find high levels of public goods provision in some very poor communities and low levels of public goods provision in some very wealthy ones. Public goods provision depends at least as much on the ability of a community to work collectively to solve its problems as it does on whether it can buy better public services by simply writing a check.

If a community's cooperative capacity is central to the generation of public goods, what accounts for this cooperative capacity? A growing literature suggests that part of the answer may lie in the community's ethnic heterogeneity. Studies conducted in communities around the world—in sites as disparate as western Kenya, northern Pakistan, central Mexico, Indonesia, and the United States—have found evidence that ethnic diversity sometimes impedes the provision of public goods by communities. The central goal of this book is to work out why this is so. Why do homogeneous communities—those where interactions are more likely to be among coethnics—seem to have an advantage in achieving collective ends? Before we answer this question, we review the evidence linking diversity and the failure of collective action and explore the arguments advanced by scholars around the world to account for this relationship.

Ethnic Diversity and Public Goods Provision

Evidence from Around the World

Roads, irrigation channels, and other forms of public infrastructure degrade quickly in the harsh weather conditions of northern Pakistan and cannot keep functioning without frequent maintenance. Some communities succeed in maintaining their infrastructure while others fail. To find out why, Asim Khwaja (2008) studied 132 community-maintained public infrastructure projects in 99 communities. He found that project upkeep—as measured by the degree of physical degradation of project infrastructure, the extent to which the project's original purpose is still being satisfied, and the amount of maintenance work carried out over the lifetime of the project—was closely related to the social heterogeneity of the beneficiary community. Controlling for other project- and community-specific factors, such as land inequality, Khwaja found that communities in the first quartile of social heterogeneity scored ten percentage points higher on the project maintenance scale than did communities in the third quartile. Given the importance of roads and irrigation in this remote, arid region, the negative impact of ethnic diversity on the maintenance of public infrastructure has severe consequences for people's well-being.

Working in a very different environment, Edward Miguel and Mary Kay Gugerty (2005) studied the determinants of school funding and quality in eighty-four primary schools in western Kenya. As in many parts of Africa, the Kenyan government pays teachers' salaries, but materials such as books, chalk, pencils, paper, desks, and even the physical school buildings themselves are funded through contributions from the local community. School quality is thus closely related to the ability of local communities to act collectively to raise funds for these purposes. Controlling for a wide range of socioeconomic, geographic, and demographic factors (including the possibility that, by generating in-migration, high school quality might increase community-level heterogeneity), Miguel and Gugerty found that communities at average levels of ethnic diversity generated 20 percent lower school contributions per pupil than homogeneous communities. As in the Khwaja study, this is a substantial effect.

The negative impact of ethnic heterogeneity on collective action has also been demonstrated in dozens of other studies conducted in cities and villages around the world. Cagla Okten and Una Okonkwo Osili (2004) demonstrated that community-level diversity in Indonesia was negatively related to contributions of labor, materials, and money to neighborhood irrigation associations, security arrangements, rice cooperatives, and local health centers.[5] Pranab Bardhan (2000) reported a negative association between caste heterogeneity and the successful maintenance of local irrigation schemes in India; Abhijit Banerjee, Lakshmi Iyer, and Rohini Somanathan (2005) and Banerjee and Somanathan (2004) reported a similar relationship with respect to the provision of schools, public transport, electricity, health centers, and water projects. Jeffrey Dayton-Johnson (2000) provided evidence for the negative impact of social diversity on the success of community irrigation schemes in Mexico. Jean-Marie Baland and his colleagues (2006) extended this work to the management of forestry resources in Nepal, where they, again, found a negative association between diversity and community-level collective action.

These findings are not limited to developing countries. Alberto Alesina, Reza Baqir, and William Easterly (1999) presented evidence that diversity was associated with lower levels of funding for schools, roads, sewers, and trash pickup in U.S. municipalities. Their findings corroborate those of James Poterba (1997) and Claudia Goldin and Lawrence Katz (1999), who reported negative associations between school funding and ethnic diversity in U.S. cities and school districts, and, recently,

those of Robert Putnam (2007), who found social diversity to be negatively associated with trust, social capital, and a variety of measures of
public goods provision. Jacob Vigdor (2004) found that racially diverse
communities had lower response rates to the 2000 U.S. census; because
the allocation of federal funds to communities is related to their response rates, he interpreted this as a failure of collective action. Julio
Videras and Christopher Bordoni (2006) found that more ethnically heterogeneous zip code areas in New York and New Jersey had lower levels of environmental protection. Xin Sherry Li (2005) extended this work
to Europe, where, using data from the European and World Values Surveys, she found that ethnic heterogeneity was negatively related to tax
compliance.

The relationships identified in these studies are all statistical relationships and thus provide evidence of correlation rather than of a determin-
istic causal relation. In specific cases, diversity may not be associated with
poor public goods provision; indeed, there is evidence in some contexts
that diversity can have powerful positive effects (Page 2007). It might also
be the case that poor public goods provision exerts a causal effect on the
level of diversity (perhaps by driving down property values and creating
opportunities for in-migration), not vice versa. Nevertheless, the consistency of the relationship documented across studies is impressive and
provides support for the proposition that, on average, diversity impedes
the provision of public goods. Summarizing the literature on the topic,
Banerjee, Iyer, and Somanathan (2005, 639) went so far as to refer to the
negative relationship between diversity and public goods provision as
"one of the most powerful hypotheses in political economy."

While the literature to date has done a reasonable job of documenting
the existence of this empirical regularity, it has been much less successful in accounting for it. Although most analyses venture hypotheses
about the mechanisms that might be at work, no study has offered a systematic enumeration of the causal channels through which ethnic diversity might undermine public goods provision, along with a test of the
comparative explanatory power of each.[6] The state of the literature
might be summarized by saying that a consensus has emerged about the
nature of the association between ethnic heterogeneity and public goods
provision, but that the micro-logic of this connection is still poorly understood. The literature provides us with a number of intuitions about
the mechanisms that might be at work, but little research that might permit us to adjudicate among them. The goal of this book is to take this
next step.

Possible Explanations

In taking on the question of why ethnic diversity impedes collective action (or, on the flip side, why ethnic homogeneity is associated with

more successful cooperative outcomes), this book departs from the typical social science concern with *whether*, rather than *why*, one thing causes another. The norm in the literature has been to focus on establishing that *x* causes *y*. Answering the question of why this relationship exists is usually secondary. Some kind of explanation is typically ventured, but such accounts tend to be post hoc attempts to explain a given result (occasionally with suggestive evidence for the plausibility of the preferred explanation) rather than the result of systematic testing of alternative mechanisms.

One reason why relatively little attention is given to causal mechanisms is that simply establishing the existence of a causal relationship is usually achievement enough. The literature we focus on here offers a good example. It is filled with studies that provide evidence for the link between ethnic heterogeneity and collective action failure, but as we noted earlier, only a relative handful employ sufficiently strong identification strategies to give us real confidence in their *causal* claims. Simply establishing that diversity impedes collective action and public goods contribution is thus a real contribution, quite apart from whether the researcher goes on to provide a comprehensive account for why.

A second reason for the relative lack of attention to causal mechanisms is the difficulty of identifying the universe of channels through which a given relationship might operate—a necessary first step in ascertaining which mechanism is actually doing the work. This is particularly so in the study of ethnicity, since there is no generally accepted framework that can be taken "off the shelf" to use in thinking analytically about how ethnic identities shape individual behavior and thus how a community's ethnic diversity affects its ability to achieve collective ends. To provide such a framework, we turn to game theory, which offers a language and a theoretical apparatus that are particularly well suited to this task.

In the language of game theory, we can describe a social interaction as a game comprising three objects: a population (the set of actors), a technology (the set of strategies available to each of these actors), and preferences (which describe how individuals value the outcomes that result once all the actors select their strategies).[7] The overall outcome of the game can be written as a function of the strategies selected by all the players, typically predicted by theorists using a solution concept.

This simple game description provides us with a set of first-order channels to investigate in order to identify how people's ethnic identities affect their behavior and the outcome of their interactions with others. Ethnicity could affect a person's behavior by changing the population playing the game, the strategies available to the players, or the players' preferences. In addition, ethnicity could affect the strategies the players decide to use, conditional on these factors. Assuming that eth-

Table 1.1   Mechanisms Linking Ethnicity to Collective Action Success

Preferences Mechanisms	
Other-Regarding Preferences	Coethnics may be more likely to take each other's welfare into account
Preferences in Common	Coethnics may be more likely to care about the same outcomes
Preferences over Process	Coethnics may prefer the process of working together
Technology Mechanisms	
Efficacy	Coethnics may be able to function together more efficiently
Readability	Coethnics may be better able to (or believe they are better able to) gauge each other's characteristics
Periodicity	Coethnics may engage each other with greater frequency
Reachability	Coethnics may be more able to track each other down
Strategy Selection Mechanisms	
Reciprocity	Coethnics may be more likely to punish each other for failing to cooperate

Source: Authors' compilation.

nicity is predicated on existence (that is, we do not treat the set of actors as a function of ethnicity), we are left with three families of mechanisms through which the outcome of a social interaction might be affected by the actors' ethnic identities: preference mechanisms, technology mechanisms, and strategy selection mechanisms. These distinct families of mechanisms can be thought of more generally as different ways in which sharing (or not sharing) an ethnic identity with others may shape the kinds of choices people make in social settings.

Each of these families of mechanisms subsumes multiple, distinct explanations. Because there is no clear way to conceptualize the universe of all possible mechanisms within each family, we examine the major arguments that have been advanced by theorists of ethnic identity, placing them within the appropriate family of mechanisms. Table 1.1 summarizes the collection of leading explanations we have identified and which we will examine in this book. We describe each in turn.

Preferences Mechanisms   To illustrate the logic of the *preferences* mechanisms, consider again the situation that Chairman Ssalongo confronts in organizing community members to maintain the drainage channels in East Nsooba. Recall that one reason why residents might shirk from this task is that each one hopes that others will do all the work, and each one fears that, if he takes part, he will be a "sucker"—the one who provides all the work but then cannot prevent others from sharing in the fruits of his labor. In some cases, this problem corresponds exactly to what game theorists call a Prisoner's Dilemma. In such cases, no matter what other people do, each individual would rather stay at home ("defect") than contribute ("cooperate"). As a result, the drainage channel remains filled with trash (and next to useless in the rainy season) even though everyone would rather see it cleared.

This unhappy outcome follows in part from an assumption that is commonly made by game theorists: that people are selfish and do not benefit from improvements in the welfare of others. But what if this assumption is wrong? What if residents in Ssalongo's zone care not only about the well-being of their own families but also about the quality of life of their neighbors? This would be a situation in which people exhibit *other-regarding preferences*. If this were the case, then residents might be willing to volunteer their labor for drainage channel maintenance regardless of what others do. Of course, the converse is equally true: if people actively dislike their neighbors and gain satisfaction from seeing them in misery, then residents are even less likely to be willing to bear the cost of maintaining the area's drainage channels. As the example makes clear, having positive (or negative) preferences for the welfare of others can help solve (or exacerbate) the collective action problem. To the extent that people specifically care more about the welfare of individuals in their *own* ethnic group—as some theorists of ethnicity assume[8]—this mechanism would lead us to predict a greater likelihood of collective action success when the members of a community share a common ethnic background.

To illustrate the second preferences mechanism, which we term *preferences in common*, suppose that the local government in Kampala's urban slums is in fact responsive to community members' requests for assistance. If residents in Chairman Kasaijja's zone can lobby together for funding to support local defense units in the area, then the likelihood of a positive response from the local government (and greater security) increases. But if community members are unable to coordinate their lobbying—if, for example, some residents want better policing but others prefer that the government allocate its resources to improve local schools or transport infrastructure—then the likelihood that the government will increase its support for local defense units diminishes. Note that here the positive (or negative) outcome for the community derives not from the degree of concern that residents have over each others' welfare but from the degree to which they share preferences about the kinds of outcomes that should be accorded the highest priority. If coethnics are more likely to have preferences in common over different public goods—as, again, some theorists of ethnicity assume[9]—then ethnic diversity can imply a diversity of preferences or tastes that, as the example illustrates, makes collective ends more difficult to achieve.

Finally, consider a very different way in which preferences might affect incentives to work together. So far we have focused on the *results* of working together. In fact, however, when choosing with whom to work on a project, individuals may also take account of the *process* of working together. People may share similar goals but refuse to work with one another because of mutual antipathy. The third preferences mechanism, which we call *preferences over process*, emphasizes explicitly these procedural features of collective action.[10] Recent work by social psychologists suggests that racism is associated with feelings of disgust that exert direct effects on the willingness of individuals to work together even for projects of mutual benefit.[11] While political scientists tend to focus on the consequences of collective action more than on the processes of participation, recent work on the politics of collective action also finds that a focus on process-oriented motivations can provide additional explanatory power, even in high-stakes settings such as civil war (Wood 2003).

Technology Mechanisms   Let us now turn to what we call *technology* mechanisms. The idea here is that ethnicity affects the set of strategies available to players. To make this idea more concrete, imagine that a local council chairman in Kampala decides to try to address the problem of flooding by applying for funds from the government to construct additional concrete drains for his zone (one option that local councils have in fact considered). He might ask two community members to take the lead in drafting the proposal to division headquarters. Under what conditions will these two invest their time in such an enterprise? Presumably, they will be more willing to do so if they think they can work together effectively. In weighing this question, one factor they are likely to consider is whether they speak the same language, share similar experiences, and can draw upon a common understanding about how to work together to facilitate their interactions. To the extent that they do, the feasibility of their collaboration will be greater and their willingness to embark upon it will be greater as well. By providing individuals with precisely this kind of reservoir of common cultural material, shared ethnicity can serve as a technology that facilitates coordination and collaboration within the community.[12] And since any "ethnic technology" is not shared across group lines, it will only facilitate collaborative endeavors—including public goods provision—in more ethnically homogeneous settings.[13] We term this the *efficacy* mechanism.

Sharing a common language or culture is not the only tool that might facilitate community members working together. The second technology mechanism we identify is the *readability* mechanism. The idea here is that coethnics may be better able to (or believe they are better able to) read cues about the positions or intentions of potential partners. As a consequence, a given partner (who is a coethnic) may be able to select a strategy conditional on information that is not available to a non-coethnic. This can be highly advantageous. For example, someone might be more willing to work with another person if she can see that he is smart or organized or has experience in the relevant area. Some of these attributes might be clearly observable, but others might not be. To the extent that sharing an ethnic background with a person makes a potential co-operating partner more "readable," coethnicity can be an important tool. In principle, for example, it is possible that individuals take actions to benefit coethnics disproportionately, not because they care more for them but because they can better target their beneficence.[14]

Whereas these first two technology mechanisms emphasize individual-level characteristics that coethnics share, the last two technology mechanisms both relate to the structure of interactions between coethnics more generally—in particular, the ways in which social networks may be structured on ethnic lines. We distinguish between two ways in which such networks can matter. The first, which we term the *periodicity* mechanism, suggests that coethnics interact with one another with greater frequency. This might matter because, as a large empirical and game-theoretic literature shows (Axelrod 1984), the advantages of sustaining cooperation into the future rise relative to the short-run benefits of defection when individuals expect to interact more frequently. Homogeneous groups might be better able to mount joint activities because members are reasonably confident that they will find themselves contemplating collective activities with others on a regular basis in the future. In the specific case of trying to reduce crime, for example, an individual may volunteer her energy for a community patrol knowing that other residents will do the same because, if they do not, she knows that she can withdraw her willingness to be an active participant later on, making other residents worse off.

A second, closely related way in which networks might matter is through what we call *reachability*. Under this mechanism, social networks are used to collect information about a potential cooperating partner's unobservable skills or experience (or deficiencies) or to facilitate the sanctioning of a person who reneges on his or her agreement (for example, by spreading information about the person's untrustworthiness so that others will know to be wary of him or her in the future).[15] Note that a key difference between this channel and the previous one is that the reachability mechanism can operate even if repeated encounters are rare.[16] To the extent that network ties are stronger between coethnics, these benefits may work disproportionately to the advantage of homogeneous communities. Returning to the obstacles faced by local leaders in Kampala's slums, this argument suggests that homogeneous communities may be better able to address shared challenges because they have a tool for disciplining the behavior of residents who do not cooperate. Community residents may contribute to the local patrol or dedicate time to garbage cleanup because they fear the costs to their reputation—which can spread through the homogeneous community, but also more broadly across the ethnic network—if they sit on the sidelines.

Strategy Selection Mechanisms   The third family of explanations focuses on what we call *strategy selection* mechanisms. While the previous mechanisms we examined highlighted the ways in which people may be playing different games when they interact with coethnics and non-coethnics, strategy selection mechanisms posit that people play the same game differently depending on the identity of their partners.[17] To illustrate how these operate, imagine that Chairman Ssalongo has organized a few young men to dedicate a Saturday morning to clearing the drainage channels. Will they show up? If it is the case that contributing to the public good makes sense if and only if all the young men participate—for example, if the task cannot be done by one person alone because large pieces of garbage obstruct the flow of water—then the rationality of showing up will depend entirely on an individual's beliefs about what the others are likely to do.

In one group of young men chosen by the chairman, each individual might expect others not to contribute and, in response, will not contribute (thereby jointly ensuring that their expectations are correct). In another group, however, each might expect the others to contribute and, in response, will also contribute (again jointly ensuring that their expectations are correct). If such expectations are related to group membership—for example, if, as a large anthropological literature suggests, people expect someone from their own ethnic group to contribute but not someone from a different ethnic group—then it is straightforward to see how ethnicity might affect the strategies that people select and the likelihood of successful collective action.[18]

The difference between the strategy selection and technology channels is subtle, particularly in the area of sanctioning. Assume for a moment that sanctioning norms exist among coethnics but not among non-coethnics (or exist more strongly among the former than among the latter). As a result, people play different strategies depending on whether they are interacting with members of their own ethnic community. Is this evidence of a technology mechanism or a strategy selection mechanism?

To answer the question, we need to know whether the technologies that facilitate sanctioning (such as reachability and periodicity) are such that reciprocity can only be sustained among coethnics, or whether these technologies could permit reciprocity among both coethnics and non-coethnics but only coethnics employ them to this end. To illustrate, suppose that we observe that two non-coethnics are less likely to cooperate on a collective task than two coethnics. A technology story might be that the non-coethnics fail to cooperate because they interact with insufficient frequency or are insufficiently connected to one another within social networks to make cooperation feasible. In a strategy selection story, on the other hand, though cooperation is feasible, neither individual cooperates because she does not expect the other to cooperate. The technology story is that everyone might like to condition cooperation on cooperation, but only coethnics can. The strategy selection story is that everyone can condition their strategies in this way, but only coethnics do.

Although we recognize that these three broad families of mechanisms may interact in complex ways—for example, the existence of ethnic technologies may reflect a group's preferences, or vice versa, and the choice of strategies may be partly determined by preferences and by beliefs about the preferences of others—we believe the set of families to be exhaustive. In particular, they subsume the major hypotheses advanced in the literature for the negative relationship between ethnic diversity and public goods provision. For example, arguments advanced by Alberto Alesina, Reza Baqir, and William Easterly (1999) and by Alesina and Eliana LaFerrara (2005) emphasizing the correspondence between ethnic groups and preferences for particular kinds of public goods are in line with our preferences mechanisms. The hypotheses proposed by Timothy Besley, Stephen Coate, and Glenn Loury (1993), Avner Greif (1993), Edward Miguel and Mary Kay Gugerty (2005), Parikshit Ghosh and Debraj Ray (1996), Marcel Fafchamps and Bart Minten (2002), and Barak Richman (2006) about the role that networks play in facilitating punishment echo our technology mechanisms, as do the hypotheses advanced by Cagla Okten and Una Okonkwo Osili (2004) and Alessandra Casella and James Rauch (2002) about the lower transaction costs of coethnic interactions and the arguments developed by Michael Bacharach and Diego Gambetta (2001) on the readability of cooperation partners (see also Gambetta and Hamill 2005). And strategy selection mechanisms are frequently invoked to explain the greater collective action we observe in homogeneous settings than in nonhomogeneous ones—particularly in situations where multiple equilibria exist and players must coordinate their choices to maximize their payoffs (as, for example, in an iterated Prisoner's Dilemma game, a Battle of the Sexes game, or an Assurance game). In such situations, the strategy is simply the rule of thumb that has emerged, perhaps through some evolutionary process, which permits the players to achieve a more desirable outcome.[19] One example is the norm among U.S. senators to lend their support to a colleague's bill in exchange for the promise of reciprocated support at a later date (Mayhew 1975), another is the norm among Italian and Jewish kids in Brooklyn to punish their own rather than risk a spiral of mutual retaliation from members of the other group (Fearon and Laitin 1996), or the norm to "live and let live" that emerged among British and German soldiers positioned within firing distance of one another in the trenches during World War I (Axelrod 1984).

Ethnic diversity might affect public goods provision through any of these three broad channels. From the standpoint of testing the relative explanatory power of each mechanism, the problem is that they all generate the same prediction: lower cooperation in a context of greater social diversity. This makes it impossible to distinguish among them simply by observing the success of homogeneous (or the failure of heterogeneous) communities to provide public goods for their members. Thus, if, in an ethnically homogeneous community, we observe that residents cooperate to pick up the trash, maintain drainage channels, and patrol the streets, we have no way of knowing whether the roots of this successful cooperation lies in a sense of other-regardingness that they feel toward one another; a calculation that their collaboration is likely to be particularly easy or fruitful; or the existence of a norm that makes not reciprocating a coethnic's cooperative overture, or not punishing a failure to reciprocate, unthinkable. Sorting out whether the pattern we observe is best explained by a preferences, technology, or strategy selection mechanism (or by some combination of the three) requires that we find a way to identify situations in which we can rule out the operation of different mechanisms. To solve this difficult inferential problem, we turn to the technique of experiments.

Empirical Strategy

The Experimental Method

Experiments are advantageous because they permit a high degree of control over the factors that might affect the outcome under investigation. Their power comes from enabling researchers to isolate and test the explanatory power of competing explanations that are difficult or impossible to disentangle in real-world settings. Their great weakness lies in their questionable external validity—that is, experiments leave researchers uncertain in extrapolating from their experimental findings to the larger world whose behavioral patterns they seek to explain. Assessing the extent of this trade-off in a given setting is critical to evaluating the merits of experimental work. While our own strategy involves bringing the laboratory into the field—in an effort to strengthen the external validity of our findings—we also believe that a great deal can be learned in highly controlled settings, as the following examples illustrate.

When evidence of the Holocaust began to emerge after World War II, it gave rise to hundreds of scholarly inquiries into how tens of thousands of "regular" Germans could have been transformed into killers. Some of these analyses were anthropological: they focused on aspects of German culture that might have facilitated the rise of the Nazis and the implementation of their "Final Solution." Others were sociological investigations that emphasized the nature of German society, the role that Jews played within it, and the rationale that this may have provided for some Germans to turn on their neighbors. Still other inquiries delved into the organizational apparatus of the German state. The best of these studies made detailed analyses of German history, society, and culture based on interviews, primary sources, and careful archival research. Yet one of the most compelling explanations for the willing participation of "regular" Germans in the execution of 6 million Jews came from a study that involved no field research, no interviews, and not a single German source.

In an attempt to understand how the Holocaust could have happened, the psychologist Stanley Milgram (1974) recruited forty subjects to participate in an experiment in the basement of a building in New Haven, Connecticut. The subjects were told that the purpose of the experiment was to study the effects of punishment on learning. They were told that they would play the role of the "teacher" while another subject (in fact a confederate of the experimenter) played the role of the "learner." After being taken to a different room from the confederate, subjects then were told to administer a series of increasingly large electric shocks to the learner (in fact, no shock was administered), who, as the voltage increased, would (pretend to) shriek in pain and beg for the experiment to be stopped. If the subject expressed a desire to stop the experiment, the experimenter would ask the subject to "please continue." If the subject continued to resist, the experimenter would push further, first telling the subject that "the experiment requires that you continue, please go on," then that "it is essential that you continue," and finally that "you have no choice, you must continue." Milgram's extraordinary finding was that about two-thirds of the subjects obeyed the experimenter's commands and continued administering the electric shocks up to the highest level, despite the fact that they were led to believe that the person receiving the shocks was, by that point, in agonizing pain. By demonstrating the power of an authority figure to compel behavior—even behavior that conflicts with a person's moral conscience—the Milgram experiment provided critical insight into how the Holocaust (and also the Rwandan genocide and other instances of mass killing) might have been possible. It also demonstrated the power of experiments to shed light on important social outcomes that are very far removed from the subjects involved or the tasks they are asked to perform.

Robert Axelrod's (1984) research on the evolution of cooperation provides another example of the power of "artificial" games to provide deep insight into real-world phenomena. Axelrod was interested in understanding how cooperation can emerge in a world of egoists—be they nations, people, animals, or bacteria—with no central authority. To gain leverage on this question, he might have conducted an in-depth study of international bargaining. He might have done a careful analysis of collusion among drug companies. Or he might have observed children playing in a park. Instead, Axelrod invited mathematicians, economists, sociologists, and political scientists from around the world to submit strategies to be pitted against one another in a computer-based, iterated Prisoner's Dilemma tournament. Remarkably, he found that all of the most cunning and sophisticated strategies proposed by these strategists were beaten by an extraordinarily simple strategy. His main finding was that a simple strategy of "tit-for-tat"—starting off by cooperating and then simply responding in kind to whatever one's partner does—works extraordinarily well. Although it might seem that nothing could have been further removed from the real-world problems that motivated his research, Axelrod's computer tournament yielded results that have contributed tremendously to our understanding of the evolution of social cooperation.[20]

Experimental Games

Our decision to employ the methodology of experimental games stems from a belief, shaped by the examples of the research of Milgram, Axelrod, and others, that progress in understanding the mechanisms through which ethnic diversity affects public goods provision can be made by uncovering the essential patterns of behavior that underlie or impede collective action among subjects playing laboratory games. We might have gone another route. We might have elected instead to conduct an in-depth qualitative study of a community that had been particularly successful or unsuccessful in providing public goods. We might have used survey data to identify correlations between observed levels of public goods provision and different kinds of preferences, different types of networks, or different kinds of norms across a broad range of communities. Instead, we decided to use experimental games.

We did this because we believe the experimental approach provides considerable leverage that is not available from alternative methods. This approach allowed us to study a set of games (described in detail in chapters 4 and 5) designed specifically to test the distinct mechanisms outlined in this chapter. As subjects played multiple rounds of each game with randomized matching—sometimes with coethnics, sometimes with non-coethnics—we were able to rule out many confounding factors and thus to assess the explanatory power of the distinct mechanisms by examining how play among coethnics and non-coethnics varied within and across games.[21]

In turning to experimental games to study the impact of diversity on collective action, we join a growing group of social scientists who have deployed similar techniques to study altruism, cooperation, bargaining, coordination, and trust (for good reviews, see Roth 1995; Camerer 2003). This literature has its roots in the pioneering work of Daniel Kahneman, Vernon Smith, and others who first used experimental methods to challenge neoclassical assumptions about the purely selfish motivations of individuals. Their experiments showed that undergraduate subjects played laboratory games in ways that contradicted the predictions of economic theory. Rather than simply trying to maximize their earnings, these subjects played the games in ways that suggested they were altruistic and cared about the fairness of the allocations to themselves and the other players. These early experiments have been replicated, expanded, and improved upon in thousands of studies, and experimental economics techniques have become accepted and embraced in a growing number of social science disciplines.

The implicit claim in the earliest foundational studies was that human beings are all the same and that we can learn something general about human behavior by studying the decisions of undergraduates in (principally American) college classrooms and experimental laboratories. A major concern of the literature that has followed has been to investigate the implications of relaxing the rather unrealistic assumptions that underlie this claim. To see where our study fits within the larger experimental tradition, it is helpful to review these efforts.

We can identify three broad branches of responses. The first has aimed to "take the laboratory out of the classroom" to investigate whether regular citizens behave differently from college students, who in terms of age, education, and other potential determinants of social behavior make up a highly unrepresentative sample of the broader population (Smith 2000; Carpenter, Burks, and Verhoegen 2005; for a key critique of the reliance on college sophomores that motivated many of these studies, see Sears 1986). A growing number of studies have attempted to test the robustness of standard experimental findings outside the university (for a good review, see Cardenas and Carpenter 2008). The most ambitious attempt in this direction is the recent Foundations of Human Sociality Project, in which researchers set up labs in the field to play standard experimental games in fifteen small-scale societies around the world (Henrich et al. 2004). Other examples include Carpenter, Daniere, and Takahashi (2004), Bohnet and Greig (2008), Marlow and others (2008), and Bahry and Wilson (2006).

A second branch of research has attempted to test whether patterns of behavior vary across subjects that possess different demographic characteristics. The issue of interest in this strand of the literature is not whether average patterns of play vary across societies, but whether they vary across players of different types in the same society. Thus, a number of studies have investigated whether altruism, trust, or reciprocity varies with gender (Eckel and Grossman 1996, 1998; Andreoni and Vesterlund 2001), race-ethnicity (Eckel and Grossman 2001; Fershtman and Gneezy 2001), age (Harbaugh, Krause, and Liday 2003), or even beauty (Andreoni and Petrie 2008; Wilson and Eckel 2006). Another set of studies have considered not just "main effects"—that is, whether women play differently from men, or whether African Americans play differently from Caucasians—but whether behavior is affected by the nature of the *dyad* or *pairing*—that is, whether men behave differently when playing with other men than when playing with women, or whether Caucasians play differently when paired with other Caucasians than when paired with African Americans. Examples of studies in this vein include Burns (2003), Wilson and Eckel (2006), Ferraro and Cummings (2007), Fershtman and Gneezy (2001), Gil-White (2004), and Petrie (2003).

The third (and newest) branch has directly taken up the issue of external validity by explicitly relating the findings derived from experimental games to patterns of behavior observed outside of the laboratory. For example, Dean Karlan (2005) exploited information gathered in trust and public goods games to predict patterns of savings, repayment, and default, up to one year later, among participants in a Peruvian microcredit organization. Jeffrey Carpenter and Erika Seki (2005) demonstrated that Japanese fishing crews composed of fishermen who exhibited greater degrees of conditional cooperation and were more willing to disapprove of shirking tended to be more productive. Others are now using experimental games to assess how levels of community efficacy and trust respond to outside efforts to inculcate democratic values and institutions in Liberia (Fearon, Humphreys, and Weinstein 2009).

The project described in this book is located at the confluence of these three branches of contemporary experimental economics research. We share with the first branch the characteristic of locating our research outside of a university laboratory as we examine how subjects behave in a context of substantive interest, an impoverished neighborhood of urban Kampala.

We share with the second branch a concern with how patterns of play vary with the characteristics of the players and the homogeneous or heterogeneous nature of the interaction. In making this move, we emphasize two different sources of heterogeneity. The first is based on membership in a given ethnic or regional group—our core interest in the book. By randomizing the partnering of players with one another, we are able to generate variation in the ethnic homogeneity or heterogeneity of the pairings we observe. The second source of heterogeneity is based on differences across individuals within groups. One of the most important contributions of behavioral economics has been to challenge the neoclassical view that all individuals respond in the same way to material incentives. Instead, as summarized by Elinor Ostrom (2000, 138), recent research suggests that "the world contains multiple types of individuals, some more willing than others to initiate reciprocity to achieve the benefits of collective action." Recognizing the existence of these different types has implications for empirical and theoretical work (see, for example, Bolton and Ockenfels 2000; Bowles and Gintis 2004b; Fehr and Schmidt 1999). If players of different types respond in different ways to a given treatment, then an aggregation problem may arise. Average behavior across types may mask systematic features of play taking place within them. To avoid this pitfall, we distinguish in our analyses between two types of players: those whose behavior is consistent with preferences in keeping with the neoclassical model (whom we term "egoists") and those who exhibit higher levels of general altruism (whom we term "non-egoists"). Although we examine the different behavior that arises across different types of individuals, we emphasize that, as with other work in this strand of the literature, we do not exercise experimental control over these types. These all exist prior to our experiments. What we do have control over, however, is how these types encounter each other in social settings. In this way, we can ensure that the interactions we examine are free of the selection effects that render much observational analysis so difficult.

With the third branch of recent scholarship using behavioral experiments, we share a commitment to demonstrating the utility of our findings for explaining outcomes outside of the laboratory. To do this, we have insisted on a methodology that, though standard in other types of research in the social sciences, is surprisingly uncommon in experimental work: we used random sampling to recruit a pool of subjects who were representative of the underlying population whose behavior patterns in the real world we were interested in explaining. There are two major advantages of random sampling. First, by producing a representative sample, it allows subjects to make inferences about other subjects based on their knowledge of the population: they are thus able to form consistent beliefs about the ethnic identities and behaviors of the individuals with whom they are playing. Second, random sampling allows us, the researchers, to make inferences from the behavior of our sample to the population from which our subjects are drawn. Matching the subject and underlying populations is especially important when the behaviors under study—in this case, how people condition play on the ethnicity of their partners—are not necessarily a universal feature of human behavior, but rather a property that may apply in different ways to different populations.

The Research Site

We located our research in the poor urban neighborhoods of Kampala, Uganda. Kampala is a good site in which to examine the impact of diversity on public goods provision. First, Kampala is not only an ethnically diverse city but also a place where ethnicity is highly salient in everyday social interactions. Yet while ethnicity matters, the political situation in Kampala is sufficiently stable and peaceful to permit questions about ethnic identifications and attitudes to be asked and for research on social interactions across ethnic lines to be undertaken. Moreover, with the devolution of responsibility for social service provision over the past decade from the central government to the financially strapped elected local councils (LCs), the supply of many local public goods—including security, garbage collection, and the maintenance of storm drains—has become a purely local affair that depends almost entirely on the voluntary contributions of local community members (Golooba-Mutebi 2003; Onyach-Olaa 2003)—a subject to which we return in chapter 2. Thus, the question of why some communities are able to generate contributions toward public goods and others are not is of real practical consequence in the area we study.

In addition, and quite importantly, we were able to confirm in Kampala the negative association between ethnic diversity and public goods provision that has been found elsewhere in the literature. Figure 1.1 plots the relationship between ethnic diversity and public goods provision across seventy-four local communities in Kawempe Division, the poorest of Kampala's five divisions.[22] We measured the ethnic diversity of each community using a fragmentation index based on the ethnic demography reported in the 2001 census, and we measured public goods provision in terms of whether, during the previous six months, residents of the local community had organized efforts in the area of crime prevention and security.[23] The data showed a negative, albeit weak, relationship between diversity and public goods provision and made it possible for us to take the next step of accounting for why.[24]

Apart from allowing us to corroborate the negative association between ethnic heterogeneity and public goods provision, the data from the Kawempe survey also put us in a position to select a narrower (and

Figure 1.1   Ethnic Diversity and Public Goods Provision in Kawempe

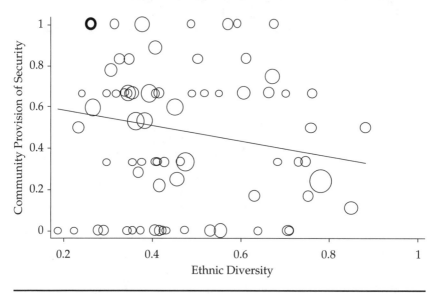

Source: Authors' calculations.

Notes: The figure reports the relationship between a community-level measure of ethnic diversity and the likelihood that the community has organized to provide security for its residents in Kawempe, Uganda. Higher levels of ethnic diversity are associated with lower levels of community security provision.

more manageable) area from which to recruit our experimental subjects. Because we were interested in studying *why* rather than *whether* diversity impedes collective action, we deliberately recruited our experimental subjects from neighborhoods of Kampala that combine high levels of ethnic diversity with low levels of public goods provision. Our study area comprises the four adjacent parishes (LC2s) of Mulago I, Mulago II, Mulago III, and Kyebando.[25] We refer to them in this book collectively as Mulago-Kyebando. Together, these parishes contain approximately seventy thousand people from whom we drew a random sample of three hundred subjects.[26] Interviews with community leaders and residents of Mulago-Kyebando (reported in chapters 2 and 6) confirmed both the difficulties of providing local public goods in this community and the highly ethnically fragmented nature of their populations.

Putting the Strategy in Perspective

As with all methods, it is important to keep in mind the limitations of our empirical strategy. The first limitation flows from our decision regarding site selection. We chose to sample our subjects from a set of communities exhibiting high ethnic diversity and low public goods provision. Although this decision put us in a strong position to evaluate the connection between diversity and the underprovision of public goods, it left us without a benchmark for each of the various mechanisms we tested. Thus, while we could determine whether a given mechanism played an important role in linking diversity to collective action failure, we could not be certain that a given mechanism worked more or less strongly in more or less heterogeneous settings. To make such a comparison, we would have had to replicate our analyses in a broader cross-section of communities.

Other limitations follow from the nature of the social interactions captured in our experimental setting. One of the many choices we faced in designing the experiments was whether to aim to replicate settings with largely anonymous interaction or to examine the operation of small-scale communities. We chose the former, sampling subjects from a large area and setting up pairings in which most interactions were anonymous. This anonymity renders our results more salient for examining interactions such as participation in urban settings and in regional or national politics—rather than, for example, in village or elite politics, a context in which subjects are almost certain to know one another.

A second choice was whether to examine interactions in which ethnicity was highly salient versus those in which it was not. We chose to study a setting in which ethnicity was not explicitly salient—in the sense that, for most of our games, we did not suggest to our subjects that ethnicity was a relevant variable to be considered in choosing how to play. Of course, ethnicity was in fact salient to many of our subjects, as evidenced in the results of our games, but ethnic patterns of play were not a consequence of any priming on our part. Thus, our results speak most directly to the ways in which identities condition everyday interaction. We cannot rule out the possibility that individuals behave differently in settings in which ethnicity is specifically emphasized as a salient category of social interaction, as in political campaigns or riots or in contexts where ongoing intergroup violence colors people's expectations about the outcome of cross-group interactions.[27]

Perhaps the most important limitation of our main empirical strategy is its emphasis on testing mechanisms through the observation of individual choices in two- and three-person experimental games. This approach gives great tractability to our design, but it has the disadvantage of implicitly reducing community- and group-level processes to an aggregation of binary or small-group interactions. We cannot rule out the possibility that homogeneous subgroups of a heterogeneous community act very differently from homogeneous subgroups of a homogeneous community (on such composition effects, see Posner 2004a).

In addition, a rich literature offers theories and empirical accounts of collective action success that emphasize aspects of social behavior that are not easily captured in this experimental setup. For example, building on the seminal work of Mancur Olson (1965), scholars such as Norman Frolich, Joe Oppenheimer, and Oran Young (1971) and Samuel Popkin (1979) have pointed to the centrality of political entrepreneurs —individuals who are willing to bear private costs in order to facilitate the production of public goods. Such entrepreneurs are absent in our study. The approach we adopted also limited our ability to speak to the importance of institutions more broadly (both formal and informal), a prominent topic in the theoretical literature on the origins and maintenance of cooperative behavior (Ostrom 1990; Cook, Hardin, and Levi 2005).

We recognize the fact that the success or failure of collective action in a community may depend on factors that we could not observe directly given our empirical strategy. But we believe nevertheless that a great deal can be learned from observations of binary and small-group interactions. Many of the prominent accounts of how informal institutions shape collective efficacy (for a review, see Sampson, Morenoff, and Gannon-Rowley 2002) depend very much on the notion that such norms exert an effect directly through the choices that individuals make in everyday interactions (for example, whether to help out a neighbor or report a crime). In principle, the effects of informal institutions should be observable in our games, even though such institutions and practices are cultivated at the community level. This question of how to link patterns of individual behavior to aggregate outcomes is clearly an important one—and one to which we return in chapters 6 and 7.

The Outline of the Book

The book is organized as follows. Chapter 2 provides a description of our research site and presents information about the variation in levels of public goods provision across our site and in the region more broadly. We explore how a wide range of public goods—roads, schools, health care, sanitation, and security—are provided in Kampala, document the erosion of the central government's role in providing these goods, and discuss the challenges faced by local communities that seek to organize their members to improve social welfare. Chapter 3 focuses on our main independent variable, ethnic diversity. The chapter provides basic background information about ethnicity in Kampala. In laying the foundation for an analysis of how ethnicity conditions behavior, we emphasize a new understanding of ethnic diversity based on how people themselves—rather than census-takers, analysts, or other outsiders—categorize the members of their own community in different informational settings. The chapter then introduces a method we have developed to measure these subjective perceptions.

Explaining how ethnic diversity undermines the ability of communities to organize the provision of public goods is the objective of chapter 4, which is in many respects the heart of our study. Here we explore the myriad arguments advanced to account for diversity's negative impact, looking for evidence in support of (or against) key preferences, technology, and strategy selection mechanisms. Drawing on the behavior of individuals from Mulago-Kyebando in a series of experimental games, the evidence tells a powerful story about why ethnically homogeneous communities are better able to act collectively than more diverse ones. The answer is simple, yet consistent with what anthropologists have chronicled about African ethnic groups for generations: shared identity makes in-group norms of reciprocity salient. What this means in practice is that individuals cooperate with coethnics at a higher rate than with non-coethnics, not because of biases toward in-group members, but because they expect coethnics to cooperate with them and because they believe that, should they fail to cooperate, they might be punished. This behavior is most prominently displayed by "egoists"—individuals who, absent the reciprocity norms made salient by shared ethnic identities, show a stronger tendency to look out for their own interests at the expense of others. Although our results point to the centrality of the strategy selection mechanism, they also suggest that ethnic technologies are at work: that is, that coethnics engage one another with far greater frequency (periodicity) and are better able to gauge the otherwise unobservable characteristics of fellow group members (readability), and that coethnics may be more effective at accomplishing joint tasks (efficacy) and have access to social networks that facilitate the sanctioning of coethnics who refuse to cooperate (reachability).

Equally important as what we did find is what we did not. Contrary to assumptions in much of the theoretical literature on ethnic diversity and public goods provision, our results suggest that preferences mechanisms cannot account for the failures of collective action in urban Kampala. Individuals in our study showed no tendency to value the welfare of members of their own ethnic group more highly than the welfare of members of other groups. We found almost no variation across groups in their preferences about what public goods should be provided. And we found no evidence that our subjects derived greater enjoyment from working with coethnics than with non-coethnics.

The empirical evidence in support of both ethnic technologies and ethnic strategies requires us to push our analysis further. In chapter 5, we ask: Is it the case that, even conditioning on how easily they are reached and sanctioned, individuals still act in a more reciprocating manner when playing with coethnics? If this is the case, it provides evidence for a distinctly coethnic norm. Or is it simply *because* they interact with coethnics more frequently and are more easily reached by coethnics that individuals reciprocate more when paired with someone from their group? If so, this might constitute evidence that coethnic cooperation arises from the uneven application of a universal norm. Although the distinction between these two mechanisms is subtle, it is essential for resolving the puzzle of why ethnic diversity undermines collective action. Evidence from additional experimental games led us to a more precise answer. More frequent interaction and greater mutual reachability were not the factors that drove coethnic cooperation. Rather, our subjects appeared to observe a distinctly coethnic norm of reciprocity—one that operated alongside a powerful universal norm that emerged when behavior was publicly observable and the threat of punishment by a third player was present. This last finding suggests that although reciprocity norms are stronger within groups than across them, it is possible to sustain cooperative norms that span ethnic groups in highly diverse societies.

Chapter 6 draws us out of the experimental setting and into the community of Mulago-Kyebando to investigate whether the patterns we observe in the games are reflected in behavior that we can measure outside the laboratory. We begin with a deeper exploration of our subject population, examining the stories they told us about how they understood the games, showing how they linked play in the lab to situations they confronted in their everyday lives, and looking to see how their game behavior correlated with their participation in community life. Moving from our subjects to the community, we then probe the sources of collective action failure in Mulago-Kyebando as described by the chairpersons of its twenty-six local councils, many of whom echo chairmen Ssalongo and Kashaija frustration at their inability to police noncontributions to community projects. Moving from the narrow to the more general, we subject our argument to tests of its external validity before turning to the implications of our argument in chapter 7.

Chapter 2

Public Goods Provision
in Kampala

O UR INQUIRY into the mechanisms that link social diversity and
collective action failure is motivated by the observation that heterogeneous communities tend to provide lower levels of public
goods for their members than homogeneous communities. This chapter
lays the foundation for our discussion by doing three things. First, we
document the underprovision of public goods in Kampala. Then, to better understand why public goods are underprovided, we describe how
roads, schools, health care, sanitation, water, and security are provided
in the city. Finally, we discuss the (mostly unsuccessful) efforts that communities have made to provide these public goods for their members.
The conclusion we draw is that accounting for the generally low levels
of public goods provision in Kampala requires understanding why communities are unable to work together to achieve collective ends.[1]

The Underprovision of Public Goods
in Kampala

Our initial examination of public goods provision draws on two
sources: a survey we conducted in 2005 and an earlier survey carried
out by the Kampala City Council in 2000. The first is a 594-respondent
public goods survey that we conducted in May 2005 in Kawempe Division, the poorest of Kampala's five divisions. The purpose of the
Kawempe Public Goods Survey (KPGS) was to identify variation in
public goods provision across local council units (LC1s) that could inform the selection of neighborhoods from which to recruit our experimental subjects. We began by randomly selecting 198 of Kawempe's 672
census enumeration areas (EAs) and interviewing three people (at least
one man or woman) in each sampled unit. Because our purpose was to
collect information about the characteristics of each local community

and the collective activities that took place there, our selection rule restricted our respondents to individuals who lived or worked in the area.[2] Our brief Kawempe public goods survey asked respondents about the quality of various public goods outcomes such as garbage collection and crime, as well as about community efforts to provide public goods in these domains. Enumerators also were asked to record their assessments of the degree of visible garbage in the area, the general wealth of the community, and the state of the neighborhood's roads infrastructure.

The second data source we draw on is the Kampala City Council Survey (KCCS), a household survey undertaken by the Kampala City Council in May and June 2000.[3] The survey was designed to collect information on residents' access to, usage of, and satisfaction with various social services in the city. Importantly for the present study, the survey collected information not just about what the city council was (or was not) doing to provide particular public goods, but also about community efforts to provide social services that the local government was not providing. Data were collected from twenty-five randomly selected households in each of eighty randomly drawn enumeration areas, for a total sample size of two thousand households.[4] To permit comparison with our own public goods survey, we limit our analysis to the sixteen enumeration areas (four hundred households) in Kawempe.

The principal inference to be made from the data collected in both the Kawempe Public Goods Survey and the Kampala City Council Survey is that levels of public goods provision in Kawempe are extremely low. Ninety percent of the LC1s surveyed in the KPGS were reported to have visible trash in the streets. Sixty-nine percent of LC1s had roads that our enumerators characterized as either "bumpy dirt" or "paved but with many potholes." Sixty-eight percent of respondents reported that either they or someone they knew had been a victim of theft in the past six months. The KCCS provided similar evidence of inadequate public goods provision. Seventy-three percent of respondents in Kawempe said that they were dissatisfied with the garbage collection in their local community; 86 percent were dissatisfied with their water source; 47 percent of those who used public health facilities were dissatisfied with the availability and quality of medical supplies (satisfaction was higher among those using private clinics); and 41 percent were dissatisfied with the storm drainage system in their neighborhood—a figure that rises to 55 percent if we limit the analysis to the 69 percent of total respondents who said that either their house or the street immediately in front of it had been flooded at some point during the past year.[5]

The generally dismal state of public goods provision in Kawempe nonetheless masked significant variation. Some communities had better roads, more regular garbage collection, superior health care access, and more reliable clean water than others. Not surprisingly, the communities

Figure 2.1   Poverty and Public Goods Provision in Kawempe

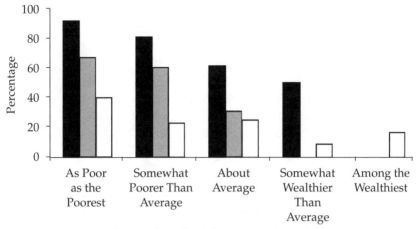

How poor are the people in this LC1 compared to other LC1s in Kampala?

- ■ Percentage saying that the roads in the area are bumpy dirt roads or paved roads with many potholes
- ▨ Percentage saying that there is some or lots of disorganized trash around in the area
- □ Percentage saying that, in the past six months, they or someone they know has been a victim of theft

Source: Authors' calculations from Kampala Public Goods Survey 2005, carried out by authors.
Notes: Although wealth is strongly related to public goods provision, not all of the poorest communities have low levels of public goods provision, and not all of the richest communities have high levels.

with the lowest levels of public goods provision tended to be the poorest ones.[6] As figure 2.1 indicates, the LC1s in Kawempe with the worst roads and the most trash tended to be as poor as the poorest in all of Kampala, and those with the best roads and the least trash tended to be among the richest. Interestingly, while the prevalence of crime also is related to poverty, the wealthiest communities were not immune to petty thievery—no doubt because they made the most attractive targets for criminals. Yet poverty is not the whole story. For as figure 2.1 also makes clear, not all of the poorest communities had problems with trash or crime (though almost all of them did seem to have bad roads). And not all of the wealthy communities were immune to having potholed roads or rubbish strewn on their streets. To get a sense of what else might be driving the variation in public goods provision in Kawempe, we need to explore in more detail exactly how public goods are provided.

Who Is Responsible for Public Goods Provision in Kampala?

In principle, public goods might be provided by one (or a combination) of three different sources: the national or local government, private individuals, or the community itself, acting collectively. Because public goods are, by definition, non-excludable, individuals have little incentive to supply them themselves. This is why public goods have traditionally been provided by governments. However, not all governments are responsive to the needs of their citizens. And many governments, particularly in developing countries, lack the resources or capacity to provide the public goods that their citizens need, even if they want to provide them. In such settings, the provision of basic social services such as health care, education, security, roads, water, and sanitation frequently falls to private individuals or local communities (or, increasingly, to aid agencies, church groups, and other nongovernmental organizations [NGOs]). Kampala is just such a place. Indeed, if the history of public goods provision in Kampala has a theme, it is of the gradual abdication by the government of responsibility for providing basic public goods and the slow but steady transfer of responsibility for supplying these services to other parties (Golooba-Mutebi 2003; Onyach-Olaa 2003). Thus, public toilet facilities in Kampala, when they exist, are frequently provided by NGOs. In many areas of the city, garbage collection is subcontracted by the city council to a private company. And in 2003, the Uganda Police Service withdrew its funding for local defense units, which had previously provided security patrols that offered at least some protection against crime. The provision of community policing in Kampala is now left almost entirely to the local communities.[7]

Part of the response to this withdrawal of the government from local public goods provision has been the emergence of privately provided alternatives. According to data from the KCCS, 77 percent of sick people in Kawempe sought treatment at private clinics. Sixty-one percent of children enrolled in school in Kawempe attended private academies. And as noted, those who could afford to do so had their garbage collected by a private truck.

Roads and water systems operate similarly. Owing to their capital intensity, roads are most often built, and taps and standpipes constructed, with the underwriting of the city council, a foreign donor, or an NGO. But once built, the maintenance of such public infrastructure is almost always turned over to private individuals or left to the local communities to handle themselves. Thus, fully 75 percent of households in

Kawempe that did not have tapped water within their own dwellings reported getting their water from standpipes that were maintained by private individuals—usually the person who lived next door to where the standpipe happened to be located—in exchange for a small fee per jerry can of water taken.[8] As anyone who has ever driven in Kampala is well aware, potholes on the most deeply rutted and heavily trafficked streets often are filled by entrepreneurial children who shovel some dirt into the holes and then beg for coins from passing motorists.

Services such as health care, education, and the maintenance of standpipes are well suited to being taken over by private individuals because they can be rationed on a fee-for-service basis—providing, of course, that people have money to pay for them (road maintenance by children is something of a special case).[9] But other public goods are less excludable (or have larger externalities) and thus are less amenable to being supplied by private individuals when the government fails to provide them. Chief among these are security, garbage collection, and the maintenance of drainage channels. Since we are particularly interested in this study in the ability of communities to overcome collective action problems, these are the public goods outcomes on which we concentrate. Of course, the wealthiest individuals simply hire private guards to defend their property, contract with haulage companies to take away their trash, or buy homes outside of low-lying areas to protect themselves against flooding. But for the vast majority of Kampala's residents, their ability to enjoy security, garbage collection, or freedom from flooding depends on whether or not their local communities have been able to organize themselves to provide these public goods collectively. Benevolent NGOs occasionally step in to help. But because the needs in Kampala's urban slums are so great, and because NGO resources are so (comparatively) small, the major determinant of public goods provision in Kampala's poorest neighborhoods is local community organization. "There are certain things you are supposed to get from the government, but it's hard," a local council chairman told us. "So you get together as a community, and you get the services yourself."

In trying to organize themselves to provide security, garbage collection, and storm drain maintenance, residents of Kampala have the advantage of a fairly well-developed system of local councils that, at least in principle, can serve as vehicles for community-level mobilization. A legacy of the village-level popular assemblies set up by the National Resistance Movement (NRM) during its insurgent struggle against the Milton Obote regime during the 1980s, the LC system emerged in the mid-1980s as the country's central institution for local administration and organization. For a few years, the LC system served this role well. Over time, however, as more and more responsibility for local public goods provision was transferred from the central government to the local councils, and as fewer and fewer resources made their way through the LC system to the councils to pay for these services, the ability of the councils to provide basic public goods was severely compromised. The problem was felt particularly acutely in Kampala, where high population density made the demand for public goods such as sanitation, functioning drainage, clean water, education, and public health particularly great. Despite the implementation of an ambitious World Bank–sponsored Local Government Development Program, under which 25 percent of the funds paid to the national government in graduated taxes were supposed to be remitted to the LC system, the local council chairmen and chairwomen with whom we spoke in Kawempe complained bitterly that resources were simply not reaching them. Starved for funds, local councils today can offer little or no financial resources to provide public goods for the communities they ostensibly serve. They do, however, provide an organizational structure through which local resources and community action might, in principle, be mobilized. Unfortunately, such community-level action and resource mobilization is often unsuccessful.

Attempts at Community-Level Public Goods Provision in Kampala

The LC1 chairpersons we interviewed told us that they spent a great deal of energy trying to raise voluntary contributions of labor and money from residents of their communities to provide public goods such as garbage collection, storm drain maintenance, and security. They made it clear, however, that this was not an easy task. "Contributions are difficult for us," one council chairman complained. "We call village meetings and decide how much is fair to collect for different programs. Then we go house to house to collect the money afterwards. . . . It is really hard to get people to pay." "We never collect money from households anymore," another council chairman told us. "People don't want to pay. In the past, this was a strategy [we] used . . . but it failed, so we stopped." Even convincing community members simply to refrain from taking actions that make problems worse, like dumping trash in the streets and drainage channels, is no easier. "People put garbage everywhere now," one council chairman grumbled. "They dump it in drains. Our committee has called on people to stop, but we have had no luck." Another agreed that trash "is a big problem in our area. People throw their trash away at night, when no one can see them, into empty plots."

The consensus among the LC leaders we interviewed was that soliciting cooperation from community members was easier two decades ago when the local council system was new. During the 1980s and early 1990s, when the LC system was first installed as the centerpiece of President Yoweri Kaguta Museveni's "Movement" system of government, constituents felt empowered. After living under decades of dictatorship, they embraced the opportunity to participate in local governance and, as Museveni himself put it, "make the decisions which affect their daily lives" (*New Vision*, January 30, 1991, cited in Kasfir 1998, 54). But by the time of our fieldwork in 2005, the enthusiasm for participation in the councils' activities had long since dissipated. "Initially people came in large numbers to village meetings," one council chairman told us. "Each month, there were between 200 and 250 people. A few years ago, there were 70 to 80 at each meeting. Now, there are between 10 and 20, and the population of the zone has markedly increased in the past few years. . . . People have started neglecting the 'Movement' system and don't want to deal with it at all." Another complained that "we used to hold village meetings, but those ended long ago. People just aren't interested. We're now just an administrative structure; there is little public involvement. People are no longer vigilant. There is very little turnout, even when we call emergency meetings."

The frustration conveyed by the LC chairmen about achieving community-level collective action was borne out in the findings of the KPGS and KCCS. Both surveys asked whether, during the previous six months, members of the local community had organized themselves to prevent crime or collect garbage (the KCCS also asked about drainage channel maintenance). As table 2.1 indicates, community organization of this sort, while not unheard of, was not a regular activity in most local communities. While more than 50 percent of respondents in both surveys reported that community efforts to prevent crime and ensure security in the area had been under way in their LC1s during the previous six months, just 25 percent of respondents in the KPGS and 32 percent of households in the KCCS reported that there had been efforts to organize garbage disposal services in their LC1s. And just 31 percent of households in the KCCS reported community efforts to clear drainage channels of debris. Given how pressing the problems of security, garbage collection, and flooding are in Kawempe (and given that the government cannot be counted on to deal with these issues), these relatively low levels of community organization provide powerful evidence for the difficulty that communities face in achieving collective action.

Before reading too much into these figures, however, a few cautionary words are in order. First, the data do not contain information on whether the government might already have been providing the local public good in question, and so we have no way of knowing whether initiatives might have been absent in some communities because they were unnecessary. Given the poor record of the city council and the Government of Uganda (GOU) in providing local security, garbage collection, and storm drain maintenance, we think this is unlikely. But we

Table 2.1   Evidence of Collective Action for Crime Prevention, Garbage
            Collection, and Drainage Channel Maintenance in Kawempe

	"In the past six months, have community members from this LC1 organized community efforts to . . . (percentage saying "yes")"	
	KPGS	KCCS (Kawempe Only)
". . . prevent crime and ensure security in this area?"	52%	62%
". . . organize garbage disposal services for this area?"	25	32
". . . organize drainage channel maintenance for this area?"	—	31

Source: Authors' calculations from Kawempe Public Goods Survey 2005, carried out by the authors, and Kampala City Council Survey 2000.
Note: Community organization, while not unheard of, is not a regular activity in most LC1s.

cannot rule it out entirely. Second, it is at least possible that a particular initiative did not exist because the local public good in question was simply not viewed as important in that area. Having well-maintained drainage channels is obviously desirable. Access to adequate security and sanitation are clearly valuable. But these local public goods and services may not be equally important in all communities. Low-lying, flood-prone neighborhoods are likely to rank drainage as their top concern and to devote most of their collective energies to solving that problem. Neighborhoods located next to markets are likely to be particularly concerned about security from petty thieves. Such community-specific preferences almost certainly have an effect on the willingness of community members to contribute to local initiatives in these areas and on the likelihood that such initiatives would have been taking place at the time of our surveys. Finally, the KPGS and KCCS provide no information about how long the various public goods–generating initiatives had been under way. If, as is reasonable to assume, cooperative communities are able to identify areas of need, organize collectively to solve the identified problem, and wrap up their efforts quickly (whereas uncooperative communities undertake initiatives that drag on indefinitely and never achieve their objectives), then the communities that have an initiative under way at a given moment may be precisely those that are *least* able to achieve successful collective action. If this is the case, then what we take to be an indicator of community success may actually be a measure of community failure.

The best way to resolve these inferential problems is to collect addi-

Figure 2.2   A Public Goods Map for Kisalosalo and Central LC1s

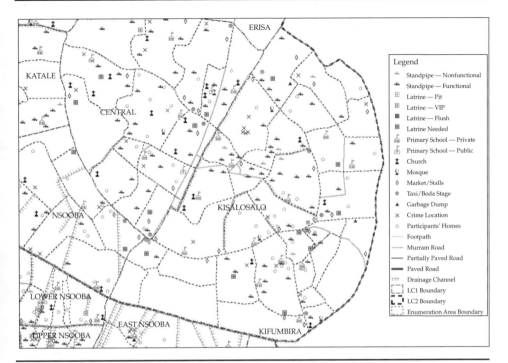

Source: Authors' compilation.

tional data. To do this, we complemented the data from the KPGS and KCCS with much more detailed information collected in the twenty-six LC1s in Mulago-Kyebando from which we recruited our experimental subjects.[10] We have already quoted from the interviews conducted with the chairmen of these local council units. In addition to these interviews, we conducted focus groups with ten randomly recruited residents from each of the twenty-six LC1s in Mulago-Kyebando. We asked participants in the focus groups to work together to draw maps of the physical locations of every school, standpipe, road, latrine, drainage channel, market, church or mosque, garbage dump, and site of (recent) crimes in the LC1 (for a sample map, see figure 2.2). After the maps were drawn, we drew up lists of every school, water tap, and latrine that had been identified and asked the focus-group participants to provide additional information about when the specific public good was built and by whom, who was currently responsible for maintaining it, and its current state of operation. We also asked focus-group participants about the maintenance of drainage channels, how garbage was disposed of, who was responsible for providing security in the LC1, whether community initiatives had been undertaken in any of these areas, and whether the levels of security, trash collection, and drainage channel maintenance that were being provided were adequate. The data collected from this exercise were then compared with the information gleaned from the LC1 chair interviews to generate an assessment of the degree of public goods provision and collective action success in each LC1. Whenever the conclusions we drew from the focus groups differed from those drawn from the LC1 chair interviews, we scheduled follow-up interviews with the LC1 chairs to try to reconcile the differences. A summary of our findings is provided in table 2.2.

As the evidence in table 2.2 makes clear, successful collective action—which we define as ongoing, widespread community initiatives that contribute to a higher quality of public goods provision in the community—was atypical in Mulago-Kyebando. Excluding those LC1s that were far wealthier than their neighbors (shaded gray in the table), only 5 percent of LC1s in Mulago-Kyebando had successfully organized to maintain drainage channels, just 10 percent had successfully organized to collect garbage, and only 20 percent had managed to organize successful initiatives to patrol the streets to prevent crime.[11] Far more common were community initiatives that had had only limited success. These tended to be stop-and-start efforts with limited community participation and a weaker impact on levels of public goods provision in the area. The general pattern of collective action failure in Mulago-Kyebando accords with that found in Kawempe more broadly (but based on less comprehensive data).

Ethnic Diversity and Public Goods Provision in Kampala

Three lessons can be drawn from the foregoing discussion. First, levels of public goods provision in Kawempe are low. Second, part of the reason for these low levels of public goods provision is that the national and local governments have ceded responsibility for supplying basic social services to private entrepreneurs (as in the areas of health care, education, and water system maintenance) and, in areas where private individuals are less willing to step in (such as security, garbage collection, and the maintenance of storm drains), to local councils, which do not have the capacity to handle the burden that has been thrust upon them. Third, when local councils attempt to provide the public goods that the government has failed to supply, they do so by trying to mobilize community initiatives. However, these initiatives are rarely successful.

In chapter 1, we suggested that a candidate hypothesis for why local communities in Kampala have by and large failed to mobilize their members to participate in public goods–generating initiatives is that ethnic diversity undermines their attempts to achieve collective action.

Table 2.2   Variation in Successful Collective Action Across LC1s in Mulago-Kyebando

LC1	Garbage		Security		Drainage	
	Effort	Success	Effort	Success	Effort	Success
Bakery	+		✓	Yes	✓	Some
Butaka Bukirwa	+		✓	Yes	✓	Some
Central	✓	Some	✓	Some	✓	Yes
Doctors	+		✓	Yes	+	
East Nsooba	✓	No	✓	Some	+	
Erisa	✓	Some	✓	Some	+	
Hospital	+		+		+	
Kafeero	✓	Some	✓	Some	✓	Some
Kalerwe	+		✓	Yes	✓	Some
Kanyana Quarters	✓	Some	✓	Some	✓	No
Katale Kyebando	+		✓	No	✓	No
Katale Mulago II	✓	Some	✓	Some	✓	Some
Kibawo	✓	No	+		+	
Kifumbira	+		+		+	
Kisalosalo	+		✓	Some	+	
Kiwonvu	✓	Some	✓	Yes	✓	Some
Lower Nsooba	✓	No	✓	No	✓	No
Nalwewuuba	✓	Yes	✓	Some	+	
National Housing	✓	Yes	✓	Some	+	
Nsooba	+		✓	Some	+	
Owen Road	✓	Some	✓	Yes	✓	Some
Triangle	✓	Yes	✓	Some	✓	Some
Tufnel	+		+		+	
Uganda Electricity Board	✓	Some	✓	Yes	+	
Upper Mawanda	+		+		+	
Upper Nsooba	+		✓	Some	✓	Some
Share with *Success* in Collective Action		10%		20%		5%
Share with *Some Success* in Collective Action		35%		50%		40%

Source: Authors' compilation.
Notes: Successful collective action is atypical in Mulago-Kyebando. Gray shading indicates wealthy LC1s (omitted from tallies in the last two rows).

We showed that this hypothesis finds much support in the literature, and in figure 1.1 we demonstrated that ethnic diversity is indeed associated with low levels of public goods provision across Kawempe. The next step is to account for why. This is the task of the chapters that follow.

Chapter 3

Ethnicity and Ethnic Identifiability

A NY CLAIM that ethnic diversity is associated with better or worse public goods provision requires some notion of what ethnic diversity means. Yet the very idea of ethnicity or ethnic diversity is itself a contentious issue. As measured by most scholars, the concept of ethnic diversity appears simple at first: if two people are paired at random in a given community, what is the likelihood that they belong to the same ethnic group? If the likelihood is high, we call this a homogeneous community. If the likelihood is low, the community is said to be diverse. All that matters for determining this likelihood is data on the community's demography. Scratching the surface of this apparently straightforward approach to measuring diversity, however, reveals a number of complications. What does it mean to say that an individual "belongs" to an ethnic group? How are we to know if two people are from the same "group"? Of the several groups in which individuals might claim membership, to which do we assign them?

When we presented the scatter plot relating ethnic diversity to public goods provision in figure 1.1, we assigned community members to ethnic group categories defined by the Uganda Bureau of Statistics (and used in the national census), and we calculated each community's diversity in terms of the relative sizes of the memberships of each of these groups. Implicitly, we assumed that the ethnic demography defined by these group categories matters for the people living in Mulago-Kyebando. We, like most scholars who use demographies based on ethnic categories officially defined by the government, assumed that people's actions are shaped by the way in which they (and others in their community) are classified by their country's national statistics department.[1] But is this a viable assumption? People living in real communities may not see themselves as fitting neatly into the categories utilized by census-takers. As we move toward a deeper understanding of how ethnic diversity can undermine collective action—and how binary and small-group interactions are shaped by the match (or not) between the ethnic backgrounds of participating individuals—we need to develop a richer understanding of the way that individuals actually perceive their own, other people's, and the broader landscape of ethnic backgrounds around them in their everyday interactions. We call this "subjective demography," and we contrast it with the "benchmark demography" that derives from census classifications.

To make a distinction between "subjective" and "benchmark" demographies is to do more than simply point out that people may categorize themselves differently from how outsiders do. It is also to recognize that a person's ethnic background cannot always be taken as an objective fact that is easily measured, as most formal and empirical work on ethnic politics usually assumes. Theorists generally assume that, at any point in time, individuals belong to some (or perhaps multiple) ethnic categories. They also assume that other individuals know these categories and have little or no problem working out the category to which any given individual belongs. Both assumptions present difficulties.

The first assumption presupposes what some might call an "objective" demography. We refer to it instead as a "benchmark" demography to reflect the fact that membership in a particular category is always subject to some form of assignment criterion—that is, relative to some necessarily subjective benchmark. We take the statement that individuals "truly" belong in a given category as nothing more than an application of some specified classification rule: *given a well-defined identification rule*, these are the categories to which each individual belongs.[2] The second assumption—that people know and use these benchmark categories—rests on an empirical claim that community members share an understanding of the relevant social categories and that they can assign people to them without ambiguity. It assumes that people's subjective demographies match a common benchmark demography. Yet, since we know so little about how people perceive the ethnic backgrounds of their fellow community members, this assumption is quite heroic.

Our goal in this chapter is to find a way to speak about ethnic identities and to measure ethnic classifications and distributions that does not depend on the existence of objective identities. Instead, we rely on something more epistemologically defensible and more strategically important: what people actually believe about their own ethnic group membership and about the group memberships of others. We begin by introducing the ethnic groups in three progressively narrower settings—Uganda, Kampala, and our study area—using the benchmark demography defined by the Ugandan government. In this respect, we start in the same place as most other scholars who are interested in the relationship between diversity and public goods provision. When we describe the benchmark demography of Uganda and Kampala, we use census classifications as the classificatory rule; when we describe our subject population, we use the categories into which people self-identified in our intake questionnaires. We describe some concerns that arise with each of these measures. But unlike many other approaches, our methodology does not stop there. Benchmark ethnic demographies are not necessarily useful in assessing the impact of coethnicity on behavior because our subjects may not know how other individuals are sorted into the benchmark categories. As an alternative, we discuss our approach to measuring the subjective demographies perceived by our subjects—including how our subjects in fact categorized others into ethnic groups, which categories they treated as being distinct from one another, and then, based on these subjective considerations, who they considered to be in-group and out-group members. Equipped with a subjective demography of Mulago-Kyebando, we are in a better position to understand how individuals condition their behavior on the identity of others and, more broadly, what ethnic diversity might mean for community life.

Benchmark Ethnic Demographies: Uganda, Kampala, and Mulago-Kyebando

Before examining how subjective demographies diverge from standard approaches to measuring diversity, we outline the ethnic demographics of Uganda, Kampala, and Mulago-Kyebando, the area in which we conducted our study. We begin with Uganda, employing a benchmark demography that uses the ethnic categories and estimates contained in the 2002 Ugandan census. For the most part, there is little disagreement in Uganda over the formal categories that should be included.[3]

The set of ethnic categories used in Uganda's national census generally mirrors linguistic divisions and, in most cases, reflects the distribution of societies that were autonomous prior to the colonial era. The major divisions, based on language groups, are between the Nilo-Saharan languages in the north, themselves subdivided into Eastern Nilotic (including the Iteso and the Karamojong), Western Nilotic (Acholi, Langi, and Alur), and Central Sudanic (Lugbara); the Bantu languages of the south, themselves divided into the Eastern Lacustrine (Baganda and Basoga) and the Western Lacustrine (Banyoro, Batoro, and Banyankole); and the smaller Kuliak languages, including the Ik and Soo. Figure 3.1 illustrates the geographic distribution of these linguistic groupings. The capital, Kampala, which is located in the center of the country, is populated by people who (or whose parents) migrated from all regions of the country. The map captures what some would consider "homelands" for each of these groups. Thus, individuals might

Figure 3.1   Linguistic Groups in Uganda

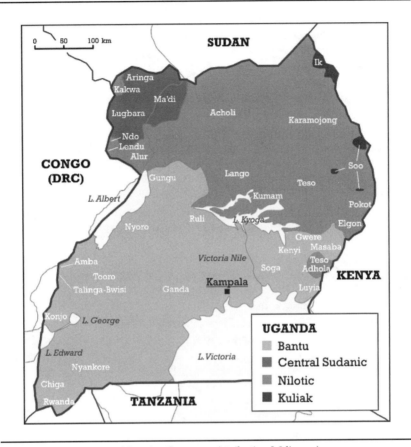

identify themselves as Banyankole, a western group, even if they were born and raised in Kampala, the central region of the country.

Individual identities are shaped not only by connections to historical homelands but also by historical rivalries between groups. The members of the Banyoro and Baganda ethnic groups, for example, are descended from the ancient kingdoms of Bunyoro and Buganda. For more than a century, the rivalry between these groups has centered on competition for control over land, with claims persisting today among Banyoro for the return of counties lost to Buganda when Uganda became a protectorate of Britain (Green 2008). In post-independence Ugandan political history, the rivalry between northern and southern ethnic groups has gained prominence. Immediately after the departure of the British, the Ugandan military was dominated by northerners, and the first prime minister of the country, Milton Obote, a northerner, deposed Uganda's first president, Sir Edward Mutesa, who was also the traditional king of Buganda. Some of the worst atrocities committed during Obote's two tenures as president were targeted against the Baganda population in the central region of the country by soldiers hailing from northern ethnic groups. The current president of Uganda, Yoweri Kaguta Museveni, who successfully unseated a northern-dominated regime in a guerrilla war, comes from the west and constructed a coalition of western and central groups in order to challenge the northerners' dominance of national politics. After more than twenty years in power, and with more than a decade-long civil war continuing in the north, Museveni now faces withering criticism for providing jobs and favors to Banyankole and other western ethnic groups while failing to end the suffering of those in the north.[4] The existence of these historical rivalries and past patterns of extreme violence between ethnic groups does not, however, imply that demographic diversity necessarily produces political divisions. Indeed, the intergroup divisions that have gained political prominence in Uganda's history represent only a tiny proportion of the ethnic dyads that might have erupted into conflict.[5]

At the national level, Uganda is extremely diverse. The census lists seventy-three different ethnic groups, while Ethnologue, an encyclopedia of world languages, lists Uganda as having forty-three surviving languages. Of these different ethnic and linguistic categories, none lays claim to more than 20 percent of the population, and only a small handful include more than 5 percent of the country's inhabitants. The six largest groups nationally (according to the official census categories) are the Baganda from the central region (16.9 percent), the Banyankole from the west (9.5 percent), the Basoga from the east (8.4 percent), the Bakiga from the west (6.9 percent), the Iteso from the east (6.4 percent), and the Langi from the north (6.1 percent). Each of another seven ethnic groups represents at least 2 percent of Uganda's population.

With so many different groups of different sizes, it is difficult to construct a simple measure of the ethnic structure of Uganda's population. One measure that is commonly used by social scientists is the index of ethno-linguistic fragmentation (ELF), which is calculated as the probability that two randomly drawn people in a given environment will be from different groups.[6] In a perfectly homogeneous society, it takes a score of zero; in a perfectly heterogeneous society, it takes a value of one. Unsurprisingly, given the large number of different ethnic groups in the country and the small size of even the largest, the figure for Uganda, calculated using the seventy-three groups enumerated in the census as the ethnic units, is 0.93. By any account, this represents an extremely high

Figure 3.2   Ethnic Heterogeneity, by District

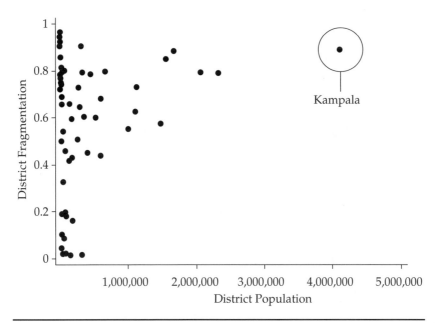

Source: Authors' calculations using 2002 Uganda census (Uganda Bureau of Statistics 2002).
Notes: This graph plots the size of the district population against a measure of district-level ethno-linguistic fractionalization calculated using data from Uganda's 2002 census. Kampala is by far the largest and among the most ethnically diverse districts.

level of ethnic diversity, placing Uganda near the top of the global ranking of ELF indices, second only to Tanzania.

A country's ethnic diversity at the national level does not, however, imply diversity at the local level. Because ethnic groups often reside in particular areas of the country, many of Uganda's districts are actually quite homogeneous. As figure 3.2 demonstrates, many districts have ELF values close to zero, and others cluster at around 0.50. There is also a substantial proportion of diverse districts, some large and some small. Among these, Kampala is clearly the largest; it is also one of the most diverse, ranking sixth in terms of ethnic diversity. The fragmentation index for Kampala, however, is below the measure calculated for the country as a whole, mainly because the Baganda are relatively dominant in the city, which is the historical seat of the Buganda kingdom.

As noted in the previous chapters, we conducted our research in the Kawempe division of Kampala in an area that we call Mulago-

Figure 3.3   Demographic Distribution of Major Ethnic Groups in Mulago-Kyebando and in Uganda as a Whole

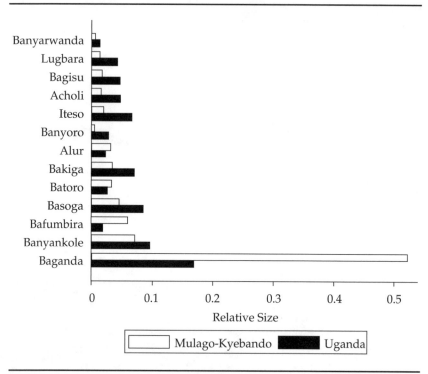

Source: Authors' calculations using Uganda census 2002.
Notes: This graph displays the relative population shares of the thirteen largest ethnic groups. The white bars represent population shares in Mulago-Kyebando; the black bars correspond to population shares in Uganda. Mulago-Kyebando has a diversity of ethnic groups, but the Baganda represent the largest group (and are disproportionately large compared to their relative share in the country as a whole).

Kyebando. The four parishes that make up Mulago-Kyebando are more diverse than other parts of the country. Yet defined more locally in terms of the twenty-six local council units (LC1s) that make up these four parishes, they exhibit less diversity than Kampala as a whole and are considerably less diverse than Uganda. Figure 3.3 again uses census data (and thus census categories) to present the relative sizes of the thirteen largest ethnic groups in Mulago-Kyebando. The white bars represent the proportion of each group in our study area; for comparison, the black bars capture the proportion of that same group in Uganda as a whole. The Baganda are the dominant ethnic group in Mulago-Kyebando, as they are throughout Kampala. They are followed in the distribution by two sizable western groups, the Banyankole and the Bafumbira, and one eastern group, the Basoga. Other western groups (including the Bakiga and Batoro) are also present, as are a small number of residents from northern groups.

The diversity of our project area, and of Kampala more generally, is the result of substantial in-migration of non-Baganda over the past twenty years. Museveni's military victory in 1986 ushered in a period of relative peace and prosperity, paving the way for people from across the country—western groups in particular—to migrate to the capital in search of new economic opportunities. Such migration has eroded the once-dominant position of the Baganda, especially in the poorest neighborhoods of the city, where migrants have been able to obtain cheap accommodation (and sometimes even land) as they make the transition from rural areas. At the same time, the combination of Obote's demise and Museveni's reshaping of the national army and police caused many northerners to flee Kampala. Aside from areas with military and police barracks, few of Kampala's parishes any longer contain sizable representations of northern ethnic groups. These patterns are clearly evident in the ethnic demography of Kawempe Division. Based on the sample of respondents in our presurvey of households (described in chapter 2), more than 50 percent have lived in the same LC1 for *less than* five years. Describing the neighborhood in which they live, nearly 80 percent of our respondents said that their community was composed of people who were born outside of Kampala and later moved to the capital.

Now let us consider the benchmark demography of an even smaller group—the set of individuals in our sample for the experimental games. We must begin by explaining how we drew our sample. When we prepared to recruit subjects in Mulago-Kyebando, we were faced with two conflicting goals. One was to draw a fully representative sample. Although not common practice in behavioral economics, a representative sampling strategy had a number of advantages for our purposes. First, it put us in a position to do something that few studies to date have been able to accomplish: to make inferences from the results of our experiments to the population in the real world that our subjects inhabited.[7] We felt that this would be especially important given that the behavior under study—how people condition play on the ethnicity of their partners—is almost certainly affected by the local environment in which people live and might not be automatically generalizable beyond the subject population. How people categorize the other people with whom they interact—an essential aspect of our experimental games that we discuss shortly—is also fundamentally shaped by the prior beliefs they have about the distribution of groups in the population of potential interacting partners. Hence, a strong mapping of subjects onto their "natural" environment was critical.

A second (and, unfortunately, incompatible) goal was to maximize statistical power. Because we were interested in exploring differences between in-group and out-group behavior, and because matching among our subjects in the experimental games was to be fully random, we wanted to ensure that our sample demographics would allow us to observe a reasonable number of both in-group and out-group pairings among members of multiple groups. Given the demographic profile of Mulago-Kyebando, a simple random sample would have resulted in many in-group pairings among the Baganda, many out-group pairings that included Baganda, and very few in-group pairings of any other groups. The second-largest group in Mulago-Kyebando, the Banyankole, represents just 7 percent of the population. With random matching, we would expect only 0.5 percent of our pairings to involve Banyankole coethnics. The next largest group is the Bafumbira, with 6 percent of the population. With random matching, expected in-group pairings among the Bafumbira would amount to only one-third of 1 percent of all pairings. A simple random sample with randomized matching would have prevented us from observing the number of pairings we needed to work out the impact of coethnicity (independent of the impact of how Baganda play with other Baganda).

One radical response would have been to abandon random sampling entirely and select subjects simply on the basis of their ethnic group—for example, by sampling such that our subject pool contained members of only three ethnic groups of equal sizes. But that approach would have created two different challenges of its own. First, it would have alerted our subjects to our interest in ethnicity—something we were extremely careful throughout the experiment not to do, since this might have influenced players' behavior in the games. Second, abandoning random sampling would have meant that the demography in our experimental games did not match any demography that our subjects were likely to encounter in the real world. Their prior beliefs about the types of people they would encounter would have matched poorly with the individuals they would actually see in the games, making our subsequent interpretation of the results more difficult.

With two worthy goals but only one sample to draw, we selected a middle ground. Using data from our public goods survey, we identified a subset of local council units (LC1s) in Mulago-Kyebando that included somewhat higher proportions of the Banyankole and Bafumbira (the second and third most common ethnic groups). We then set sampling targets for each LC1 such that random sampling techniques within each LC1 would yield a sample population with a slightly smaller share of Baganda and slightly larger shares of Banyankole and Bafumbira (and also Banyarwanda, a group considered similar ethnically to the Bafumbira).

Figure 3.4   Sample Demography and Site Demography in Mulago-Kyebando

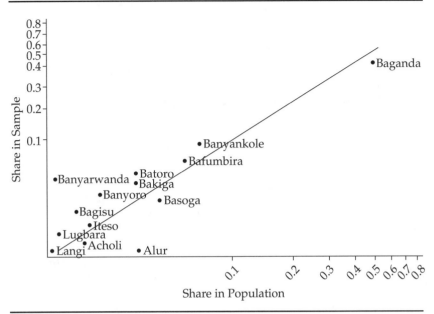

Source: Authors' calculations using intake survey data and Uganda census 2002.
Notes: This graph plots the share of each ethnic group in our sample (y-axis) against the share of the ethnic group in Mulago-Kyebando (x-axis). The former is calculated based on self-identifications in our intake survey, the latter based on data from the 2002 Ugandan national census. Our sample closely approximates the population in the study area, with a slight overrepresentation of the medium-sized groups that were targeted in our sampling.

Using this technique, we drew a random sample of three hundred subjects.[8] The ethnic demography of our subject population is shown in figure 3.4. The horizontal axis indicates the share of the group in Mulago-Kyebando (based on census data), and the vertical axis indicates the share of the group in our sample (based on the self-identification of subjects in our intake questionnaire). We see that our sampling strategy was successful in generating a slight underrepresentation of the largest group, the Baganda, and a slight overrepresentation of the smaller groups, notably the Bafumbira and Banyankole. For example, the Banyarwanda amount to 5 percent of our sample (sixteen subjects), whereas they make up only 1.5 percent of the population of Mulago-Kyebando. The Alur, on the other hand, make up 3 percent of the Mulago-Kyebando population, but only 1 percent of our sample (three subjects). Overall, the distribution of ethnic groups in the sample population closely mirrors the true population. Consequently, we can be confident that the subjects playing our games encountered other subjects in proportions nearly identical to those they would have encountered in random everyday interactions in their local environment.

Subjective Ethnic Demography

Now that we have a good understanding of the benchmark ethnic demographies of Uganda, Kampala, Mulago-Kyebando, and our study sample, we turn to the measurement of subjective demography. How do individuals *in practice* perceive the ethnic landscape of the world in which they operate? How were our subjects identified by others? How accurate or inaccurate were our subjects in placing each other into ethnic categories? To what extent did our subjects perceive different groups to be similar or dissimilar?

To answer these questions, we examine how our subjects categorized each other and compare these categorizations to how the subjects classified themselves. For the purpose of this analysis, we say that an individual correctly identified another person if he or she identified that person as belonging to the same category that the person used to identify himself or herself. Thus, person 1 is said to correctly identify the ethnic background of person 2 if person 1 classifies person 2 in the same way that person 2 classifies himself or herself. We use this notion of correct identification to generate measures of the ethnic "identifiability" of an individual (or group) under different informational conditions.[9]

Using this framework, the identifiability of an individual can be expressed as a probability: specifically, the identifiability of person 1 for person 2 is the probability that person 2 will correctly identify person 1 under a given informational condition. Note that this notion of correct identifiability is pairwise. This pairwise notion serves also as a microfoundation on which to make more abstract statements about the identifiability of groups. Thus, the identifiability of a particular group can be conceived as the probability that any given individual will correctly categorize an arbitrary member of that group.[10]

An aspect of identifiability that follows directly from these definitions is that the correct identification of both individuals and groups depends not just on the benchmark demography underpinning our notion of "correctness" but also on the informational environment under which empirical estimates of identifiability are assessed. Thus, not only are the specifics of our empirical frame important for interpreting our results, but in principle we can seek to make more general statements about identification processes *as a function of the empirical frame employed*. In particular, we can examine how the identifiability or distinctness of groups changes as a function of the set of categories used, the criteria for membership in groups, the population under consideration, and, most germane for our work here, the information made available to—and made available by—individuals.

As our primary interest is in working out how—rather than why—people categorize one another, our experimental design was relatively straightforward.[11] We began by generating a benchmark demography (which, like many censuses, used information about how subjects identified their own ethnic group membership) in a pre-experiment questionnaire. We then invited subjects to guess the identities of a set of randomly selected partners, rewarding them when their guess corresponded with how the partner identified himself or herself in the pre-experiment questionnaire. Importantly, we manipulated experimentally the information that subjects had about the people they were trying to identify. We took five digital images of each subject, each one providing a different level of information about the subject's ethnic background.

Information level 1 was a simple photograph of the person's face. Information levels 2 and 3 were two short videos in which the subject greeted the camera, respectively, in Luganda (Kampala's lingua franca) and in the respondent's primary language. At information levels 4 and 5, subjects spoke in video images in Luganda and the primary language, as in those at levels 2 and 3, but they also provided their given and family names.[12] By exposing participants to an image of a partner at a randomly selected level of information and asking them to guess that individual's ethnic background, we were able to measure the impact of informational contexts on ethnic identifiability and to examine how identifiability depended on observer characteristics and ethnic group membership.

Note that these images were only partially ordered with respect to the level of information they provided about the subject's ethnic background. Information level 5 provided more potentially relevant information than level 3, which in turn provided more information than level 1. Similarly, information level 4 provided more information than level 2, which offered more information than level 1. Whether or not the information contained in level 5 was more useful than the information contained in level 4, however, depended on the ability of an observer to extract a name from a statement even if he or she did not understand the language spoken. And whether information level 4 provided more information about a person's ethnic background than information level 3 depended on whether a name carried more information than the use of a primary language.

The structure of the exercise worked as follows. (Further details, along with the specific proctor instructions, are available in the online appendix, at https://www.russellsage.org/publications/Coethnicity Appendix.) Participants were told that they would see a random sample of about fifty images or videos of people drawn from the project's subject pool. In most cases, subjects saw images of partners they had been matched with in the experimental games they had played previously. We explained that the distribution of ethnic backgrounds of the individuals whose images they would see matched the distribution of ethnic groups in Mulago-Kyebando. To ensure that all subjects had the same prior beliefs about what this distribution looked like, we told them explicitly the approximate ethnic sizes of each of the ethnic groups in Mulago-Kyebando according to the benchmark demography. We then assigned subjects to computers and randomly paired them with enumerators. After (privately) seeing each image on a computer screen, subjects were asked to guess how that person would have classified himself or herself if asked to do so.[13] For every correct guess, subjects received 100 Ugandan shillings; total potential winnings were 5,000 shillings. In all, 274 of our subjects participated in the identification exercise, producing a total of 15,265 guesses.[14]

Patterns of Identifiability

We begin here with the issue of how our subjects understood the demographic environment in which they lived. In particular, we ask whether the subjective ethnic demography of Mulago-Kyebando, as measured by the way our subjects perceived and classified one another, corresponds to the benchmark demography, based on how our subjects identified themselves. A striking finding is that, *in the aggregate*, our subjects' estimations of the ethnic demography approximated the benchmark demography very closely.

Figure 3.5 shows how the benchmark share of each of the ethnic groups in our sample compares with the relative frequency with which subjects guessed others to be members of that group. It is clear that, in many cases, the distribution of subjective guesses across ethnic groups corresponds with their relative share in the population, as determined by the self-identification criterion. In a number of cases—including the Baganda and the Bafumbira—the share of guesses for these groups corresponds almost exactly to the actual self-reported share of these groups in the sample. There is more variation in other cases: subjects self-identifying as Banyoro accounted for 4 percent of our sample but just 1.4 percent of guesses—a figure that more closely approximates their 2.3 percent population share in Mulago-Kyebando according to the census. The Bagisu are also underrepresented relative to our sample benchmark demography: they represented 2.8 percent of our sample according to self-reports, but only 1.5 percent of guesses. As with the Banyoro, the guesses of Bagisu track their population share of 1.5 percent according to the census. Interestingly, people guessed Banyankole with a slightly higher frequency than their share in the sample, despite

Figure 3.5   Group Sizes Based on Benchmark and Subjective
Demographies

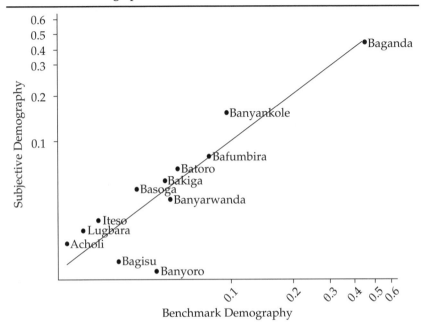

Source: Authors' calculations.
Notes: This graph plots the share of each ethnic group in our subject population according to self-reported group memberships (the benchmark demography) against its share in the population according to the subjective perceptions of our subjects. The distribution of subjective guesses across ethnic groups corresponds closely with their relative share in the population.

the fact that the Banyankole are already overrepresented as compared to their actual share as recorded by the census.

It would be wrong, however, to conclude from figure 3.5 that subjects were perfectly or even near perfectly identifiable. It is possible for subjective demographies to approximate the benchmark demography on average while individual guesses are consistently way off base. For example, if all individuals mistakenly assume that every individual they encounter is a coethnic, then the average subjective demography would reflect exactly the benchmark demography, even though each individual's subjective demography would diverge radically from the benchmark. Alternatively, each subject could have completely ignored the information from the video imagery and guessed randomly but in proportion to what we had just told them about the distribution of groups in our sample, and the aggregate outcome would have been the same.[15]

Tables 3.1 and 3.2 suggest that one or both of these things was almost certainly taking place.

Table 3.1 reports how individuals from different ethnic groups were classified (on average). Each cell entry shows the percentage of viewings in which an individual of a row type was classified as an individual of the column type. A quick look at the diagonal provides evidence of the extent to which people miscoded. If classifications were always correct, this matrix would be what we call an identity matrix—each of the diagonals would contain a one and the off-diagonals a zero. The difference between this matrix and the identity matrix is a measure of the degree of misclassification. For example, a Munyankole was correctly classified as a Munyankole 41 percent of the time (upper-left cell).[16] When mistakes were made, Banyankole were most likely to be classified as members of the most populous group, the Baganda (17 percent of the time). Banyankole were also often thought to be members of other western groups, including the Bakiga (14 percent of the time), the Batoro (8 percent of the time), and the Bafumbira (10 percent of the time). In a number of cases, individuals from one group were misclassified as members of another group more often than they were classified correctly. The Bakiga and the Batoro, for example, were guessed to be Banyankole more frequently than they were classified correctly as Bakiga and Batoro. The Banyarwanda were coded as Bafumbira about as often as they were classified as Banyarwanda.

While table 3.1 offers a picture of how individuals were misclassified, table 3.2 provides detail about who did the misclassification. The cells report the frequency of correct identification, averaged across all information levels and for each pairwise combination of groups. Consider first the final column on the right-hand side of the table. The numbers in this column reflect how often, on average, individuals in each of the benchmark ethnic categories correctly identified others—about 50 percent of the time. Interestingly, there is not much variation across groups in their ability to identify correctly the ethnic backgrounds of others. The Banyankole and Batoro were most successful, and the Basoga were least successful, but these differences are not substantively large. (Indeed, from a statistical point of view, we cannot reject the null hypothesis that there are no differences across groups in their guessing ability—results not shown.) There is significantly more variation across the bottom row of the table. This row captures the likelihood that an arbitrary member of each of the column types would be successfully identified. The Banyoro, for example, almost never were identified correctly as Banyoro. The group that was most commonly identified correctly was the Baganda—68 percent of the time.

Table 3.1   Patterns of Ethnic Identifiability: Classifications and Misclassifications

	Banyankole	Baganda	Bagisu	Bakiga	Banyarwanda	Basoga	Batoro	Banyoro	Iteso	Bafumbira
Banyankole	0.41	0.17	0.01	0.14	0.04	0.03	0.08	0.01	0.01	0.10
Baganda	0.09	0.70	0.01	0.03	0.03	0.05	0.04	0.01	0.01	0.03
Bagisu	0.13	0.36	0.16	0.04	0.02	0.10	0.06	0.02	0.04	0.06
Bakiga	0.34	0.20	0.01	0.22	0.03	0.03	0.07	0.01	0.01	0.08
Banyarwanda	0.19	0.34	0.01	0.07	0.16	0.02	0.05	0.01	0.01	0.14
Basoga	0.11	0.45	0.02	0.03	0.03	0.23	0.06	0.02	0.02	0.04
Batoro	0.25	0.25	0.01	0.06	0.06	0.02	0.24	0.04	0.01	0.05
Banyoro	0.21	0.35	0.01	0.07	0.05	0.06	0.14	0.06	0.01	0.04
Iteso	0.07	0.33	0.02	0.04	0.02	0.09	0.03	0.02	0.31	0.08
Bafumbira	0.17	0.17	0.01	0.06	0.10	0.04	0.06	0.02	0.02	0.34
Total	0.17	0.48	0.01	0.06	0.05	0.05	0.07	0.02	0.02	0.08

Source: Authors' calculations.

Notes: This table reports the likelihood that a row type will be classified by an arbitrary player as a column type. The gray shading indicates the likelihood that a player from a given group will be identified correctly. Individuals often are misidentified as members of other ethnic groups.

Table 3.2   Patterns of Ethnic Identifiability: Correct Guesses

	Banyankole	Baganda	Bagisu	Bakiga	Banyarwanda	Basoga	Batoro	Banyoro	Iteso	Bafumbira	Total
Banyankole	0.50	0.70	0.07	0.15	0.16	0.18	0.34	0.10	0.11	0.47	0.49
Baganda	0.39	0.70	0.16	0.20	0.17	0.19	0.23	0.03	0.20	0.27	0.46
Bagisu	0.38	0.71	0.14	0.19	0.09	0.24	0.14	0.05	0.56	0.23	0.47
Bakiga	0.28	0.67	0.04	0.38	0.18	0.21	0.16	0.03	0.31	0.37	0.46
Banyarwanda	0.56	0.58	0.24	0.31	0.24	0.19	0.36	0.00	0.17	0.33	0.45
Basoga	0.34	0.61	0.13	0.13	0.00	0.60	0.23	0.05	0.31	0.46	0.43
Batoro	0.46	0.70	0.11	0.19	0.16	0.37	0.23	0.20	0.35	0.36	0.50
Banyoro	0.30	0.62	0.11	0.33	0.17	0.21	0.29	0.33	0.31	0.32	0.45
Iteso	0.44	0.70	0.30	0.00	0.00	0.15	0.18	0.00	0.33	0.33	0.44
Bafumbira	0.39	0.64	0.13	0.28	0.22	0.24	0.33	0.13	0.27	0.55	0.47
Total	0.41	0.68	0.14	0.21	0.16	0.22	0.25	0.06	0.23	0.35	0.47

Source: Authors' calculations.

Notes: This table reports the probability that a row type will correctly classify a column type. Gray shading indicates the likelihood that a player from a given group will be identified correctly by a coethnic. Individuals are generally more likely to be identified correctly by coethnics than by non-coethnics.

How is one to evaluate a 68 percent rate of correct identification for the Baganda? Is it high or low? How high is it, for example, relative to the 48 percent rate of successful identification of the Banyankole? One way to answer the question is to ask how much visual information contributed to correct identification. The probability that a randomly selected individual in our sample self-identified as Baganda was 44 percent. Thus, if players were to make guesses based on what they knew about the distribution of self-identifications in our sample and simply guessed Baganda 44 percent of the time, then, conditional upon the person whose ethnic group membership they were being asked to ascertain actually being Baganda, they would have correctly guessed Baganda to be Baganda 44 percent of the time.[17] The additional information provided by the images improved the rate of successful categorization from this 44 percent baseline to 68 percent, or just over 50 percent. By contrast, a subject using only what he or she knew about the distribution of self-reported Banyankole in our sample might have correctly categorized Banyankole as Banyankole about 10 percent of the time. The fact that Banyankole actually were categorized correctly 40 percent of the time indicates that information increases the accuracy of guesses by a factor of four.

So far we have focused only on how groups varied in how easily they could be identified and on how well others could identify them, on average. But the variation *within* table 3.2 is perhaps more interesting. First, compare the numbers in the diagonal of the table (shaded gray) with those located off the diagonal. We can see immediately that individuals were more likely to be correctly identified by members of their own group than by those who were not coethnics. Reading down each column, the number on the diagonal is consistently one of the highest. For five groups, it is the highest; in two others, it is the second highest. Statistically speaking, this pattern is strong. For a member of the largest group, the Baganda, the probability of correctly identifying another group member was 70 percent, while the probability of correctly coding an out-group member was just 20 percent. For the Bafumbira, the probability dropped from 55 to 42 percent. For the Banyankole, it went down from 50 to 43 percent. For some groups, there was no difference, and a few groups experienced greater success in coding out-group members than in-group members. The *average* effect of coethnicity, however, was a forty-three-percentage-point increase in the probability that a given individual would correctly place his or her partner.[18] This effect derives in part from the fact that most people were likely to guess the Baganda correctly, and so Baganda subjects (of whom we had many in our sample) were more likely to be correct when guessing the group membership of coethnics. To take account of this, we can ask a related question: what is the effect of coethnicity on the probability that a given individual will be correctly identified? This effect, it turns out, is much weaker, though still statistically strong. The average treatment effect was six percentage points, an effect that is significant at the 99 percent level.[19] This finding that coethnics were significantly better at correctly placing each other is one that will prove important as we interpret our findings in subsequent chapters.

There is much to be learned as well from those cases in which members of one group seemed to do particularly well at identifying members of another. Consider the Bafumbira, who correctly identified other Bafumbira 55 percent of the time. But some other groups also did quite well identifying Bafumbira, most notably the Banyankole (a success rate of 47 percent). As we saw in table 3.1, the Banyankole are "close" to the Bafumbira in the sense that others often misidentify them as Bafumbira. It appears that not only do coethnics have an advantage in identifying members of their own groups, but also that members of groups that are often confused with one another are particularly good at sorting themselves into their correct categories.

As we noted earlier, any assessment of the degree of correct identification depends on the informational environment. As one might expect, people are much more successful in the identification exercise as they gain access to more information about the people whose group memberships they are trying to discern. Beyond the obvious impact of more information, it is natural to ask how different types of information affect the likelihood that individuals will code others correctly. Recall that our information levels are not strictly ordered. As shown in the top panel of figure 3.6, average levels of identification success generally moved monotonically across the five information levels. Overall identification success was higher under information level 3 than under information level 2, indicating that the use of a primary language carried more information than the use of Luganda, the local lingua franca. Identification success rates were similar at information levels 3 and 4, suggesting that providing one's name, but doing so in Luganda, had a similar impact to using one's primary language. Success rates were highest at information level 5. This indicates that the information contained in subjects' names and subjects' primary language were complementary rather than direct substitutes. In all, moving from the lowest information level (the still photograph) to the highest (the video in which the subject greeted the camera in his or her local langauge and provided his or her full name) led to a near doubling of success rates, from an average of about 0.29 to 0.59. However, there was important variation across groups in the impact of information. Figure 3.6 demonstrates that the key piece of information used to recognize a member of the Bafumbira group was primary language, which was revealed at levels 3 and 5. Names appear to have provided relatively little additional information to aid in classify-

Figure 3.6   The Impact of Information on Identification Success

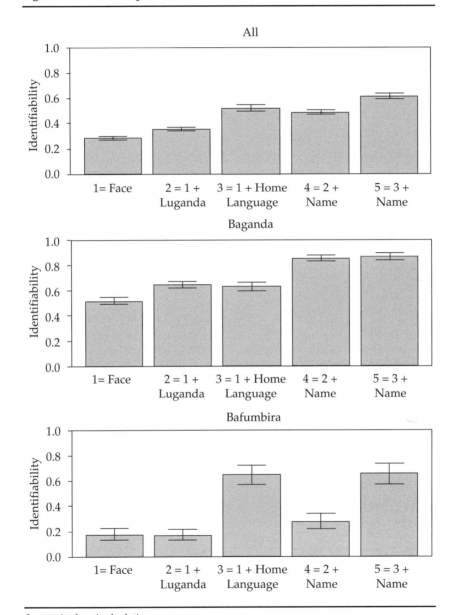

Source: Authors' calculations.
Notes: This graph shows average rates of successful identification at different information levels. The top panel corresponds to overall success rates, the middle to success rates for the Baganda, and the bottom to success rates for the Bafumbira. Average levels of identification success generally increase with additional levels of information, although the impact of information varies across groups.

**Figure 3.7   Variation in Individual Identifiability Across Groups, by
Ethnic Category with Which Player Self-Identifies**

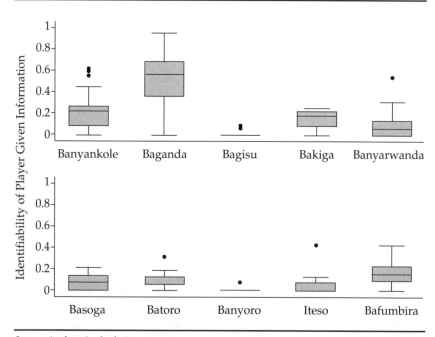

Source: Authors' calculations.
Notes: The box plots show the distribution of identifiability for players self-identifying as
members of ten major ethnic groups. Each distribution is represented by a shaded box of
different heights. The dashes represent the limits of the outliers; any dots beyond the
dashes are extreme outliers. The height of each box shows the inter-quartile range. The
line through the box corresponds to the median level of identifiability for the group. The
average identifiability of individuals within each ethnic group varies across groups in the
sample.

ing Bafumbira. For those viewing Baganda, the reverse was true: since
Luganda is the lingua franca in Kampala, all the gains in classification
success came from providing viewers with the subject's name.

Although we have focused on the degree to which different groups
are identifiable, identifiability can also be thought of as a property of individuals. Variation in identification success occurs not just across groups
or information levels, but also across individuals within groups. Some
individuals are highly identifiable as members of their group even
though, on average, members of their groups are poorly identified;
other individuals are correctly identified rarely even though, on average, their groups are highly identifiable. Figure 3.7 captures this variation in individual identifiability across the major ethnic groups in our
sample. Among the Baganda, for example, some individuals are per-

fectly identifiable while others are never correctly identifiable. For the Banyarwanda, the story is quite different. Although average identifiability for Banyarwanda is below 10 percent, at least one individual has an identifiability score of around 50 percent—significantly higher than the scores of others in the same group.

Group Boundary Errors in Classification

Why focus so much on differences across and within groups in patterns of identifiability? The fact that some people or groups can be easily slotted into their correct ethnic categories and others cannot is perhaps obvious (although no matter how obvious, the assumption of perfect identifiability has been embedded in much of the work on ethnic politics). Yet if we recognize these patterns of imperfect classification, and understand that they vary across groups, we must take seriously the fact that individuals are often confused about who is or who is not a coethnic. The errors we observe reveal information about the lines that individuals draw between groups—both between in-group members and out-group members and between different types of out-group members.

To examine these errors further, we consider two specific types in more detail. First, we consider the case in which someone codes another individual as a coethnic even though the other individual self-identifies as a member of a different ethnic group. We call such an error an *error of inclusion*. Conversely, an individual may mistakenly classify an in-group member as an out-group member. We refer to such an error as an *error of exclusion*.[20] The extent to which individuals are likely to make such errors may be thought of as an indicator of the degree to which they police group boundaries.

Table 3.3 reveals just how often errors of exclusion occur. Each cell records the likelihood that an individual of a row type will code someone of a column type as a coethnic. The entries in the diagonal cells are the same as in table 3.2, but the off-diagonal elements are different. If subjects identified the people whose images they were shown perfectly, this matrix would be the identity matrix: each cell on the diagonal would be one and all the off-diagonal cells would be zero. In some ways, the matrix is close to the identity matrix. The diagonal is "strong" in the sense that the number on the diagonal is the largest number in each row and in each column. This means two things: that a player from a given group is more likely to say that a coethnic is a coethnic than is a guesser from any other group, and that a guesser is most likely to say that someone is a coethnic when that person is indeed a coethnic.

In some ways, however, the matrix is quite unlike the identity matrix. The diagonal elements are often lower than one, sometimes substan-

Table 3.3   Patterns of In-Group Coding

	Banyankole	Baganda	Bagisu	Bakiga	Banyarwanda	Basoga	Batoro	Banyoro	Iteso	Bafumbira	Errors of Inclusion
Banyankole	0.50	0.10	0.19	0.44	0.14	0.10	0.23	0.19	0.08	0.14	0.13
Baganda	0.14	0.70	0.27	0.17	0.32	0.46	0.22	0.35	0.25	0.16	0.20
Bagisu	0.00	0.01	0.14	0.00	0.00	0.00	0.00	0.00	0.00	0.00	0.01
Bakiga	0.20	0.02	0.00	0.38	0.09	0.07	0.00	0.10	0.00	0.05	0.04
Banyarwanda	0.05	0.04	0.00	0.06	0.24	0.07	0.09	0.15	0.00	0.27	0.06
Basoga	0.02	0.05	0.25	0.00	0.00	0.60	0.03	0.00	0.08	0.08	0.05
Batoro	0.07	0.02	0.11	0.17	0.00	0.03	0.29	0.17	0.04	0.04	0.04
Banyoro	0.00	0.00	0.11	0.00	0.00	0.00	0.05	0.33	0.00	0.00	0.01
Iteso	0.00	0.02	0.10	0.00	0.05	0.00	0.00	0.07	0.33	0.04	0.02
Bafumbira	0.06	0.03	0.08	0.02	0.16	0.00	0.02	0.08	0.04	0.55	0.04

Source: Authors' calculations.
Notes: This table reports the likelihood that a row type will classify a column type as a coethnic. The final column reports the overall frequency with which people of a row type incorrectly classify out-group members as in-group members. Individuals often mistakenly code coethnics as out-group members and non-coethnics as in-group members. Gray shading indicates the likelihood that a player from a given group will be correctly identified by a coethnic.

tially so, because individuals frequently failed to recognize coethnics as coethnics. These errors of exclusion can be computed for each group as one minus the shaded value in the diagonal. The Baganda, for example, made this mistake 30 percent of the time; the Banyarwanda committed errors of exclusion 76 percent of the time. Across our sample, players incorrectly coded in-group members as out-group members about one-third of the time. Mistakes of this form, we find, were most common among smaller ethnic groups. Larger groups had higher prior beliefs about the probability of encountering members of their own group; for smaller groups, encountering a coethnic was a rare event. As a result, the possibility that someone was a coethnic was discounted, even if he was in fact a coethnic. The likelihood of making these errors also depends on the information available. Based only on the information contained in a still photograph, the overall likelihood of committing an error of exclusion is 75 percent. These errors drop to just 15 percent of viewings at the highest level of information.

The matrix also differs from the identity matrix in the structure of its off-diagonal elements. A positive number in an off-diagonal cell has a simple interpretation: it means that people are coding out-group members as in-group members. For example, Banyankole classified Bakiga as Banyankole about 44 percent of the time, only slightly less than their rate of classifying other Banyankole as Banyankole. Bakiga also tended to confuse Banyankole for Bakiga, but not to the same extent—they coded Banyankole as Bakiga 20 percent of the time. In Uganda, Bakiga and Banyankole are often considered related groups, and these patterns of misclassification are consistent with this fact. Banyarwanda coded Bafumbira as Banyarwanda slightly more often then they coded self-declared Banyarwanda as Banyarwanda. In effect, it appears that Banyarwanda did not tend to discriminate between Banyarwanda and Bafumbira when coding in-group members. Self-declared Bafumbira, however, were three times more likely to code Bafumbira as Bafumbira as they were to code Banyarwanda as Bafumbira. Again, these two groups are considered closely related and speak the same language, and the patterns of misclassifications we observe in our data seem to reflect this.

Other groups that are closely related also made such errors, although, as with the Banyarwanda and Bafumbira, there were often asymmetries. The Basoga, for example, rarely confused Baganda for Basoga, but the Baganda often classified Basoga as Baganda. Indeed, across the board, the Baganda were more likely to incorrectly classify non-Baganda as Baganda than people from other groups were to misclassify Baganda as members of their own communities. In contrast with errors of exclusion, the incidence of these errors of inclusion is relatively low (see the last column of table 3.3). Overall, they occurred just 11 percent of the time in our sample. Errors of inclusion tended to be most common among larger groups: the Baganda miscoded out-group members as coethnics approximately one in every five viewings. Among smaller groups, the incidence was much lower: Bafumbira or Banyarwanda, for example, made this mistake in only 5 percent of their viewings. More generally, it is clear that the nature of boundary errors is correlated with group size. Whereas errors of exclusion were more common among smaller groups, errors of inclusion were much more common among larger groups. Again, as we would expect, the incidence of these errors declined substantially with increases in information.

No matter the size of the group, however, subjects were more likely to misclassify an in-group member as an out-group member than they were to classify an out-group member as an in-group member. What differs is the extent to which this was the case across groups. The Baganda were 50 percent more likely to commit errors of exclusion than errors of inclusion. The Banyankole, however, were nearly four times as likely. The relative propensity to make one type of error rather than another was again closely related to group size: as one would expect of Bayesians, individuals from smaller groups were relatively more likely to commit errors of exclusion than errors of inclusion relative to larger groups.

To calculate the total frequency of these two types of errors, we must take into account the likelihood that each can actually occur. For example, although the Banyankole committed errors of exclusion 50 percent of the time when they encountered in-group members, they encountered coethnics only about 10 percent of the time. Thus, the overall likelihood that they would make an error of this form in a given encounter was only 5 percent. The Baganda, although they made such errors only 30 percent of the time when they encountered coethnics, actually encountered in-group members nearly 50 percent of the time. Their overall frequency of committing errors of exclusion was therefore approximately 13 percent —higher than that of the Banyankole.

The frequency of errors of exclusion and errors of inclusion for each group appears in figure 3.8, which shows both the probability of making each type of error when the opportunity arises and the total frequency. Two patterns stand out. The first is that, for most groups, although errors of exclusion were more likely than errors of inclusion when the opportunity occurred, the total frequency of both types of errors was approximately the same. Typically, for any miscoding of an in-group member as an out-group member, there was another coding of an out-group member as an in-group member. This suggests that individuals, in general, did not have an inclusionist or exclusionist bias. The most important exception to this was among the Banyankole, who committed errors of inclusion more frequently than errors of exclusion. The second notable feature is that the magnitude of the errors increased with the

Figure 3.8   Relative Frequency of Errors

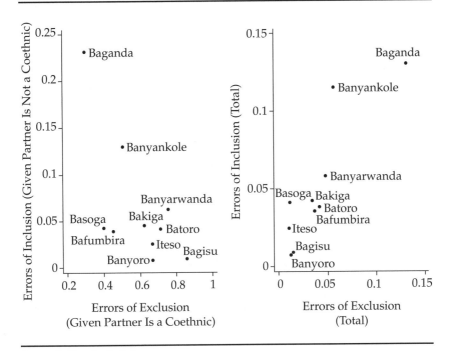

Source: Authors' calculations.
Notes: This graph plots the frequency of errors of inclusion against the frequency of errors of exclusion. Errors of exclusion are more likely than errors of inclusion (when the opportunity occurs), but the frequency of the two types of errors is about the same overall, suggesting that individuals do not have an inclusionist or exclusionist bias.

size of the group. Larger groups were generally less accurate in their in-group and out-group classifications; small groups, though they also made mistakes, did so with a lower frequency.[21]

Group Distinctness

We focus very carefully on how our subjects miscoded one another because the errors they made form the basis for an empirical assessment of the distinctness of groups. In particular, for a given subjective demography, measures of group distinctness reveal the extent to which members of particular groups, on average, are often (or never) confused for one another. We define the distinctness of two groups, groups A and B, for a given individual as the (expected) probability that the individual will code an individual from group A as a member of group A, given that he classifies that individual as a member of A or B, plus the (expected probability) that he will code an individual from group *B* as a member of group *B*, given that he classifies that individual as a member of *A* or *B*, minus one.[22]

The measure ranges from minus-one to plus-one. If members of groups *A* and *B* are never confused with one another, then our measure of distinctness equals one. If guesses are independent of the true identity of the subjects—for example, if group classifications are decided by a coin toss—then our measure of distinctness equals zero. Values between zero and minus-one may arise if players do worse than chance. The score is undefined if players always classify members of *A* or *B* as members of groups other than *A* or *B*. Note that two groups may not be highly distinct, yet individuals from group *A* may still find particular individuals from *B* highly identifiable.[23]

Table 3.4 shows these distinctness measures for each pair of groups in our sample (for example, Banyankole-Baganda, Banyankole-Bagisu, and so on). Strikingly, we find that all the cell entries in table 3.4 are positive: the ability of our population on average to distinguish any two groups is better than chance. The lowest scores are for pairs of groups that share regional connections. The Bakiga and the Banyankole are consistently confused for each other (even by their own members). So too are the Banyankole and the Banyarwanda, the Banyarwanda and the Bafumbira, and the Batoro and Banyoro. These groups—all western—have distinctness scores below 0.2. The score of 0.14 for the Banyankole-Bakiga pairing corresponds to a situation where if choosing between the two, an individual would code a Munyankole as a Mukiga and vice versa 57 percent of time—little better than chance. These measures of distinctness clearly pass a test of face-validity; they quantify, from the aggregation of binary actions, relationships among groups that correspond to historical and geographic patterns. Forming the exception to this rule are the three main eastern groups, the Bagisu, the Basoga, and the Iteso, which are largely distinct from all other groups and from one another. In each case, they are most likely to be confused with the dominant group, the Baganda, but otherwise almost always have distinctness scores above 0.5.

Alternative Objective and Subjective Demographies

We are now in a position to take one last step toward a purely relativist conception of identity. The errors in classification that we have discovered are, of course, only errors with respect to a particular set of benchmark categories—in this case, the self-identification by individuals as members of groups defined by national census categories. From a subjective perspective, they may simply reflect the fact that at least some of

Table 3.4   Group Distinctness

	Banyankole	Baganda	Bagisu	Bakiga	Banyarwanda	Basoga	Batoro	Banyoro	Iteso	Bafumbira
Banyankole		0.60	0.53	**0.14**	**0.36**	0.62	**0.32**	**0.20**	0.79	0.47
Baganda	0.60		**0.30**	0.48	**0.28**	**0.27**	0.44	**0.13**	0.47	0.62
Bagisu	0.53	**0.30**		0.77	0.80	0.51	0.69	0.79	0.77	0.69
Bakiga	**0.14**	0.48	0.77		0.56	0.75	0.56	0.44	0.83	0.58
Banyarwanda	**0.36**	**0.28**	0.80	0.56		0.79	0.55	0.48	0.90	**0.31**
Basoga	0.62	**0.27**	0.51	0.75	0.79		0.69	0.44	0.70	0.76
Batoro	**0.32**	0.44	0.69	0.56	0.55	0.69		**0.16**	0.86	0.66
Banyoro	**0.20**	**0.13**	0.79	0.44	0.48	0.44	**0.16**		0.80	0.59
Iteso	0.79	0.47	0.77	0.83	0.90	0.70	0.86	0.80		0.75
Bafumbira	0.47	0.62	0.69	0.58	**0.31**	0.76	0.66	0.59	0.75	

Source: Authors' calculations.
Notes: Entries in the table show the empirical distinctness of row and column types based on the likelihood that a random member of the sample mistakenly classifies a column type as a row type and a row type as a column type. A score of one indicates that a row type is never confused for a column type. A score of zero indicates that classification is no better than chance. Although individual guesses are better than chance, some groups are more frequently confused with one another (indicated in bold). These indistinct boundaries between groups tend to correspond with regional divisions.

the formal divisions defined in the census lack meaning for our subjects. We have seen, for example, that players routinely confuse Bafumbira and Banyarwanda. Even the Bafumbira and Banyarwanda make these "errors" with great frequency. One reason for this might be that, although individuals who self-identify as a member of one or the other of these groups consider the differences between them to be important, their identification skills do not match their cognitive categorizations. Another possibility is that errors reflect the use of a benchmark set of categories that poorly reflect the categorizations that individuals in our study area view as salient. Perhaps the interchangeable coding of people as Bakiga or Banyankole simply reflects the fact that both are "westerners" and that this shared regional identity is seen as more salient than the distinction that the national statistics office insists on making between them.

To the extent that this is the case, then it is possible that by using census categories, we are coding identification success using a taxonomy that poorly reflects the identities that are salient in the communities in which we are working. Indeed, in our earlier discussion of the history of Uganda's ethnic cleavages, we slipped easily into the language of regional divisions, emphasizing the political conflicts pitting northern ethnic groups against those in the center and west. Perhaps regional identities matter more than ethnic identities when individuals condition their behavior on information about others in everyday social interactions. The findings in table 3.4 suggest that, if this is the case, a more salient taxonomy might focus on regional affiliation or perhaps something located between the fine-grained census ethnicity categories and broader regional affiliations—something that combines groups that our subjects treated as part of the same broader grouping. For this reason, in all of our subsequent analyses of the impact of coethnicity, we consider how players conditioned their actions not only on the ethnic group memberships of their partners (as defined by the census categories) but also on shared regional affiliation. Table 3.5 shows the extent to which measures of identifiability produced on the basis of region are more permissive: successful identification is easier and miscodings less common. Correct identification rises to 62 percent in our sample from 42 percent, and successful in-group identifications rise to 37 percent from 23 percent. If regional identities are politically salient (and we believe they are, at least at the national level), *and* if individuals are more successful at correctly locating their partners in a set of regional categories, then the use of regional identities represents an important additional test of the ways in which coethnicity conditions behavior in social interactions.

Table 3.5   Identifiability and In-Group Coding by Region

	Correct Identifications					In-Group Identifications				
	Center	East	North	West	Total	Center	East	North	West	Total
Center	0.70	0.30	0.44	0.72	0.65	0.70	0.32	0.14	0.21	0.43
East	0.69	0.38	0.48	0.63	0.62	0.08	0.38	0.25	0.07	0.12
North	0.58	0.22	0.57	0.56	0.53	0.04	0.11	0.57	0.05	0.08
West	0.66	0.27	0.53	0.70	0.62	0.23	0.26	0.09	0.70	0.40
Total	0.68	0.29	0.49	0.69	0.63	0.42	0.29	0.16	0.37	0.37

Source: Authors' calculations.
Notes: The left panel ("correct identifications") reports the probability that a row type will classify a column type into his or her correct region. The right panel ("in-group identification") reports the likelihood that a row type will code a column type as an in-group member. Patterns of correct identification are much higher when individuals are identified in terms of their regional affiliations.

Conclusion: Implications for the Study of Ethnic Politics

This chapter has described the ethnic demography of Uganda, Kampala, Mulago-Kyebando, and our sample using the formal categorization of ethnic groups employed in the national census of Uganda. These measures highlight the diversity of ethnic groups in our study area; further, they allow us to document the same empirical relationship linking high levels of diversity to poor public goods provision found elsewhere in the world. But since we are interested in uncovering the micro-foundations of this relationship, we have not been willing to assume that the existence of a formal set of categories implies that individuals are easily able to sort one another into those categories. Such questions of ethnic identification, we argue, are fundamentally empirical questions.

Taking seriously the notion that ethnic identifiability may be imperfect and that the errors people make may have an underlying structure, we designed techniques to produce "subjective" demographies for each of our subjects. For each individual in our sample, we collected measures of how he or she perceives the ethnic group memberships of others and how others in turn perceive his or her's. We showed that the divergence between the official ("benchmark") demography and the subjective demographies is striking. Although aggregate outcomes may appear similar, we showed that individuals make errors with great frequency. People consistently confuse in-group members for out-group members, and out-group members for in-group members. Some individuals are particularly likely to be identified correctly by others; others interact with a much higher degree of ethnic anonymity.

We found a number of underlying patterns that help to account for the errors that individuals commit. First, individuals are in general more likely to be correctly identified by coethnics than by non-coethnics. Coethnics identify their own members relatively well, but when engaging with non-coethnics, they are less able to correctly identify that person within the benchmark classificatory scheme. Second, there is substantial variation across groups in the extent to which group members make errors. Smaller groups are less likely to confuse out-group members for in-group members, or in-group members for out-group members. Larger groups, the Baganda in particular, commit these errors with great regularity. In approximately 30 percent of their encounters, they make one of these types of errors. Third, when one individual misidentifies an in-group member, we found that we could estimate *how* he misidentifies him. Misidentifications are confined to a relatively limited set of categories; in particular, when errors are made, they tend to be made within and not across a set of broader regional categories.

Our analysis of subjective demographies in Mulago-Kyebando challenges the relevance of census categories for subjects in our sample. In particular, it seems inappropriate to think of each of the ethnic groups represented as being, like billiard balls, "uniformly equally distinct." Given the set of benchmark categories in the census, some groups are clearly much "closer" to each other in terms of identification behavior than others. Ethnic groups from the same region are especially likely to be confused with each other. The "closeness" we describe here, however, is simply a statement about perception. The proximity of groups in perceptual space does not necessarily imply similarities in behavior or in treatment. Given the proximity we have identified here, we opt to examine patterns of experimental play using both "ethnic" and "regional" benchmark demographies. Whether regional categorizations provide greater leverage in explaining actual behavior is a question that we turn to in the next chapter.

As we turn to the experimental games, we build on what we have learned here about identifiability in one additional way. Measuring how individuals condition their behavior on the identities of others is a task complicated by patterns of misidentification. In assessing the relative power of the different mechanisms hypothesized to account for the impact of diversity, our attention turns to how individuals condition their play on sharing a group membership (either ethnic or regional) with a partner. Standard approaches code coethnic or co-regional pairings based on a match between individuals' self-identification as members of benchmark categories. Recognizing that individuals often do not know the identities of their partners, we code shared identities in a supplementary way as well. Using information from the identification exercise (contained in table 3.3), we explore how behavior is shaped by the likelihood that a subject codes his or her partner as an in-group member—a measure that reflects the imperfect nature of these classifications.

Chapter 4

Testing the Mechanisms

ACROSS Mulago-Kyebando, local council chairs bemoan the lack of cooperation from members of the community when they launch initiatives to fight crime, collect garbage, and maintain drainage channels. Their frustration is shared by people living in other ethnically diverse communities around the world. The problems these communities face are clear: crumbling infrastructure in Pakistan, low levels of school funding in Kenya, poor maintenance of irrigation channels in India, and little support for community groups, health centers, and agricultural cooperatives in Indonesia. Everyone would be better off if the community could organize itself to address these problems. Yet, in Mulago-Kyebando, as in other heterogeneous environments, community members are often unable to come together to improve their welfare.

This book began with the premise that ethnic diversity provides part of the explanation for these failures. But our goal is more ambitious: we seek to understand *why* diversity impedes collective action. This requires confronting a difficult inferential problem. Simply observing that heterogeneous villages are unable to maintain functioning water wells tells us little about why this is the case. It might be that villagers care only about the welfare of people from their own ethnic group, or that groups disagree about the nature of the public goods that should be provided. It could also be that villagers from different ethnic groups have difficulty working together, or that, if someone from a particular group elects not to participate, members of other groups have no means to punish him for not contributing. Perhaps the collective action failure can be traced to the absence of a norm that makes not cooperating unthinkable. Or perhaps such norms exist but only for cooperation among members of the same group, in which case the absence of a general cooperative norm is the culprit. Distinguishing between these various stories—examples of what we call preference, technology, and strategy selection mechanisms—is the central aim of our research and the process we begin in this chapter.

To resolve this puzzle of collective action failure, we introduced an empirical strategy rooted in the methodology of experimental economics. Experiments are powerful because they enable us to observe real people making real choices in an environment where we can control the context in which they make their decisions. They are useful for a project concerned with distinguishing otherwise observationally equivalent stories because they allow us to examine, evaluate the strength of, and even rule out the operation of different mechanisms. This chapter begins with a description of the experimental design we employed. We then describe the games themselves, each designed to test a specific mechanism drawn from the three families of mechanisms first introduced in chapter 1. Our results demonstrate that shared ethnic group membership among players mattered quite a lot for some mechanisms but not for others—evidence that helps us understand why coethnicity facilitates cooperation and why diversity, more generally, impedes collective action.

The Experimental Treatment: Information About Coethnicity

Our empirical strategy relied on a central experimental manipulation: we had our subjects play multiple rounds of multiple games, but in each case we randomly determined whether, in any given round of a game, they were playing with a coethnic or a non-coethnic partner.[1] We then compared patterns of behavior not just across pairings but also across games. For this approach, it was critical to devise a means for subjects to be able to form judgments (if they chose to) regarding the ethnicity of other players in the game without at the same time cueing them to our interest in how ethnicity shapes behavior. In three of the games that we describe here, subjects interacted face to face with one another, so inferences about other players' ethnic backgrounds—if made at all—could be made based on appearance, accent, and other visible cues. The other games were played using a computer interface. Recall from chapter 3 that, for each subject, we recorded a series of five digital images, including a still photograph and brief video greetings. In the computer-based games, players could make inferences about the ethnic backgrounds of the other players in each round of each game through the information they gleaned from the pictures and/or videos that were made available to them in what we call the Public Information Box (PIB).[2]

The key attribute of the PIB is that, as its name suggests, the information it provides about the players in the game is provided publicly. Before each round of each game, all the players in the round were shown the same PIB, which contained images of all of the players in that round,

Figure 4.1   Public Information Box with Non-Anonymous Offerer

Source: Authors' images.
Notes: Player 2, the offerer, is seen by all players. The images used in this figure are for illustration purposes only and are not the images of actual subjects.

including themselves, with the images of the players ordered in the same way. Underneath the PIB, each player saw a note telling them which player number they were for that round (for example, "In this round you are player 2"). Figures 4.1 and 4.2 provide sample screen shots of the PIB.

The PIB played three roles in the computer-based experiments. First, it made the interaction more realistic by increasing the credibility of the existence of the other players. Second, it provided the conditions needed for common knowledge about the information provided to all players in the game: each player was provided with information not just about who the other players were, but also about what the other players knew about him or her; each player was also informed that the other players knew what he or she knew about them, and vice versa. Third, the design of the PIB allowed us to manipulate the anonymity of the players in the game. Compare, for example, figures 4.1 and 4.2. In figure 4.1, the middle player's picture is shown to the other players. He will therefore play the game knowing that the other players can see who he is. But in figure 4.2, the middle player's picture is not shown. He still has information about the other players, but he knows that they have no information about him. He will therefore play the game knowing that he is doing so anonymously. As we will show, exploiting this manipulation turns out to be extremely valuable for distinguishing behavior motivated by preferences from behavior motivated by strategy.

Although subjects were shown images of (or interacted face to face with) the other players in the game, the games were designed to simu-

Figure 4.2   Public Information Box with Anonymous Offerer

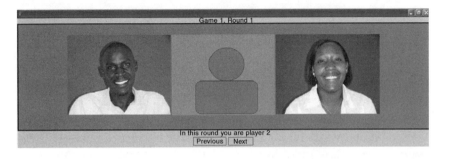

Source: Authors' images.
Notes: Player 2, the offerer, is anonymous. The images used in this figure are for illustration purposes only and are not the images of actual subjects.

late interactions between strangers. Therefore, after viewing the PIB, subjects were asked to report if they knew either of the other players in the round personally. On average, about 6 percent of all rounds involved partners who knew each other. The results we report are robust to the exclusion of such rounds.

Each subject played all of the games multiple times but never played more than once with the same player. Furthermore, although players played multiple times (with different partners), they were not given feedback about play until they had completed all games. This limited learning but also prevented players from using repeated interaction to establish coordination procedures, norms, or different forms of other-regarding preferences within the context of the game.[3]

Note that the design of the games imposed no structure based on our beliefs about what the ethnic identities of players "really were." Beyond the selection of our site area (which entailed a deliberate focus on ethnically heterogeneous communities), our sampling of subjects at the LC1 level was undertaken randomly (with some adjustments, as described in chapter 3) and, in all cases, independently of how subjects identified themselves ethnically. The pairings for the games also were constructed randomly and without reference to the ethnic identities of players.[4]

Coding Coethnicity

Although ethnic information was not used in the structuring of the games, information about the coethnicity of each pairing is central to our analysis. As we discussed in chapter 3, coding in-group members is a much more difficult task than it at first appears. Following standard practice in the literature, and for comparison purposes, we begin with the assumption that subjects were able to distinguish coethnics from non-coethnics perfectly. We therefore first present results with co-ethnicity defined in terms of benchmark demographies. In these analyses, we code an interaction as a coethnic pairing if both players identified themselves as members of the same ethnic group in our pregame questionnaire.

But we know from our investigation of identifiability in Mulago-Kyebando that this assumption does not always hold: subjects often miscoded the identities of others in systematic and predictable ways. Using data from the identification exercise discussed in chapter 3, we generated a second indicator of coethnicity based on the likelihood that a player from a given group would code a player from another group (in each case defined in terms of the benchmark identities) as an in-group member.[5] While the benchmark measure is discrete, this subjective measure of perceived coethnicity is continuous (between zero and one). This allowed us to assess more precisely how behavior in games responded to changes in the likelihood that a given individual would code his or her partner as an in-group member.

In keeping with our discussion in chapter 3, we also explore how regional identities shape play in the experimental games. Our finding in that chapter that patterns of misplacement in the identification game corresponded closely with the regional origins of different ethnic groups suggests that the census categories used to classify ethnic groups may not have been salient (in terms of how people perceived the identities of others) for individuals in Mulago-Kyebando. Groups from the west were often confused with one another; the same went for groups from the east. Moreover, we suggested that regional divisions are politically salient in Uganda—political conflict has often been structured along regional lines. For these reasons, rather than assuming that we, the researchers, knew what the salient lines of ethnic cleavage were for our subjects, we presented two different "cuts" at ethnic division: one where we coded coethnic pairings as those between members of the same "tribe" (as described earlier), and a second where coethnicity was defined in terms of region of origin (that is, central, eastern, northern, or western Uganda). We also examined these pairings using both benchmark and subjective measures of shared identity.

Play Among Different Types

Before turning to the games, one final issue must be addressed. We could manipulate many of the basic elements of the games that our subjects played, including the set of players in each round of each game, the strategies available to each player, and the material rewards associated with each strategy profile. There was one part of the game, however, that we could not control: the preferences of players over outcomes. That was beyond our reach.

Neoclassical economics assumes that human behavior is driven purely by self-interest. Behavioral economics challenges this view by demonstrating that individuals are often motivated by other-regardingness, reciprocity, and norms of fairness and inequality aversion. Recent research in the experimental field demonstrates that much of the variation we observe in individual behavior in laboratory games cannot be explained with reference to a purely self-interested model of behavior. The behavior of some individuals more closely approximates the rational, self-interested model, while other individuals do not appear to maximize their material gains: they give away money in anonymous settings, prefer to accept nothing rather than accept low offers of money made to them by others, and respond to cooperative overtures in public goods games even when they cannot be sanctioned and would benefit materially from defection. In Fehr and Schmidt (1999), bargainers are either neutral or rational; in Bolton and Ockenfels (2000), individuals are either egoists or relativists; in Murnighan, Oesch, and Pillutla (2001), individuals are classified as "rational dictators," "equals," or "reluctant dictators"; while in Bowles and Gintis (2004b), players are "selfish," "reciprocators," or "cooperators." Recognizing the existence of these different types has important implications for empirical and theoretical work. If players of different types respond in different ways to a given treatment, then an aggregation problem may arise. Average behavior across types may mask a systematic feature of the play taking place within them.

To avoid this pitfall, we distinguished in our analyses between two types of players: "egoists" (whose behavior was consistent with preferences in keeping with the neoclassical model) and "non-egoists" (who exhibited higher levels of general altruism).[6] To classify players into one of these two categories, we used their play in a version of the Dictator game (described in more detail later in the chapter). In this game, one player (the "offerer") is provided with two 500-Ugandan-shilling coins and given the opportunity to decide how much she wishes to keep for herself and how much she wishes to give to each of two other players. The only constraint is that no player, including the offerer, can be allocated more than one coin. We call this version of the Dictator game the Discrimination game, because offerers are forced to choose which of the two other players should benefit—providing that, as expected, they elect to keep a coin for themselves. Of course, a subject could choose to reward both of the other players and keep nothing for herself.

We used information about how individuals played the Discrimination game to identify different types of players in our sample. If a subject always kept at least one of the two coins for herself across all rounds of the Discrimination game, we coded this person as an egoist.[7] Egoists always took the maximal permissible amount for themselves; they preferred to discriminate between partners rather than forgo a benefit for themselves. Otherwise, the subject was coded as a non-egoist. While dividing the population into just two types is obviously a simplification (we do not claim that the world is made up of only two types of people), the binary structure allows for a particularly crisp examination of patterns in the data. This coding rule yielded 124 egoists in our sample (40 percent) and 182 non-egoists (60 percent).[8] On average, non-egoists chose not to discriminate (that is, they chose to give away both coins) in 41 percent of their games. Only eighteen subjects always gave both coins away, accounting for only 20 percent of the total games played without discrimination. Most other non-egoists varied their strategies, sometimes giving away both coins, sometimes keeping one. In our subsequent analyses of the games, we explore how egoists and non-egoists responded differently to the introduction of coethnic partners. These distinctions are relevant for games designed to capture other-regarding preferences and reciprocity, where differences in the degree of self-interest among players are likely to shape behavioral outcomes.

Assessing Preferences Mechanisms

Other-Regarding Preferences: The Dictator Game with an Anonymous Offerer

We begin with one of the simplest explanations linking coethnicity to cooperation. It is found prominently in journalistic accounts of ethnic politics: individuals behave differently with in-group (or out-group) members because they care more (or less) about them. In social science research, this mechanism has its origins in the work of social psychologists. The field of "social identity theory" has established that patterns of intergroup behavior reflect the fact that individuals often assign a positive utility to the welfare of in-group members and a negative utility to that of out-group members. A series of famous "minimal group" experiments have demonstrated that such in-group bias exists when group membership is arbitrarily determined (Tajfel et al. 1971).[9] This tells us a lot about how easily group identification may form in some settings, but it says little about which types of group identification will be more or less important in different settings. If, in practice, other-regarding preferences are stronger within groups than across group lines—or indeed, if individuals actually feel better when people from other groups do badly, that is, they have a "taste for discrimination" (Becker 1957)—then this may provide the answer to our puzzle: having multiple ethnic groups in a community may lower the willingness of individuals to contribute to collective action and lead to lower levels of public goods provision simply because individuals do not sufficiently internalize the benefits to other individuals of their actions (Alesina and LaFerrara 2005).

To measure other-regarding preferences of this form, we had subjects play a version of the standard Dictator game in which the offerer was anonymous and the receivers' identities were known (as in figure 4.2).[10] The Dictator game is perhaps the most commonly used tool of experimental economics; in its fully anonymous version, it represents a measure of baseline altruism (Kahneman, Knetsch, and Thaler 1986; for a review of Dictator game results, see Camerer 2003).[11] We build on experiments that manipulate the information available to offerers (Bohnet and Frey 1999), enabling us to measure how altruism is conditioned by the characteristics of the receiver. In the game we had our subjects play, any observed difference in patterns of play between situations where the offerer and receiver were coethnics and where they were from different ethnic groups was plausibly a reflection of differential levels of altruism vis-à-vis in-group and out-group members (Fershtman and Gneezy 2001).

Each round began with subjects (who in this game played only the role of offerer) being shown a PIB containing pictures and/or videos of themselves and two other randomly selected players (the receivers). Subjects were then given ten 100-Ugandan-shilling coins (about sixty cents, approximately equal to the per capita daily income in Uganda) and asked to divide it between themselves and the two other players in any way they pleased. They were told to put the amount they decided to keep directly into their pockets and to put the amount they wanted to allocate to the other players into envelopes, which were then deposited in ballot boxes located directly below the pictures in the PIB of the players in question. Subjects were told that the envelopes would be delivered to their intended recipients at a later date, and in fact they were (unopened!).[12] An enumerator manipulated the computer to show the PIB for the given round and handed the subject the money, but then stepped away and waited behind a screen while the subject completed his or her allocation. When the subject was finished making the allocation, he or she signaled to the enumerator, who returned from behind the screen and set up play for the next round.[13] In a second version of the game (described earlier), subjects were given two 500-Ugandan-shilling coins. This time they were instructed that no player (including the subject himself or herself) could be awarded both of the coins. The 500-Ugandan-shilling-denomination game therefore forced subjects to discriminate (although they were free to discriminate against themselves and to treat their two partners equally).

As with most other games described in this book, the assignment of players into trios was random. Consequently, the probability that any given individual would encounter a coethnic was approximately equal to the relative size of his or her group in our sample.[14] Each subject played multiple rounds (an average of 2.7) of each of the 100-Ugandan-shilling- and 500-Ugandan-shilling-denomination games. In all, we have data from 801 rounds (and 1,602 individual choices) in the 100-Ugandan-shilling-denomination games and from 782 rounds (1,564 individual choices) in the 500-Ugandan-shilling-denomination game.

In the 100-Ugandan-shilling-denomination game, subjects exhibited a substantial degree of other-regardingness. The modal strategy, employed in 25 percent of the rounds, was to retain 400 Ugandan shillings and to allocate 300 Ugandan shillings to each of the other players. The next most common strategy was to keep 600 Ugandan shillings and to allocate 200 Ugandan shillings to each of the other players (21 percent of rounds). In the vast majority of allocations, subjects appeared to adhere to a norm that the two receivers should be treated equally. On average, subjects retained 540 shillings and allocated 230 shillings to each of the other players.

Because the 500-Ugandan-shilling-denomination game forced subjects to discriminate, it produced a clear measure, first, of whether individuals discriminated in favor of themselves (enabling us to generate our measure of egoism from this game), and second, of whether they favored players from one group over players from another. The downside is that, since this game involves only binary choices, it cannot provide a sensitive measure of the *degree* to which players favored other players based on their in-group or out-group status. The modal strategy in this game (played in 73 percent of rounds) was to keep one 500-Ugandan-shilling coin and allocate the other to another player. Nonetheless, in 23 percent of the rounds, subjects allocated both coins to other players, and in one round a subject, contrary to rules, gave both coins to one of the other players. These offers can be compared with a baseline strategy of random allocation under which subjects would keep one coin two-thirds of the time.[15]

We now turn to the question of whether subjects displayed different degrees of other-regardingness toward coethnics and non-coethnics. Our first finding is that, although we observed high levels of other-regardingness in the 100-Ugandan-shilling-denomination game, there is no evidence that it was directed more at in-group members than at out-group members. Figure 4.3 shows the average effect of coethnicity on offers under four different definitions of shared group membership (benchmark versus subjective coethnicity, with coethnicity defined, for each, over both ethnic groups and region), for both the egoist and the non-egoist subgroups.[16] For each specification, the magnitude of the av-

Figure 4.3   Effect of Coethnicity on Average Offers in the 100-Ugandan-Shilling Dictator Game with an Anonymous Offerer

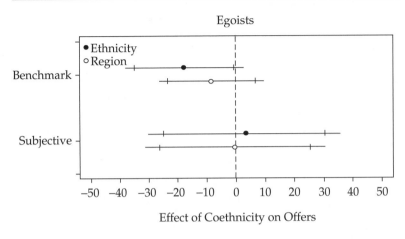

Egoists

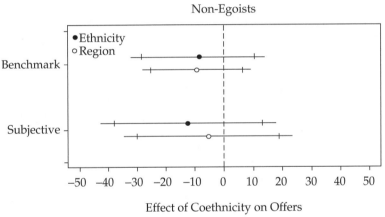

Non-Egoists

Source: Authors' calculations.
Notes: The figure reports the estimated effects of coethnicity on average offers in games where the offerer is anonymous, broken down by player type. Horizontal lines and ticks show 95 percent and 90 percent confidence intervals, respectively. Players exhibit no tendency to favor coethnics when playing anonymously.

erage effect is represented by the placement of the corresponding point; uncertainty about these estimates is represented by horizontal lines and ticks. The horizontal lines show the 95 percent confidence interval for these estimates, and the ticks indicate the 90 percent confidence intervals. Whether these are contained to one or the other side of the zero effect vertical line is an indication of whether the estimated effect is significantly different from zero at the corresponding level.[17]

For the non-egoists, we find that, in all four specifications, the difference in offers to coethnics and non-coethnics is negative on average; moreover, in none of these cases can the effect be distinguished from zero (that is, in each case the horizontal lines cross the zero mark). Egoists also gave less to coethnics (in three of four specifications).[18] None of these effects among egoists, however, is significant at the 95 percent level, although the impact of benchmark coethnicity is significant at the 90 percent level. We conclude that there is no evidence that subjects in this context exhibited any "taste" for discrimination toward in-group members.

It is possible that the (non-) finding with respect to ethnic discrimination might be due to the high degree of general inequality aversion among our subjects and the difficulty, given such inequality aversion, of detecting differential altruism in the 100-Ugandan-shilling game. Because the 500-Ugandan-shilling games rendered equitable distributions more costly, it is likely to have been more sensitive to even slight preferences for the welfare of in-group members over out-group members.

We restrict our analysis of the 500-Ugandan-shilling-denomination game to rounds in which a player was playing (or believed he or she was playing) with one coethnic partner and one non-coethnic partner and in which he or she also elected to discriminate.[19] In effect, we condition upon egoism and ask: when facing a coethnic and a non-coethnic, is a player more likely to favor the coethnic? In figure 4.4, we show the marginal effect of coethnicity on the likelihood that players would discriminate in favor of in-group members. We see in all cases that the estimated effect is close to zero and that the horizontal bars cross the zero line. As in our analysis of the 100-Ugandan-shilling-denomination game, we find no evidence of a coethnic effect. Even when players elected to discriminate and had to choose between a coethnic and a non-coethnic, they exhibited no propensity to act along ethnic lines.

Preferences in Common

A second preference-based explanation emphasizes that members of a given ethnic group have correlated preferences over outcomes. This argument has been offered most commonly as an explanation for lower levels of public goods provision in racially fragmented American cities. Examining outcomes as diverse as the composition of public budgets (Alesina, Baqir, and Easterly 1999), levels of spending on education (Goldin and Katz 1999), and the implementation of redistributive policies (Alesina and LaFerrara 2005), scholars have suggested that ethnic heterogeneity implies a "diversity of tastes"—which, by creating disagreement about which goods should be provided or where they should

Figure 4.4   **Effect of Coethnicity on the Probability of Discrimination in the 500-Ugandan-Shilling Dictator Game with an Anonymous Offerer**

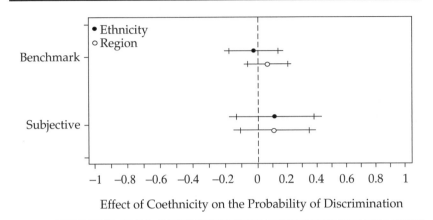

Effect of Coethnicity on the Probability of Discrimination

Source: Authors' calculations.
Notes: The figure reports the estimated effects of coethnicity on the probability of discrimination in games where the offerer is anonymous. Horizontal lines and ticks show 95 percent and 90 percent confidence intervals, respectively. Players who discriminate in allocating benefits exhibit no tendency to favor coethnics when playing anonymously.

be located, leads to the underprovision of public goods. Applied to the African context, scholars have emphasized how the geographic segregation of ethnic groups induces conflict over the location of public investments (Bates 1973) and how the diversity of languages undermines the ability of heterogeneous communities to generate contributions for public schools, which ultimately are forced to select a principal language of instruction—thereby lowering the value of education for members of the community who speak another language (Miguel 1999). Surprisingly, in spite of how common this explanation is, we do not know of a single empirical test of this mechanism. The argument is certainly plausible, but is it right?

To probe the plausibility of this explanation, we used simple survey techniques with our random sample of community members.[20] We examined two types of questions. First, to what types of public goods did individuals of different groups attach the highest priority? Second, how did they believe these goods should be provided? For example, should private or public means be used? Asking these questions allowed us to examine whether there was in fact a diversity of preferences over public goods among residents of Mulago-Kyebando, and if so, whether these varying preferences were structured along ethnic lines.

When asked to describe their top priority in terms of public goods provision, individuals from our sample exhibited considerable variation in their responses. For example, 21 percent claimed that drainage was the biggest issue, 35 percent said security, and 43 percent highlighted garbage. However, although there was considerable variation in preferences, there was little or no variation across ethnic groups in the priority accorded to these three outcomes. Indeed, six of the ten largest ethnic groups ranked these three outcomes in the same order as the population as a whole. There was somewhat less variation in the responses to the attitudinal questions. We found overwhelming support across ethnic groups for a fee-for-service program to collect garbage. At the same time, members of most ethnic groups expressed a willingness to contribute time or money to support community efforts to provide security and channel maintenance if the alternative was worse public goods provision. In each case, only between 8 and 16 percent of respondents took the opposite position. Again, these differences, though small, were not structured along ethnic lines. We identified variation in responses within all groups, and among the seven largest ethnic groups there were always individuals on both sides of the issue. Although variation in attitudes existed, there seemed to be little evidence of "ethnic preferences."[21]

After also testing more systematically for group-specific differences in preferences (see figures 4.5 and 4.6), using ordinary least squares (OLS) regression with dummy variables for each of the major ethnic groups in our sample, we find little evidence that ethnic group differences were associated with differences in either preferences for particular public goods or opinions about how they should be provided.[22] Although the results point to some small differences in opinion, only four (of fifty-four) ethnic group pairs provided responses that differed at statistically significant levels. Table AB.3 in the appendix also reports a measure of the amount of variation explained by these ethnic group dummies, the adjusted R-squared, which takes a value close to one if the variables explain most of the variation and a value of zero or possibly even a negative number if the variables explain no variation. By this measure, we find that ethnic group variables account for at least 1 percent of the variation in only one of six cases. For half of the questions, the statistic actually takes on a negative value.

A second test we can perform asks the question: what is the likelihood that we would observe data like these if preferences were not in fact structured along ethnic lines? The answer is given by an F-test and its associated p-value. For each question, the data we observe are consistent with the hypothesis of no ethnic group effects. Finally, the group-specific effects that show up as significant (for example, the Bafumbiras' interest in drainage channel maintenance—see the large, significant coefficient in the first column of the ninth row of figure 4.5) are rendered

Figure 4.5   Variation in Policy Preferences Across Ethnic Groups: Priorities

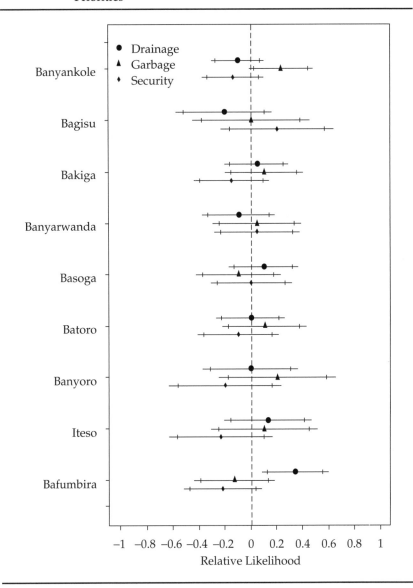

Source: Authors' calculations.
Notes: The figure reports the relative likelihood that each ethnic group will rank a given issue as a priority, as compared to the ranking by the Baganda. Horizontal lines and ticks show 95 percent and 90 percent confidence intervals, respectively. There is no difference observed across ethnic groups in the priority that people afford to different public goods.

Figure 4.6   Variation in Policy Preferences Across Ethnic Groups: Policies on Service Delivery

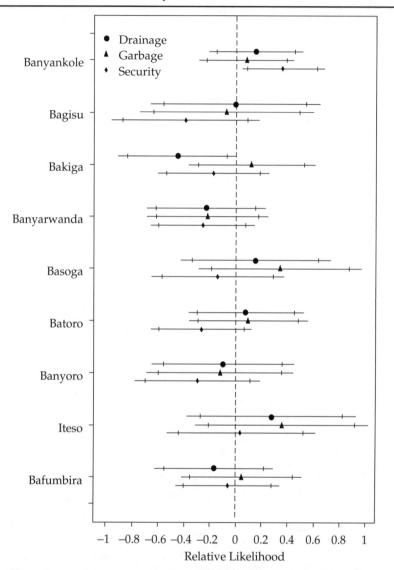

Relative Likelihood

Source: Authors' calculations.
Notes: The figure reports the relative likelihood that each ethnic group expressed a willingness to pay fees for public goods, as compared to the ranking by the Baganda. Horizontal lines and ticks show 90 percent and 95 percent confidence intervals, respectively. There is no difference observed across ethnic groups in the willingness of people to pay for different public goods.

insignificant once we account for location-specific features, suggesting that what looks like a finding with respect to membership in a particular ethnic group was being driven by factors specific to the area in which members of that group happened to predominate. The Bafumbira live in a particularly low-lying, flood-prone area and so understandably were concerned with drainage channel maintenance. In short, there is little empirical support for the argument that ethnic groups share preferences in common in Mulago-Kyebando.

Preferences over Process

The final preferences mechanism we examined emphasizes preferences over processes. Individuals may choose to work with coethnics, not because they care about the same things or because they care about each other's welfare, but instead because they simply enjoy working together. The argument that participation in collective action is explained by preferences over process rather than over outcomes has been made convincingly by Elisabeth Wood (2003) in her study of insurgent participation in the civil war in El Salvador. But can this argument account for specifically coethnic cooperation?

To examine the possibility that coethnics prefer to work together independent of the outcomes they expect to achieve by doing so, we asked a sample of our subjects to self-select into teams to complete a joint task. The key challenge here was to distinguish player motivations: if players elected to work with coethnics, was it because they preferred the process of working with them (a preference-based explanation) or because they expected to be more successful working with them (a technology-based explanation)? To distinguish between these two possibilities, we randomly varied whether a given individual would have the opportunity to select a partner. Comparing outcomes between those who had the opportunity to select a partner and those who did not enabled us to examine the ability of individuals to estimate the implications of partner choice for achieving a successful outcome. These results, in turn, could be used to estimate the players' *non*-consequentialist motivations (that is, their preferences about process).

The game we examined here—the Lockbox game—involves two people working together to open a combination lock that has been affixed to a box containing cash. Pairs of players who successfully open the box share the money. Partners were matched by randomly dividing six subjects in a given session into two groups of three[23]: one group was designated to play the role of player 1, and the other to play the role of player 2. Player 1 was taught how to open the combination lock; he or she then provided oral instructions to player 2, who actually manipulated the lock. After receiving instructions about how the game would be played, one subject was selected at random from the player 1 pool, shown pictures of the three subjects in the player 2 pool, and asked to select one to be his or her partner in the game. A second subject was then selected at random from the player 1 pool, shown pictures of the two remaining subjects in the player 2 pool, and asked to select one to be his or her partner. The final subject in the player 1 pool had no choice and was simply assigned to play the game with the last remaining subject in the player 2 pool. Each subject played the game only once, so only half of our subjects played in the position of player 1. Thirty-one subjects could choose a partner from among three partners, fifty-one chose from among just two, and sixty-six had no choice at all.

A first question is whether, when players had the opportunity to choose their partner, they were more likely to choose coethnics. Table 4.1, which presents data on partner selection for those cases in which a player could select a partner from a pool of coethnics and non-coethnics, provides an answer. Although the n is low for all these cases, we see that player selection was as close as possible to random given integer constraints. The same pattern emerges from a more general analysis (not shown) that used an alternative-specific multinomial probit model to check for coethnicity effects. This model is appropriate for settings in which an individual chooses one option from a set of alternatives (with the number of options possibly varying) for which each option has distinct characteristics. In this analysis, we looked to see whether *any* ethnic cues were used. It is possible (and consistent, for example, with the findings of Fershtman and Gneezy 2001) that individuals find it optimal to work with particular ethnic groups not necessarily their own. Again, we find no evidence to support this view and fail to reject the null hypothesis that the selection is independent of the ethnic composition of the pool of potential partners.

That players did not select partners on the basis of ethnicity is striking, especially since we expected that the prospect of higher success rates (or even the expectation of higher success rates) among coethnics would bias us toward finding a selection effect. However, such selection concerns might have still persisted. In principle, it is possible that players preferred to work with coethnics but also believed that their success rates would be *lower* with coethnics—although, given the nature of this game, the possibility seems remote. We reserve our analysis of the impact of shared ethnicity on success until the next section, where we discuss the results of the Lockbox game from the perspective of its implications for the technology mechanism. Here we explore the broader question of whether selection of *any* form affected success rates. Table 4.2 reports success rates in the Lockbox game based on whether players were able to choose their partner. It is clear that having the option to se-

Table 4.1   Partner Selection in the Lockbox Game

	Share of Players Who Selected In-Group Members		Expected Share Given Random Selection
Case	Ethnicity (n)	Region (n)	
One coethnic, one non-coethnic	0.55 (11)	0.53 (19)	0.50
One coethnic, two non-coethnics	0.39 (8)	0.33 (12)	0.33
Two coethnics, one non-coethnic	0.60 (5)	0.67 (6)	0.67

Source: Authors' calculations.
Note: Players exhibit no tendency to prefer working with coethnics.

lect a partner had no appreciable impact on the likely success of the pairing. In fact, the best-performing pairs were those in which player 1 had no choice at all (although the difference is too small to be of statistical significance).

Our results suggest, then, that the selection of partners is also not driven by objective determinants of success. Of course, there are some correlates of selection: men, for example, were more likely to be selected, especially by other men, and middle-aged partners were more likely to be chosen than the very old or the very young. These selections might have been driven by preferences to work with such individuals independent of expected success rates, but if any such preferences over process exist in Mulago-Kyebando, they do not appear to account for successful coethnic cooperation.[24]

Table 4.2   Impact of Partner Choice on Success Rates

Number of Partners to Choose From	Success Rate (n)
1	0.62 (66)
2	0.57 (51)
3	0.61 (31)

Source: Authors' calculations.
Note: Players are not more successful at completing joint projects if they have a greater opportunity to choose their partner.

Assessing Technology Mechanisms

We have not found much evidence for the preference-based explanations—our subjects' preferences over outcomes did not appear to be structured on ethnic lines, their preferences over the welfare of others did not appear to have an ethnic coloring, and they did not appear to prefer working alongside coethnics. As noted earlier, however, it is still possible that coethnics work better together or treat one another differently because they have access to various "technologies" that they do not share with out-group members. There are multiple types of technology that we might examine, but we focus here on four: efficacy, readability, periodicity, and reachability.

Efficacy: The Lockbox and Puzzle Games

Whereas we examined the other-regarding preferences mechanism with a version of a standard experimental game taken "off the shelf," we used two new games—the Lockbox game and the Puzzle game—to examine the ease with which coethnics can work together. One scholar has identified efficacy as the defining feature of ethnic groups: unlike other identity groups, their ability to quickly and effectively transmit complicated messages makes them "communities of communication" (Deutsch 1966). These games, played face to face rather than via a computer interface, reward players based on their ability to complete a joint task in which effective communication is a critical determinant of success.

As detailed in the previous section, in the Lockbox game player 1 was taught how to open a standard combination master lock. (These locks are not used in Uganda—no subject reported ever having seen one—so opening them was a novel task.) The player was given twenty minutes to practice opening the lock and then tested to ensure that he or she could open it without difficulty. After player 1 had demonstrated mastery of this task, the lock was affixed to a lockbox containing 6,000 Ugandan shillings. Player 1 was then matched with a partner (player 2), according to the procedure described earlier, and the pair was given ten minutes to work together to open the locked box. The two players were permitted to communicate, but player 1 was not permitted to touch the lock.[25] The players were instructed that they would share the money in the box if they succeeded in opening it before the ten minutes elapsed and that they would receive an additional bonus of 1,000 Ugandan shillings each if they were able to open the box within three minutes. All of our subjects played the Lockbox game once, in the role of either player 1 or player 2.[26]

Fifty-nine percent of the pairs in the Lockbox game managed to open the chest within the ten-minute time limit and received the reward of

Table 4.3   Success Rates in the Lockbox Game

	Non-Coethnic Pairing (*n*)	Coethnic Pairing (*n*)	Difference (standard errors)
Ethnicity	0.624 (80)	0.625 (32)	0.000 (0.10)[0.11]
Region	0.61 (83)	0.59 (51)	–0.02 (0.09)[0.09]

Source: Authors' calculations.
Notes: Differences are average treatment effects on the treated (ATT) using exact matching to average over the treatment effects obtained for offerers in each ethnic or regional group. For the analysis of ethnicity, smaller ethnic groups are grouped together according to the probability of assignment to treatment in order to minimize the loss of observations. Standard errors in parentheses are calculated using weighted OLS regression (with weights to account for different assignment probabilities across groups). Standard errors in brackets are heteroskedastic-consistent standard errors that assume independence across all observations. Coethnics are not more successful than non-coethnics at opening the lockbox in the time allotted.

6,000 Ugandan shillings. Almost one-third of these successful pairs were able to complete the task in fewer than three minutes and thus received the bonus. As the results reported in table 4.3 make clear, however, whether the two players were members of the same ethnic or regional group cannot account for the variation in success rates.[27] Coethnic pairings were no more successful (62.5 percent) than non-coethnic pairings (62.4 percent). Success rates among players from the same region were also virtually identical to those of pairings from different regions; indeed, pairs from the same region did marginally *worse* on average. In both cases, the differences were not statistically different from zero.[28]

As discussed in the previous section, the absence of a difference in success rates between in-group and out-group pairs does not seem to be related to whether subjects had an option to choose their partners. If subjects anticipated that communication with their partner would be critical for completing the task successfully, we might have expected that those who were given the opportunity to choose their partner would have selected a partner from their own group. We might also have expected these coethnic pairings to achieve higher success rates. Yet we find no evidence that subjects selected their partner along ethnic lines, and we observe no increase in success rates when we limit the sample to those who could choose their partner.[29]

Although we found no evidence of a technological coordination effect in the Lockbox game, one might be concerned that the failure of coethnics to work more efficiently on one task does not imply that there are no efficiency gains for any tasks. To further examine the issue, we studied a second, more symmetric game, the Puzzle game.

Figure 4.7   The Puzzle Game

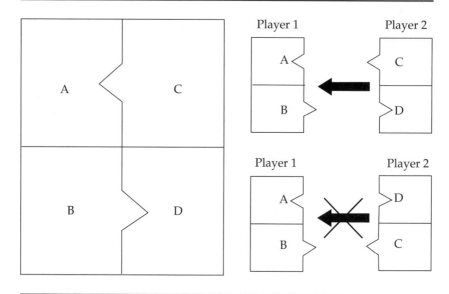

Source: Authors' illustration.

The Puzzle game was played with a four-piece jigsaw puzzle (see figure 4.7). Before play began, subjects were given the opportunity to practice assembling a sample puzzle. They were then randomly divided into pairs and seated on either side of a small table. A low partition between the subjects prevented them from seeing what their partner was doing with his or her hands but permitted communication over the top of the partition. Each player was given two of the four pieces of the puzzle and instructed to work together with his or her partner to complete the full puzzle.

To solve the puzzle, the players each had to work together to decide, based on information they held collectively but not individually, which of their two pieces should go on the top and which should go on the bottom. Thus, in the example provided in figure 4.7, the players had to communicate to make sure that, if player 1 put piece *A* on the top and piece *B* on the bottom, player 2 would place *C* on the top and *D* on the bottom. Players were permitted to talk to their partner, but they were not allowed to show their partner their pieces. The players were given three minutes to complete the task, at the end of which an enumerator checked to see if the two halves of the puzzle fit together. If they did, the players were paid 1,000 Ugandan shillings each. Subjects played the

Table 4.4   Success Rates in the Puzzle Game

	Non-Coethnic Pairing (n)	Coethnic Pairing (n)	Difference (standard errors)
Ethnicity	0.36 (457)	0.48 (146)	0.12 (0.07)[0.05]
Region	0.37 (421)	0.42 (234)	0.05 (0.06)[0.04]

Source: Authors' calculations.
Notes: Differences are average treatment effects on the treated (ATT) using exact matching to average over the treatment effects obtained for players in each ethnic or regional group. For the analysis of ethnicity, smaller ethnic groups are grouped together according to the probability of assignment to treatment in order to minimize the loss of observations. Standard errors in parentheses are calculated using weighted OLS regression (with weights to account for different assignment probabilities across groups), and disturbance terms are clustered for each player across all of his or her games. Standard errors in brackets are heteroskedastic-consistent standard errors that assume independence across all observations. Coethnics are marginally more successful than non-coethnics at completing the puzzle.

Puzzle game three times, each time with a different (randomly assigned) partner and with a slightly different puzzle. One of the three puzzles was "easy" (ordering the pieces randomly generated a 50 percent chance of solving the puzzle correctly), and two were "hard" (the success rate from a random ordering of pieces was 25 percent).[30]

Subjects found the Puzzle game to be more difficult than we anticipated. Just 40 percent of pairs completed the puzzle successfully. We can easily reject, however, the null hypothesis that success rates are no better than chance (the associated p-value for a one-sample t-test is .006). Table 4.4 summarizes the success rates in terms of the in-group or out-group characteristics of the pairings.[31] Here we find some evidence that coethnic pairings succeeded at a higher rate in completing the task. Whether defined on the basis of ethnicity or region, players had on average a 33 percent better chance of completing any given puzzle when playing with a coethnic than when playing with a non-coethnic. Further investigation reveals that this effect was driven by the Baganda in the sample and was not observed within other groups; nevertheless, the coethnic effect for the Baganda was such that the average treatment effect is substantively large and significant at the 90 percent level.

Readability: Guesses About Education

We found weak evidence for the first technology mechanism, efficacy. We now consider readability. While the efficacy logic suggests that the greater ability of coethnics to communicate complicated messages facilitates coethnic collaboration, readability refers to the idea that coethnics may be better able to read (or believe they are better able to read) cues about unobservable characteristics of their partners that are relevant to their decisions about whether or not to engage in cooperative activities in the first place. While some individual qualities are directly observable to anyone (age, gender, height, weight), other characteristics are harder to discern (one's willingness to work hard, intelligence, level of education). But knowing whether a potential partner is dedicated or smart may make an enormous difference in an individual's willingness to cooperate. Coethnics may be better able to pick up on these unobservable characteristics, perhaps because some observable traits carry signs that coethnics are more adept at deciphering. Take the practice of scarification, for example. One could imagine that, for a particular ethnic group, scarification is practiced as a rite of passage, but only for those male youth deemed ready to advance into adulthood. Within this hypothetical group, age is a very noisy sign about whether a young man is educated, responsible, and trustworthy. Scars, however, are a clear sign, but only to those who understand what a scar means. In this case, the coethnic advantage is technological: coethnics are better able to discern the unobservable characteristics of people they encounter. Can coethnics in fact "read" each other better?

To assess the readability mechanism, we employed data gathered in the identification exercise discussed in chapter 3. Recall that all of our subjects were invited into the lab at the end of the project, after every game had been played, to view images of some of the players with whom they had been matched in the experimental games. After viewing each image, subjects were asked to record their guess about the person's ethnic identity and level of education and to indicate their level of certainty. A response scored a 0 on the certainty scale if subjects reported that their guess was no better than chance, 0.5 if they were somewhat certain, and 1 if they said they were very certain.[32]

We reported earlier the greater facility of coethnics in identifying members of their own groups: coethnicity increases the likelihood of correct identification by six percentage points. To the extent that a person's self-identification with an ethnic group is an unobservable characteristic, this finding is consistent with the story that coethnics are better able to decipher signs about the unobservable characteristics of their partner. Here we explore how our subjects performed in what may seem a still more difficult task: guessing the education levels of those they viewed. Being able to guess the socioeconomic characteristics of other individuals (such as their level of education) may play an important technological role. For example, suppose that individuals wish to support others who are needy. If they can identify neediness more accurately among coethnics than among non-coethnics, then they may be systematically more likely to support coethnics—not because of a coeth-

Figure 4.8   Effect of Coethnicity on Success and Confidence in the Education-Guessing Game

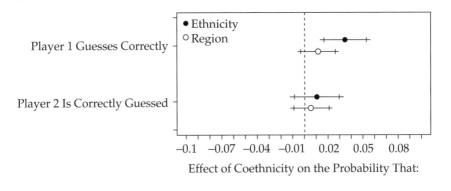

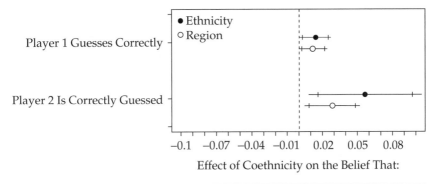

Source: Authors' calculations.
Notes: The figure reports the estimated effects of coethnicity on the likelihood of correct guessing and the belief that the guess is correct. Results are presented both for the guesser (top row of each panel) and the person being guessed (bottom row). Horizontal lines and ticks show 95 percent and 90 percent confidence intervals, respectively. Subjects are weakly better able to guess the education of a coethnic. However, they are much more likely to believe they are better able to infer a coethnic's education level.

nic preference, but simply because of their greater ability to assess need in this group.

Figure 4.8 presents the results of our investigation. We find that, as with the identification of a partner's ethnic group, coethnics appeared to have done much better in discerning a person's level of education, based only on what they could see in a photograph or short video image. Matching at the individual level, we find that success rates were three and a half percentage points higher on average when an individual was paired with a coethnic, and just over one percentage point higher when the subject was paired with someone from the same region.

Figure 4.9   Coethnicity and Frequencies of Interaction

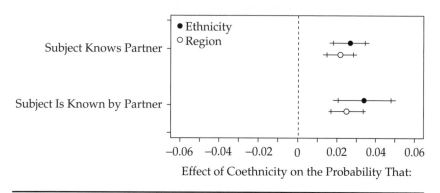

Effect of Coethnicity on the Probability That:

Source: Authors' calculations.
Notes: The figure reports the estimated effects of coethnicity on the probability that a given subject knows his or her partner and is known by his or her partner. Horizontal lines and ticks show 95 percent and 90 percent confidence intervals, respectively. Subjects are significantly more likely to know coethnics than non-coethnics.

The coethnic effect is strongly significant, but the co-region effect falls short of significance at the 90 percent level.

As with the identification game, however, it is possible that coethnicity improves the chances that an average subject in our sample would read his partner's education correctly without that implying that a partner's education would be more correctly read by a coethnic. This could arise, for example, if all players found the Baganda easier to read.[33] In response to this concern, we also show the effect of coethnicity on the likelihood that a partner's education would be correctly inferred. The data suggest that this effect is essentially zero.

Because decisions about whether to invest one's effort in a cooperative task depend not so much on whether one *correctly* codes the type of another person as on how *certain* one feels about that coding, we looked at the determinants of an individual's level of certainty as well. These results are also shown in figure 4.8. Here we find that coethnicity exhibited a powerful effect. When the guesser was from the same group as her partner (according to benchmark demographies), she was significantly more likely to express confidence in her guess. Similarly, a coethnic partner was more likely to be confident in her reading of another person's education than a non-coethnic partner.[34] So, while the evidence on whether coethnics can better sort out unobservable characteristics is mixed, coethnics were consistently more likely to believe that they were better able to make such judgments.

Periodicity: Frequency of Interactions

A third way in which ethnicity may provide a technology is highlighted in the analysis of intra- and interethnic cooperation offered by James Fearon and David Laitin (1996). Fearon and Laitin's analysis (and more generally, the extensive literature on repeated games) suggests that an important condition for the sustenance of a cooperative equilibrium is a minimal *frequency* of interactions between individuals. Indeed, the "periodicity" of interactions—how long it might be until the next interaction with a member of a given population—is embedded in the discount factors used in standard, formal models of cooperation in repeated games. Fearon and Laitin's contribution emphasizes the impact of ingroup or out-group membership on periodicity. For each of the two families of equilibrium they analyze, they argue that "intraethnic cooperation . . . requires that interethnic interactions not be too frequent [relative to intraethnic interactions]" (Fearon and Laitin 1996, 723).

We do not have the data we need to measure the extent to which typical interactions in Mulago-Kyebando are more or less likely to involve coethnics. But we can get close to this idea by generating an estimate of the degree to which subjects in our sample were more or less likely to *know* coethnics relative to non-coethnics. Knowing an individual is an indicator of past contacts and serves in our analysis as a proxy for the likelihood of future contacts. Recall that when subjects were shown the image of their partner at the beginning of each round of the computer-based games, they were asked whether or not they knew the individual.[35] We collected this information so as to be able to exclude interactions that were not between strangers. However, the data also provide a rich picture of the structure of relations among our three hundred subjects. Because our subjects were a random sample of the population, and because the set of interactions we observed was a random sample of all possible interactions, our data represent the likelihood that a given resident of Mulago-Kyebando would know another resident (or would believe that he did on the basis of photographs and videos). On average, individuals claimed to know about 6 percent of the other subjects in the sample. The question is: were these relationships structured along ethnic lines?

The results in figure 4.9 suggest that the answer is yes. A given individual was approximately two and a half percentage points more likely to know another randomly selected person if that person was a coethnic—an effect that is statistically significant and robust to multiple specifications. This represents close to a doubling in the probability of knowing a given individual. Similarly, recognizing that claims to "know" somebody might not have been symmetric, the data show that an individual was more likely to be known by another if that person was a coethnic.[36]

Is this effect substantively large? In terms of its implications for the periodicity of social encounters, this doubling of frequencies turns out to be surprisingly small. The reason is that, in a heterogeneous population, a near doubling of the likelihood of knowing a coethnic relative to a non-coethnic does not imply that an individual's associates are highly concentrated within his ethnic group. To estimate the ethnic concentration of acquaintances, we need to condition on the number of acquaintances of each individual and estimate the probability that a given acquaintance is a coethnic. When we do this, we find a close relationship between the size of a subject's group and the share of acquaintances from his or her group, indicating relatively little clustering (see figure 4.10). With a random distribution of acquaintances, 22 percent of acquaintances would be coethnics; with ethnic enclaves, this number would approach 100 percent. The actual share in our sample is 30 percent. The Baganda were the only group for whom a majority of their acquaintances were coethnics, but even this proportion corresponds to only a 5 percentage points higher likelihood that a given acquaintance was a coethnic than we would expect from a random distribution of acquaintances.

As a result, the evidence is mixed. Empirically, an individual's acquaintances are significantly more likely to be coethnic, but whether these effects can account for the functioning of different strategies of reciprocity is unclear.[37] We return to this question in chapter 5.

Reachability: The Network Game

A final way in which coethnicity may provide a "technology" is through the existence of social networks that potential cooperating partners can draw upon to increase the likelihood of successful collaboration. Networks are useful in providing access to information about a partner's unobservable skills and attributes. But they may also be important in making possible the sanctioning of partners who defect in the context of collective activities. If individuals are "reachable" through social networks, then these networks can be used either to spread the word about those who do not cooperate or by engaging others (within the network) in an effort to apply punishment in the event of noncooperation. If the structure of networks follows ethnic lines, then networks may provide part of the answer for why cooperation is greater among coethnics. Are social networks especially useful for tracking down coethnics?

To examine this causal channel, we designed a game that would permit us to measure the extent to which coethnics were able to benefit from the existence of a shared social network. To put the reachability aspect of the network front and center, the task involved finding a stranger. We began the network game by randomly selecting 148 Mulago-Kyebando residents from outside of our regular subject pool.

Figure 4.10   Group Size and Coethnic Acquaintances

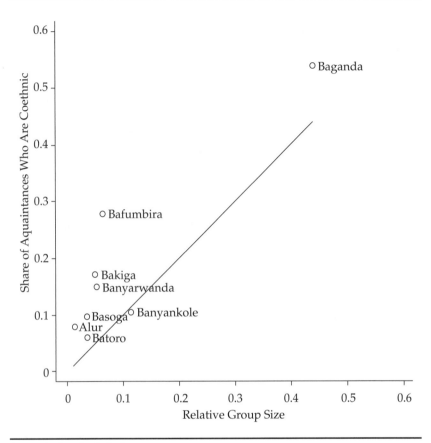

Source: Authors' calculations.
Notes: Bivariate scatterplot of the size of major ethnic groups in our sample and the share of coethnics among reported acquaintances. The larger one's group, the more likely one's acquaintances are to be coethnics.

These were the "targets" we would send our subjects to try to find. We collected a small amount of background information about each target, including the person's ethnicity and birthday. We also took a digital photo of each target person. We told the target that, within the next two weeks, someone might come looking for him or her and asking for a message. The message was simply the target's birthday (or a parent's name for those targets who did not know their birthday). We asked the targets to provide this message to the person who came looking for them, and we gave them 3,000 Ugandan shillings for their participation.

Then, in waves of four or five per day, we sent out 148 "runners," randomly drawn from our regular subject pool, to find the targets. We selected runners on a day-by-day basis to ensure balance in the treatment and control groups, but without using information on individuals other than their benchmark ethnicity. The runners were shown the target's photograph and given a sheet of paper with the target's name and the parish (LC2) in which the target resided. We instructed the runners to phone us when they found the target and to tell us the target's message. This provided a check that the runner calling in had actually found the person he or she had been sent to find. Runners were given 5,000 Ugandan shillings to defray the cost of hiring a boda boda (motorcycle taxi) to take them around the parish and to pay for the phone call. We told the runners that we would pay them 20,000 Ugandan shillings—a very large sum, equal to about $12, or more than one-half of Ugandan per capita monthly income—if they managed to find the target in three hours and that this sum would decline at a rate of approximately 1,000 Ugandan shillings per hour until it reached zero in twenty-four hours. This provided runners with a strong incentive to find their assigned targets and to do so as quickly as possible.[38]

The results in this game reflect a noisy process. Serendipity was likely to play an important role for the runners, and we anticipated that generating statistically significant results would be difficult. What we found is therefore striking. First, a relatively large number—49 of the 148 runners (or just over 33 percent) managed to track down their targets.[39] Second, the success rate among runners whose targets happened to be coethnics was higher (43 percent) than the rate among runners whose targets were from other ethnic groups (28 percent). A simple comparison of means is significant at the 90 percent level.[40] A more reliable estimate of the average treatment effect, however, is given by weighting observations to take account of the different assignment probabilities of ethnic groups to coethnic pairings. The results of this exercise are shown in table 4.5. After taking account of these weights, the coethnicity effect is diminished, falling to ten percentage points and just below conventional levels of statistical significance (with an associated p-value of just over 0.20). The same analysis yields somewhat weaker results for the co-regional pairings. Importantly, however, the qualitative effect obtains across ethnics groups, rather than being concentrated in any one group. These findings provide weak evidence for the idea that ethnic groups possess social networks that facilitate the flow of information useful for the tracking down of fellow group members.[41]

Assessing Strategy Selection Mechanisms

So far we have found no evidence for the preferences mechanisms but some evidence for all four technology mechanisms. The final way in

Table 4.5   Success Rates in the Network Game

	Non-Coethnic Pairing (n)	Coethnic Pairing (n)	Difference (standard errors)
Ethnicity	0.33 (97)	0.43 (51)	0.10 (0.08)[0.10]
Region	0.33 (84)	0.38 (61)	0.05 (0.08)[0.09]

Source: Authors' calculations.
Notes: Differences are average treatment effects on the treated (ATT) using exact matching to average over the treatment effects obtained for players in each ethnic or regional group. For the analysis of ethnicity, smaller ethnic groups are grouped together according to the probability of assignment to treatment in order to minimize the loss of observations. Standard errors in parentheses are calculated using weighted OLS regression (with weights to account for different assignment probabilities across groups). Standard errors in brackets are heteroskedastic-consistent standard errors that assume independence across all observations. Coethnics are slightly better than non-coethnics at tracking one another down.

which ethnicity might condition behavior is through what we have called the family of strategy selection mechanisms. Many social environments are marked by the existence of multiple equilibria—that is, given a solution concept (such as the Nash equilibria, or "each does the best he or she can, given what the others are doing"), the choice situation produces many possible solutions. In such contexts, ethnic information may be used by players to select one set of solutions over another.[42] The example we gave in the introduction is illustrative. Two non-coethnics may be less likely to cooperate than two coethnics, not because they are less able to reciprocate cooperation with cooperation, but because neither expects the other to cooperate in the first place. With different expectations in place, cooperation can perhaps be maintained by all parties. Strategy selection mechanisms may reflect, then, the existence of norms that make particular strategies (like reciprocity) more likely to be used. If such norms exist among coethnics and not among non-coethnics, patterns of reciprocity—which are more apparent in within-group interactions—may help explain why homogeneity facilitates collective action and better public goods provision.

The Dictator Game with a Non-Anonymous Offerer

To find out whether a reciprocity mechanism is at work, we added a twist to the Dictator game, which we used earlier to test for other-regarding preferences. Recall that when we played the Dictator game, we varied the amount of information that receivers had about the offerer. Earlier, we analyzed the games in which offerers were anonymous (and knew that they were anonymous) in their actions (as in figure 4.2). We found that they did not discriminate in favor of coethnics. Would this also be the case when we removed their anonymity (as in figure 4.1)? What would happen when receivers were given (and offerers knew that receivers were given) information about who the offerer was and what actions he or she had taken?[43]

Variation in this information is critical for working out how people play strategically. It is relatively easy to show that (in principle) even egoists can be made to cooperate in repeated games through the use of social sanctions—but only if others receive information about the actions taken by the egoists. Such information is a necessary condition for the utilization of targeted punishment strategies. We argue that, in this version of the game, an offerer's behavior vis-à-vis a receiver can be interpreted as a joint product of the offerer's other-regardingness toward that receiver and the offerer's concerns about being seen to violate social norms and/or opening himself or herself up to the possibility of social sanctions. If reciprocity norms are such that coethnics are expected to play more cooperative equilibria with each other, then we would expect to observe this as a difference in patterns of play across Dictator games with one-sided and two-sided information.

In interpreting this game, it is important to emphasize that the Dictator game, by construction, does not allow for the possibility of punishment *within the context of the game*. We were interested in whether subjects, entering a laboratory environment, would act *as if* punishment were possible or *as if* enforceable norms against shirking applied (for a discussion of this approach, see Hoffman, McCabe, and Smith 1996). Playing the Dictator game with an anonymous offerer excludes the possibility of extra-game punishment, since the offerer is anonymous. The Dictator game played with a non-anonymous offerer, however, does not make any such exclusion. We used this version of the game to test whether patterns of play in coethnic and non-coethnic pairings differed when the threat of sanctions in response to norm violation obtained.[44] If our reading of play in this game seems implausible, read on to chapter 5, where we introduce the possibility of punishment *within* the context of a game and show that players do in fact anticipate punishment for their actions and modify their strategies accordingly.

For this version of the Dictator game, we had each subject play approximately two rounds of the 100-Ugandan-shilling-denomination game and approximately four rounds of the 500-Ugandan-shilling-denomination game. This yielded a total of 672 rounds (and 1,344 individual choices) in the 100-Ugandan-shilling-denomination game and 1,226 rounds (2,452 choices) in the 500-Ugandan-shilling-denomination game.

On average, patterns of play were similar to those found in the Dictator game with an anonymous offerer. The modal strategy (employed in

23 percent of rounds) in the 100-Ugandan-shilling version was to retain 600 Ugandan shillings and allocate 200 Ugandan shillings to each of the other players. The next most common strategy was to keep 400 Ugandan shillings and allocate 300 Ugandan shillings to each other player (22 percent of rounds). Again, a strong norm of inequality-aversion was evident. On average, players retained 548 Ugandan shillings and allocated 226 Ugandan shillings to each of the other players.[45] In the 500-Ugandan-shilling-denomination game, aggregate results were again similar to those reported in the previous section: in 70 percent of cases, subjects kept one 500-Ugandan-shilling coin and allocated the other coin to another player, and in 24 percent of cases they gave both coins away.

Strikingly, however, while there were few differences in average play, there were consistent differences in how subjects played with different kinds of partners. Once their actions became observable to others, the players in our sample—and in particular the egoists—started to exhibit a bias toward coethnics.[46] Figure 4.11 presents estimates of the impact of coethnicity on behavior in the 100-Ugandan-shilling game, coding coethnicity using measures of benchmark and subjective coethnicity (defined over ethnic groups and region). As in the anonymous version of the game, non-egoist players offered somewhat *less* to coethnics, though this effect is small and statistically weak. However, when we focus on the behavior of egoists, a very different pattern emerges. Egoists, while offering considerably less on average, offered significantly more to coethnics in these non-anonymous games—between 20 and 50 Ugandan shillings more, depending on the particular measure of coethnicity we used.[47]

Similar results obtain in the 500-Ugandan-shilling game (figure 4.12). As before, we focused only on the sample of subjects who actually discriminated (including all egoists and some non-egoists) when faced with a choice between a coethnic and a non-coethnic. Again, we find strong evidence that our subjects favored coethnics. Using a coding based on benchmark demography, we find that coethnicity increased the chances that a partner would be favored by about twelve percentage points. Our estimates of the impact of coethnicity increase in magnitude and improve in precision with finer definitions of coethnicity, using subjective guesses. These results suggest that a perceived in-group member was twenty-eight percentage points more likely to be favored in the Discrimination game than a perceived out-group member. Results for shared group membership defined by common regional background were similarly large and significant at conventional levels.

The contrast between these findings and those reported in figures 4.3 and 4.4 is striking. When they were making their offers anonymously, (egoist) subjects gave no more to coethnics than to non-coethnics. But when they knew that they could be seen, they gave significantly more.

Figure 4.11   Effect of Coethnicity on Average Offers in the 100-Ugandan-Shilling Dictator Game When Offerers Are Seen

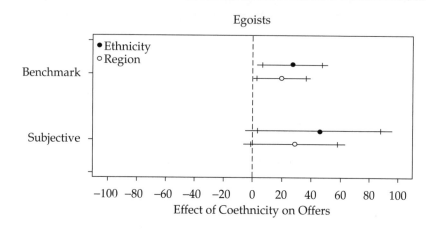

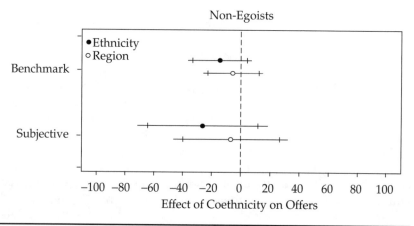

Source: Authors' calculations.
Notes: The figure reports the estimated effects of coethnicity on average offers in games where the offerer is not anonymous, broken down by player type. Horizontal lines and ticks show 95 percent and 90 percent confidence intervals, respectively. Egoists exhibit a tendency to favor coethnics when their play is not anonymous.

These results suggest that cooperation-facilitating norms operate especially strongly within ethnic groups but are required only for a subset of players. To further explore the role of information, we can estimate the joint effect of coethnicity and offerer anonymity in a single framework. We pool the data from all Dictator games and compare the impact on offerers' behavior of being seen, being paired with a coethnic, and the interaction of these two conditions. This interaction term is especially use-

Figure 4.12   **Effect of Coethnicity on the Probability of Discrimination in the 500-Ugandan-Shilling Dictator Game When Offerers Are Seen**

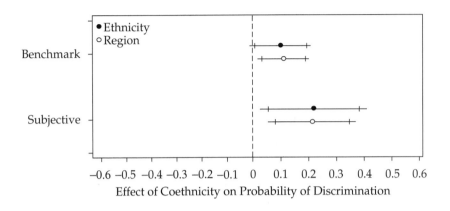

Source: Authors' calculations.
Notes: The figure reports the estimated effects of coethnicity on the probability of discrimination in games where the offerer is not anonymous. Horizontal lines and ticks show 95 percent and 90 percent confidence intervals, respectively. Players who discriminate in allocating benefits exhibit a tendency to favor coethnics when their play is not anonymous.

ful because it provides a direct test of the impact of social norms on within-group cooperation while controlling for the possible effects of within-group altruism.

When we do this for the 500-Ugandan-shilling game, we find qualitative support for the claim that players exhibited an in-group bias if and only if they were observed. But the interaction terms in this case do not reach significance at conventional levels. While we are confident that individuals discriminated if they were observed, our confidence that they did so *only if* they were observed is weakened somewhat by our uncertainty regarding how players behaved when they were not observed in the Discrimination game.

By contrast, the evidence from the 100-Ugandan-shilling game suggests clearly that the in-group effect (among both coethnic and co-regional benchmark pairings) is due to information and cannot be accounted for by other-regarding preferences. This interaction term is illustrated in figure 4.13. Egoists favored coethnics *if and only if* they were seen to do so. Taken together, these findings offer support for this strategy selection mechanism as an important source of the variation in public goods provision across ethnically homogeneous and heterogeneous settings.

Figure 4.13   The Importance of Being Seen

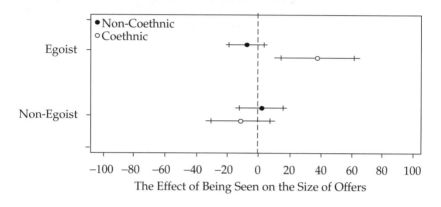

The Effect of Being Seen on the Size of Offers

Source: Authors' calculations.

Notes: The figure reports the estimated effects of the loss of anonymity on average offers to coethnics and non-coethnics (using benchmark measures for ethnicity) in the 100-Ugandan-Shilling-denomination Dictator game, broken down by player type. Horizontal lines and ticks show 95 percent and 90 percent confidence intervals respectively. Egoists exhibit a tendency to favor coethnics *if and only if* their play is not anonymous.

Confounding Factors

The methods we used in our analysis are very different from those typically used to study ethnic politics. By turning to experimental methods, we have benefited from the fact that the pairing of players is determined randomly. By virtue of our design, we can rule out in most cases the possibility that the individual characteristics of the offerer or receiver (or the runner or target in the Network game, or player 1 or player 2 in the Puzzle and Lockbox games) were correlated with our assignment to a pairing. For this reason, we generally present simple statistical tests—tests that compare the mean value of what we want to explain in coethnic pairings and non-coethnic pairings and that look for a difference.

Nonetheless, we are frequently asked whether individual characteristics affect patterns of behavior in our games: whether older people behave differently than younger people, whether women behave differently than men, and whether the educated use different strategies than the uneducated. To answer these questions, we explored the robustness of our results to the inclusion of a battery of control variables, including age, gender, education, and a host of others. We find that, for the Dictator game, older people did tend to give more on average, women offered slightly more than men, and the educated gave less than the uneducated. But we find that our results regarding the differences between coethnic and non-coethnic pairings were unaffected by the inclusion of these controls. This should not be surprising since, by design, coethnic and non-coethnic pairings did not differ in expectation in terms of the observable characteristics of the subjects.

Of potentially greater concern is how the demographic structure of our sample might have shaped the experimental results. Given the dominance of the Baganda within the ethnic demography of Mulago-Kyebando (the Baganda constitute approximately 50 percent of the population while no other group makes up more than 10 percent), we could not avoid a situation in which assignment to a coethnic pairing, though random for any individual, would nonetheless be correlated with self-identification as Baganda. We account for this by examining the effect of coethnicity within each ethnic group and taking the averages of these effects across groups, weighting by the relative size of the group among the "treated" observations. This ensures that we were truly estimating average treatment effects on the treated. Nevertheless, it is still the case that our estimates of the average effect of coethnicity heavily weighted the effects among the largest group, in this case, the Baganda.

In some cases, this poses a challenge for interpretation: Do dominant group members act in a particular way toward other in-group members because those others are members of the dominant group or because they are members of the *same* group? For some cases in which we felt that this issue of interpretation was particularly important, we supplemented our analysis by reversing the treatment group—that is, we looked not at the effect of coethnicity on how successful a given individual was at guessing the education of a randomly selected partner, but at how coethnicity shaped the likelihood that a given partner's education was correctly guessed by the individuals making a guess. Similar analyses can be undertaken with our other results. In doing so, we generally find our results strengthened. Thus, for example, while coethnicity increased the offers made by a given egoist offerer if and only if that offerer was seen, so too did coethnicity increase the offer received *by* a given receiver from egoist offerers if and only if those offerers were seen. These checks help to rule out the possibility that the coethnic effect derives from the dominant group being in general more likely either to give or to receive under various conditions.

Interpretations

Our results are informative, both for what we found and for what we failed to find. We found no evidence for the other-regarding preferences, the correlated preferences, or the preferences over process variants of the preferences mechanism. If coethnics are more effective at producing public goods, it is not simply because they value more highly the happiness of other group members, care about the same things, or simply prefer working with people from their own ethnic group.

There is stronger evidence in support of the technology mechanisms we investigated. We found some evidence for the efficacy variant of the technology mechanism: coethnics do appear to be more effective than non-coethnics at working together on one of the two joint tasks we studied. We also found evidence for the readability mechanism: individuals are better (and believe they are better) at "reading" people from their own group—they are more accurate not just in their guesses about the ethnic identity of coethnics but also about features such as coethnics' level of education. Individuals are also more likely to know coethnics than non-coethnics, suggesting a periodicity effect, although the substantive magnitude of this result makes it unlikely as a candidate explanation for patterns of ethnic cooperation. We found weaker evidence for the role of reachability: coethnics do appear to be more closely linked through network structures in our project area, although the statistical case for this tendency is not very strong.

Finally, we found compelling evidence that players condition their strategies on the ethnicity of the other players in the game. Our findings suggest that ethnically homogeneous communities may have an advantage in providing public goods because those individuals least likely to contribute are also particularly sensitive to threats of retaliation should it be known that they have failed to contribute to collective endeavors.

In our earlier discussion of the rival channels through which ethnicity might operate, we highlighted the difficulty of distinguishing between the strategy selection and technology mechanisms. Given the results of our investigations, we are confronted by precisely this inferential problem. We have found that egoist players use more cooperative strategies with coethnics only when they are exposed to threats of punishment. This finding is consistent with two distinct stories. On the one hand, it may be that a pure ethnic strategy selection mechanism is at work. It may be that interactions are sufficiently frequent and players sufficiently reachable that reciprocity norms can be sustained in general, but that, in practice, these norms have been established (or have been more strongly established) only among coethnics. An alternative explanation, however, is that this norm of cooperation under the threat of sanction is not specific to ethnic groups but is universal, conditioned only on the ease with which individuals can be punished. It simply may happen that, as a practical matter, the application of the universal norm is more commonly observed in coethnic interactions, since coethnics are easier to identify, more frequently encountered, and (somewhat) more "reachable." The distinction between these two stories is subtle. Disentangling them is a task of the next chapter.

Chapter 5

A Closer Look at Reciprocity

OUR EXAMINATION of differences in how coethnics interact has pinpointed a number of mechanisms that could account for the higher levels of cooperation we observe in ethnically homogeneous communities. In the last chapter, we found evidence for a number of technological advantages. Coethnics are more likely to know one another directly, and even if they do not, they are better able to identify ingroup members, to infer otherwise unobservable characteristics about one another, and to locate a randomly selected group member in the community. In addition, there is some evidence that coethnics can perform joint tasks more efficiently. All of these advantages can make it easier for coethnics to cooperate for mutual gain. We also discovered evidence that the strategies people use are conditioned on identity: egoistic players treat coethnics better *if and only if* they are seen to be doing so, suggesting the existence of a norm that sustains cooperation among ingroup members.

In this chapter, we push our investigation further in an effort to explore how these findings, taken together, might provide a coherent answer to the puzzle of why more homogeneous communities are more successful at providing public goods. We deepen our investigation in four ways. First, whereas most of the games we have analyzed so far capture *aspects* of a collective action dilemma, we now explore behavior in a game that captures the challenge of public goods provision directly. Using a classic public goods problem studied by game theorists, the Prisoner's Dilemma, we examine how behaviors differ across types of players and how play is structured by coethnicity—an important check on the consistency of our results in chapter 4. The evidence from these analyses confirms three of our main findings: egoists cooperate at lower rates in collective action dilemmas, coethnics succeed at higher rates, and coethnicity drives more cooperative behavior among egoists (and only among egoists), thereby making up for the collective action failures that egoistic behavior would otherwise induce.

Second, we examine the plausibility of a sanctioning account more directly, focusing on how in-group reciprocity norms might work in practice to support more cooperative behavior. To do this, we examine play in a version of the Prisoner's Dilemma in which we introduce the possibility of sanction by a third player who observes how others play the game. We explore the data for evidence that players anticipate punishment, that they act more cooperatively when sanctioning is possible, and that they do in fact engage in costly punishment. We find strong evidence that players do all of these things.

We then take an additional step and try to sort out how exactly in-group reciprocity norms function. Recall that, in the last chapter, we emphasized the difficulty of disentangling the technology and strategy selection mechanisms. In the third part of this chapter, we investigate whether coethnics act in a more reciprocating manner even among players who know one another or who can be easily found—that is, while controlling for periodicity and reachability. This analysis permits us to separate out two distinct logics for how ethnicity figures in the solution of collective action problems. The first is purely about strategy selection: players condition their behavior on the ethnicity of the other player, ceteris paribus. The second emphasizes technology: players condition their behavior on particular characteristics of others that happen to be correlated with coethnicity, such as reachability or periodicity. Our evidence suggests that patterns of coethnic cooperation cannot be explained simply by the technological advantages that groups possess. A specifically coethnic reciprocity norm exists among our subjects in Mulago-Kyebando.

Finally, we examine whether coethnic reciprocity norms (which are powerfully in evidence in binary interactions between egoists) extend to a different strategic context, one in which information about behavior is publicly observable and norm enforcers are empowered (whether they are coethnic or not) to sanction. To do this, we return to the data on play in the Prisoner's Dilemma with a third-party enforcer. In this case, external actors can play a role in supporting cooperation. We ask whether there are conditions under which a universal reciprocity norm—which is in evidence when punishment is possible—is sufficiently powerful to erase the coethnic advantage in cooperation. We find that, in environments where actions are publicly observable and all players are equally able to sanction, reciprocity norms can function effectively across group lines.

Before turning to these tasks, we provide a more concrete description of a public goods problem—in this case, a Prisoner's Dilemma—and use the example to illustrate how a number of the different mechanisms we have described (and some rival explanations) can provide solutions to the problem.

Decentralized Solutions to Collective Action Problems

The collective action problem most studied by game theorists is called the Prisoner's Dilemma (PD) (Davis and Holt 1993; Colman 1995; Ledyard 1995; Sally 1995). In the classic account, two prisoners face interrogation separately for their role in a crime. Each must decide whether to provide information about the other prisoner. The tragedy of the dilemma is that, although both would be better off if they could keep quiet, each has a private incentive to provide information about the other. Both end up providing information even though they would have been better off saying nothing. An example of a PD is given in figure 5.1.

Dramatic as it may seem, the logic of the PD is the same as that underlying the real-world, everyday decisions faced by community members in Mulago-Kyebando. Many rotating credit and savings organizations—a key source of financial capital for business in the informal sector—have the structure of a public goods game. Individual decisions about whether to report suspicious behavior in the neighborhood, to serve on committees, or to show up for a community initiative to clear drains provide other examples.

To see the strategic logic of the dilemma illustrated in figure 5.1, consider the example of two individuals contemplating an investment in some public good. Each has $100 available to invest. Assume that every $100 invested yields a benefit worth $75 for each person, but that this benefit is *public* in the sense that it can be enjoyed by both people whether they make an investment.[1] In this case, while the private cost of contributing $100 is $100, the total (social) benefit of a $100 investment is $2 \times \$75$, or $150. Privately, this is a costly investment, but socially it is profitable.

Now imagine that both individuals are egoists in the sense that the direct benefits that accrue to each individual fully capture how they value the outcome. If both invest, the value of the good to each person is $150. Each then receives a net benefit of $50, having invested $100 already. If neither invests, then they are both where they started and no one experiences any gains or losses. But what if only one person invests? In this case, the dollar value of the good is $75 to each person. The net gain to the one who invests is then –$25, while the one who did not invest has a net gain of $75. Game theorists call one a "sucker" and the other a "free-rider." The sucker suffers from having contributed, while the free-rider does well from *not* having contributed. The tragedy of games of this form, as has long been recognized, is that no matter what

Figure 5.1   A Prisoner's Dilemma

		Person 2	
		Not Invest	Invest
Person 1	Not Invest	0 0	−25 75
	Invest	75 −25	. 50 50

Source: Authors' illustration.
Notes: The figure shows payoffs from different investment decisions. The payoff for person 1 is given in the lower-left corner of each cell; the payoff for person 2 is given in the upper-right corner.

one player does, the other is better off not investing. As a consequence, everyone ends up worse off.

There are well-known solutions to this problem that rely on the ability of players to sanction each other for failing to contribute (or to reward one another's decisions to contribute).[2] For example, if players replay this game many times with one another, then each can agree to cooperate in expectation that the other will too, but with the knowledge that, should one of them fail to cooperate, the other will not cooperate in the future (Axelrod 1984). Thus, although individuals cannot punish one another for failing to cooperate with them in a given instance, they can ensure cooperation if they expect to interact with one another in the future. This is the logic that underpins the *periodicity* mechanism.

This sort of behavior can emerge within communities even if individuals do not often interact with each other directly but still belong to a broader community of individuals who interact with one another (Kandori 1992). Two individuals might choose to invest in a public good if each is afraid that his decision not to invest would be broadcast to friends and relatives—some of whom might respond with a variety of sanctions, such as excluding them from social events or reducing the amount of trade credit they are offered. Conversely, they might choose to invest if they feel that such behavior will be rewarded. This is the logic that underpins the *reachability* mechanism.

Under either logic, failing to cooperate can be costly—but only if one is seen to fail to cooperate. In addition, even if people do interact frequently or can track one another down, this allows only for the *possibility* of cooperation; it does not guarantee it. It could be that, in such an environment, individuals follow norms of cooperation. But it could also be that people expect others not to cooperate and so do not cooperate themselves, even if interaction is frequent or people are easily reachable. Under such circumstances, whether the collective action problem is solved is a matter of *strategy selection*. These solutions, which emphasize the utility of sanctions, are the focus of the remainder of this chapter.

Other possible solutions exist, none of which rely on sanctioning. The simplest one is that people are not egoists and actually value the accrual of benefits to others. For example, if each individual counts the benefits to others as gains for himself or herself, the game illustrated in figure 5.1 would really be one in which all individuals have an incentive to contribute no matter what the other person does. The collective action problem is then solved by *other-regarding preferences*. Our evidence from chapter 4 suggests that people in Mulago-Kyebando do exhibit preferences of this form and that this could provide a basis for cooperation among our subjects. However, the data also indicate that other-regarding preferences are not structured along ethnic lines, making it unlikely that this logic accounts for coethnic cooperation in particular.

Also, PDs can be resolved if norms of generalized reciprocity are present (Ostrom 1990; Rabin 1993). Players may elect to cooperate with their partner because they like to cooperate with people who cooperate with them. Notice that the threat of sanction does not figure into this story at all. Cooperation is possible simply because players have expectations that others will cooperate. With those expectations *and* a preference for cooperating with those who are cooperative, egoistic players could, in principle, overcome collective action problems without any sanctioning behavior whatsoever.

Finally, players may achieve cooperative outcomes because of something that social scientists have termed "quasi-magical thinking" (Shafir and Tversky 1992). The idea here is that individuals believe, because of the symmetry of the situation, that if they choose to cooperate, then so will the other person and both will end up better off. The "magical" part of this thinking is the implicit belief that one's actions exert a *causal* effect on the actions of others, even if such an effect is impossible when actions are taken simultaneously. This explanation may seem a bit far-fetched at first, yet economists and psychologists have identified examples of magical thinking in everyday human behavior. Although we do not provide direct tests for either of these alternative mechanisms, we do provide evidence that the threat of sanctions, not just expectations of cooperation or magical thinking, is a key part of what explains patterns of coethnic cooperation in Mulago-Kyebando.

Coethnicity and Cooperation in a Prisoner's Dilemma

To examine behavior around an actual public goods problem, we had subjects play a PD game like the one described earlier and illustrated in figure 5.1.[3] Each round began with subjects being shown a public information box (PIB) containing pictures and/or videos of themselves and a single partner. The amount of information provided about players varied, as in the Dictator games described earlier, although for the PD game the information level was always symmetric (that is, no information for both, head shot for both, and so on). Subjects were given a 1,000-Ugandan-shilling note and asked to decide whether to invest the money or to keep it for themselves. In front of each subject, we placed two boxes—one labeled "self" and the other "group."[4] To invest, a subject simply placed the 1,000-Ugandan-shilling note in a sealed envelope and put it into the group box. If the subject wished not to invest, she placed the 1,000-Ugandan-shilling note in a sealed envelope and put it in the box marked "self." Any contributions put into the group box were increased in value by 50 percent and then divided equally between the two players at the end of each round.[5] (Note that this division of interest plus capital produced exactly the payoffs described in figure 5.1.) Each subject played approximately four rounds of this game. In all, we have data from approximately six hundred rounds (and since two players played each round, twelve hundred individual choices).

The informational treatment (varying whether players could see who their partners were) is again central to the experimental design. Observing how individuals played with different types of partners and different levels of information about them told us something about their beliefs about the likelihood that others would cooperate. Subjects might, for example, have inferred from the information provided that a player looked "trustworthy," which might have increased the likelihood that they would cooperate. Subjects might also have been cued to the ethnic identity or gender of a partner. If subjects believed, for example, that individuals from their ethnic group would behave in a more cooperative way, then we would have observed this in higher rates of coethnic cooperation.

The outcome of primary interest is the frequency of cooperation across pairings and, in particular, the likelihood that two matched players from the same ethnic group would cooperate. As before, in addition to exploring the impact of the ethnic composition of partners on cooperation rates, we examine the extent to which a player's type (egoist versus non-egoist) affected his or her behavior.

We begin with the impact of a player's type on patterns of cooperation. The left-hand panel of figure 5.2 shows the overall level of coopera-

Figure 5.2   Cooperation in the Prisoner's Dilemma Game

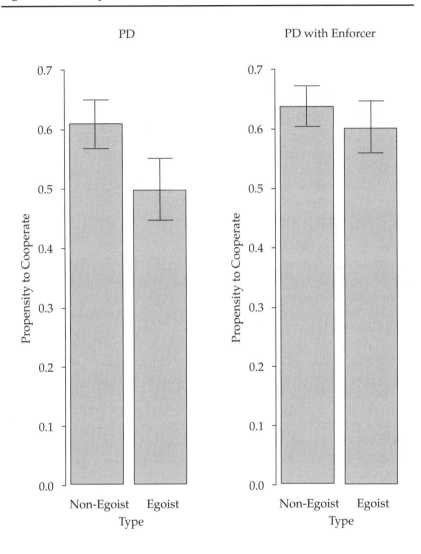

Source: Authors' calculations.
Notes: The figure reports mean levels of cooperation by player type in games without and with a third-party enforcer. The bars represent 95 percent confidence intervals. Non-egoists are more likely to cooperate than egoists. The presence of an enforcer raises the co-operation rate among egoists to the level achieved by non-egoists in the absence of poten-tial punishment.

tion broken down by player type. Egoists cooperated about 50 percent of the time, whereas non-egoists cooperated at a substantially higher rate—approximately 61 percent of the time. This finding is consistent with our earlier discussion of other-regarding preferences among our subjects and similar to results found elsewhere (Andreoni 1990; Camerer, Lowenstein, and Rabin 2004; Sally 1995). The eleven-point difference in rates of cooperation between egoists and non-egoists is significant at the 99 percent level and provides added confidence that our categorization of types, developed on the basis of play in the Discrimination game, captures consistent features of our subjects.

Figure 5.3 presents evidence on the effect of coethnicity on cooperation in the PD game.[6] Players were more likely to cooperate if they were playing with coethnics regardless of player type (the center result in each panel).[7] From a statistical point of view, we can be more confident of this finding for co-region than coethnicity. The result is also statistically stronger when we examine subjective beliefs rather than our benchmark measure of coethnicity. Most importantly, disaggregating the results for egoists and non-egoists, we find that the coethnic effect is driven almost entirely by self-interested players. For the benchmark measures of coethnicity, the coethnic effect is observed only among egoists. For our subjective measures, the effect is weak among non-egoists but strong among egoists. Note that, just as in the Dictator game discussed in chapter 4, we find that, when people know that their behavior will be observed, coethnicity induces higher levels of cooperation specifically among the individuals who would otherwise be least likely to cooperate—the egoists.[8]

The PD game is instructive. In contrast to the experiments discussed in chapter 4, the PD game captures directly the challenge of collective action faced by residents of Mulago-Kyebando. Our findings confirm that coethnics resolve collective action problems with greater facility than non-coethnics. Consistent with the story we developed earlier, it appears that the advantage of coethnicity comes from its ability to induce egoistic players to act more like non-egoistic players, at least when they interact with coethnics. But the results do not yet tell us how ethnic groups discipline the behavior of noncontributors. Is there evidence of sanctioning at work in Mulago-Kyebando? We turn to this question next.

Do Individuals Really Sanction Each Other for Violating Norms?

When we first introduced the idea of sanctioning in chapter 4, we suggest that changes in Dictator game behavior that resulted from the loss of anonymity could be attributed to the impact of expectations of sanc-

Figure 5.3   Coethnicity and Cooperation in the Prisoner's Dilemma Game

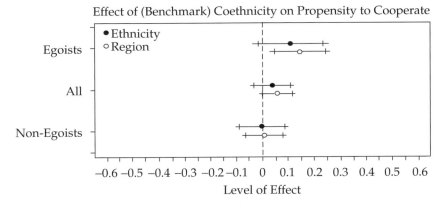

Effect of (Benchmark) Coethnicity on Propensity to Cooperate

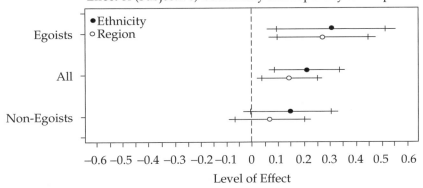

Effect of (Subjective) Coethnicity on Propensity to Cooperate

Source: Authors' calculations.
Notes: The figure reports the estimated effects of coethnicity on cooperation broken down by player type. Horizontal lines and ticks show 95 percent and 90 percent confidence intervals, respectively. Coethnics exhibit a tendency to cooperate at higher rates than non-coethnics, especially if they are egoists.

tions for norm violation (or rewards for norm compliance). To examine sanctioning behavior more directly, we employed a version of the PD game with a third player (the "enforcer") who observed the actions of the first two players in the PD and could choose—at a cost to himself or herself—to punish either one or both of them for their behavior (for a related game, see Fehr and Fischbacher 2004).[9]

In these games, the enforcer was first given the opportunity to observe whether each of the two players in the PD game cooperated or defected. Then, with two 500-Ugandan-shilling coins provided as an endowment, the enforcer was invited to decide whether to punish either player (or neither or both) at a cost of 500 Ugandan shillings each. To do this, the enforcer placed one of the 500-Ugandan-shilling coins in a sealed envelope in a box corresponding to the player to be punished. Any player who was punished lost his or her entire payoff in the round. Of course, if the enforcer chose not to punish anyone, he or she was able to keep the 1,000-Ugandan-shilling endowment. In these games, the players in the PD game also knew whether a third party was observing their play (via the addition of a picture of the enforcer in the upper-right corner of the PIB). This enabled us to explore how the threat of sanctioning conditioned play in the games. Each subject played approximately six rounds of the PD game with an enforcer. In all, we have data from approximately 900 rounds (approximately 1800 individual choices).

One might expect that punishment of this form would be highly unlikely. Since there were real, material costs to sanctioning but no obvious material gains to the enforcer, it would be reasonable to imagine that our subjects might not expect enforcers to punish and that the existence of an enforcer would have no impact on their behavior in the PD game. We find, however, that the presence of an enforcer mattered a great deal. The right-hand panel of figure 5.2 shows the impact of the enforcer on baseline rates of cooperation. Overall levels of cooperation increased from 56 to 62 percent when an enforcer was present, a difference that is statistically significant at the 95 percent level.[10] Turning to how the threat of punishment affected play among different types of players, we find that the impact of the enforcer varied across types. Egoists increased their rates of cooperation substantially when an enforcer was present, while non-egoists became only slightly more cooperative. The presence of an enforcer increased rates of cooperation among egoists to the same level observed among non-egoists when they played without an enforcer (and only a few points below the rates of the non-egoists with an enforcer). Once punishment was permitted within the game, the difference in cooperation rates between egoists and non-egoists almost completely disappeared. This result is strongly suggestive that expectations of sanctioning contribute substantially to cooperation among our subjects, especially among the egoists.

Now let us turn to the behavior of enforcers. Incurring a cost to punish and deter undesirable behavior is also a public good since effective deterrence helps all of those who interact with players facing the threat of punishment. We have already observed that our subjects changed their behavior in anticipation of punishment, but did enforcers in fact punish? Moreover, was punishment a response to defection on the part of players?[11] The results presented in figure 5.4 are reassuring.

Enforcers punished defectors, and they did so at high rates. Again, the fact that we observed *any* punishment—whether of defectors or not—may be surprising to some. Enforcers bore costs to punish even

Figure 5.4   Punishment Behavior by Type and Player Action

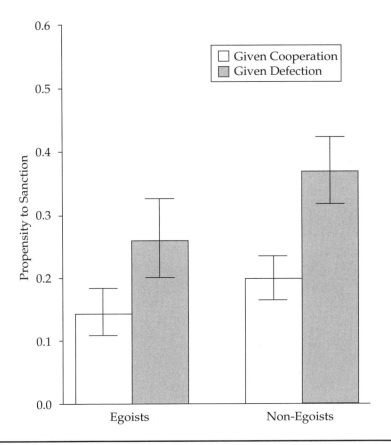

Source: Authors' calculations.
Notes: The figure reports the mean likelihood of punishment by player type broken down by whether the player cooperates or defects in the PD game. The bars represent 95 percent confidence intervals. Non-egoists punish at a higher rate than egoists; punishment is re-sponsive to defection regardless of player type.

in the absence of direct benefits for doing so; moreover, enforcers could not expect to be punished themselves if they failed to punish since their actions went unobserved. Consequently, punishment in this game represented nonrational behavior, at least in terms of short-run material rewards.[12] Yet players punished nearly 25 percent of the time. In addition, enforcers responded systematically to how subjects played.[13] They punished PD game players who defected one-third of the time and players who cooperated slightly more than one time in six.[14] Consistent with the logic of rational egoists, the egoists punished at lower rates than the non-egoists. Egoists did sometimes punish co-operators, but at a rate five percentage points lower than that for non-egoists. And although they punished defectors more than they punished cooperators, they did so at a rate twelve percentage points lower than that for non-egoists.

The fact that we observed punishment, although difficult to reconcile with egoist incentives, is consistent with our account of how subjects played the PD game when they knew an enforcer was present: they cooperated at significantly higher rates because they understood that there was a substantial risk that they would be punished if they did not. The risk of punishment rendered cooperation in the PD game rational even for egoistic players.

Evidence from our analysis of a public goods game thus provides further support for the existence of in-group reciprocity norms sustained by the threat of punishment in Mulago-Kyebando. Subjects in our sample anticipated punishment and responded by cooperating at higher rates. They also engaged in the sanctioning of uncooperative behavior, even at a cost to themselves. While other strategy selection mechanisms cannot be ruled out, the sanctioning account appears to rest on strong foundations.

Is Collective Action Supported by Ethnic or Universal Norms?

With added confidence that sanctioning sustained the reciprocity norms we observed in the non-anonymous Dictator and PD games, we now turn to a closer investigation of how these norms work. There are two distinct pathways through which coethnicity may account for the sanctioning strategies we observe in Mulago-Kyebando.

The first is that there could be a universal norm to cooperate with *any* individual with whom cooperative behavior can be sustained. For example, individuals could seek to engage cooperatively with people with whom they interact frequently or who they can access along social networks. Periodicity and reachability can thus sustain this universal norm. However, because both the periodicity mechanism and, possibly, the reachability mechanism operate more strongly within coethnic pairs, the *application* of this universal norm is uneven: although the norm does not specify cooperation with coethnics, in practice cooperation with coethnics will be more common.

The second possibility is that there exists a specifically coethnic norm stipulating that cooperation *with coethnics* should be employed whenever it can be sustained. Again, periodicity and reachability can sustain

Figure 5.5   Universal and Coethnic Norms

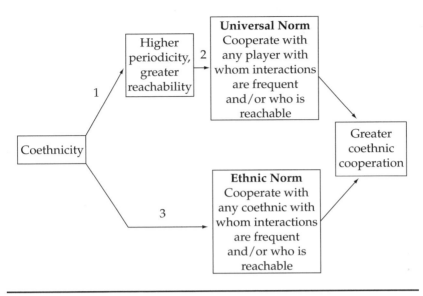

Source: Authors' compilation.
Notes: If coethnics encounter each other with greater frequency or can locate each other more easily through shared membership in an ethnic network (path 1), this could lead to universal norms being applied more consistently with coethnics (path 2). Alternatively, there may exist specifically coethnic norms of cooperation (path 3).

this coethnic norm, but whereas ethnic differences in periodicity and reachability account for cooperation under the first mechanism, strategy selection accounts for cooperation under the second.

These two paths to coethnic cooperation are illustrated in figure 5.5. If individuals play according to a universal norm in which they cooperate with those with whom cooperation can be sustained through repeated play or networks, they will, empirically, cooperate more with coethnics (paths 1 and 2). If, however, the norm is a specifically coethnic norm (path 3), then we will also observe greater cooperation among coethnics (so long as coethnics engage in repeated interaction or are accessible on networks), but even if they are not *more* accessible in these ways than non-coethnics. Of course, it is also possible that coethnic effects work through both channels.

To distinguish among these accounts, we derive some observable implications from each. In particular, we search for observable patterns that would be consistent with one story but inconsistent with the other.

Observable Implication 1: If coethnic cooperation results from the greater frequency of interaction of coethnics (the periodicity mechanism) and not from strategy selection, then the frequency of interaction among co-ethnics should account for the coethnic effect. Moreover, greater periodicity should predict the differences we observe between the anonymous and non-anonymous versions of the Dictator game, irrespective of whether the other players are coethnics.

Observable Implication 2: If coethnic cooperation is a result of reachability, and not of strategy selection, then the ease with which someone can be found should predict the differences we observe between the anonymous and non-anonymous versions of the Dictator game, irrespective of whether the other players are coethnics.

To test the first observable implication, we return to the Dictator game from chapter 4 and examine how knowing partners affected behavior in that game: Did the loss in anonymity have different effects when partners were previously known to the players? Moreover, did such effects work differently when the players were coethnics? To examine the second implication, we generate a measure of the likelihood that an individual can be found using data drawn from the network game. We then examine the relationship between this measure and offers in the anonymous and non-anonymous Dictator games, looking to see whether players who were more easily found responded more to a loss of anonymity regardless of whether their partner was a coethnic.

Periodicity and Cooperation

In chapter 4, we found that coethnicity strongly predicted whether players knew one another. In fact, subjects were about 50 percent more likely to know a randomly selected partner if that partner was a coethnic. We take this not just as a measure of whether partners had interacted in the past but also as an indicator of the likelihood that they would encounter each other in the future. Furthermore, players typically offered more to people they knew in the Dictator game, and there is some (weak) evidence that, on average, players were more responsive to a loss of anonymity when they were playing with partners they knew personally.[15] Plausibly, then, one might suspect that the coethnic effect we observed in the non-anonymous Dictator game was simply an artifact of the greater likelihood that players knew their coethnic partners.

This is not the case. When we take account of whether a subject knew her partner, we continue to find powerful evidence of a coethnic effect across our specifications. So coethnicity is not simply a proxy for per-

Figure 5.6   Periodicity and Offers

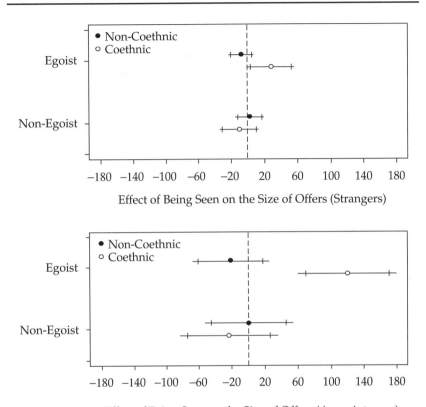

Effect of Being Seen on the Size of Offers (Strangers)

Effect of Being Seen on the Size of Offers (Acquaintances)

Source: Authors' calculations.
Notes: The figure reports the estimated effects of being seen on average offers in the 100-Ugandan-shilling-denomination Dictator game broken down by coethnic and non-coethnic pairings and by player type. Horizontal lines and ticks show 95 percent and 90 percent confidence intervals, respectively. Being seen drives egoists to increase what they give to coethnics, but especially to coethnics they know. It has no impact on the behavior of non-egoists.

sonal knowledge. In fact, the real story, captured in figure 5.6, is more intriguing.

Figure 5.6 shows the effect of losing anonymity on the size of the offers that players of different types made in the Dictator game to partners they knew and partners they did not know, for both coethnic and non-coethnic pairings. Let us begin with non-egoist subjects. The figure shows that the loss of anonymity had no discernible impact on the behavior of non-egoists. These players made large offers to their partners whether their partner was a coethnic, whether they knew their partner, and whether or not they were observed in their actions.

The situation is very different among egoists. We already know that egoists offered less than non-egoists in general (about 100 shillings less). They also tended to offer more to partners they knew than to those they did not know (although they still offered 50 shillings less than non-egoists). So while non-egoists shared universally, egoists were more targeted in their generosity, whether they were seen.

But a very striking pattern emerges when we examine how the loss of anonymity affected behavior among egoists. In non-coethnic pairings, the loss of anonymity had no impact on the size of their offers, whether these players knew their partner. Among coethnics, however, a strong relationship is observed. Being seen drove egoists to give more to coethnics (the result we saw in chapter 4), and to give still more to coethnics they knew. So egoists were especially likely to treat a coethnic acquaintance well when their behavior was observed, but they were no more likely to treat a non-coethnic better just because the person was known to them personally.

This evidence strongly suggests that knowing partners—which we take as an indicator of repeated interaction—cannot *account* for the coethnic effect, but rather seems to *complement* it. Coethnic norms of cooperation (in contexts where players are observed in their actions) operate even more strongly when players know one another.

Reachability and Cooperation

In the Network game, we found some evidence that coethnicity made it easier for individuals to physically locate a randomly selected partner: individuals were ten percentage points more likely to find a coethnic than a non-coethnic, an effect that is statistically weak but substantively large. Can this difference in reachability account for the coethnic effect? Unfortunately, we do not have the statistical power to conduct an analysis of reachability like the one we did for periodicity. Whereas we had measures of whether players knew each other for every round of the Dictator game, we had no direct measures of whether players in our sample were reachable. (Recall that the "targets" in the Network game were selected from outside of our regular subject pool.) Nevertheless, we can explore this question through a related test.

While our interest is in reachability through shared ethnicity, other characteristics may also render a person more or less reachable. Individual markers such as gender, age, skin color, dress, or religious affiliation may make it easier to identify, describe, and locate someone. If reachability matters as we hypothesize, then individuals who possess such highly visible traits may behave differently than individuals who lack them. Our exit interviews with players in the Network game suggest that visible characteristics were indeed utilized by runners as they sought to locate their targets. One player described seizing on a target's name as an indicator that she was probably a westerner and thus probably located in a particular neighborhood.[16] Others focused on skin tone. Another reported that he could tell that the target was Muslim, and so he started his search at a mosque. We might also expect that age or the length of residence in a given area would have made people easier to find, though of course, not all of these characteristics were observable from simple photographs to the same extent.

Several of the accounts we collected in our Network game debriefings suggested that individuals may also be easier to locate if they are connected to local political institutions. Players often reported that they turned to the LC1 system in an effort to locate their partner. This is perhaps not surprising, since LC1s are responsible for maintaining a list of all community members. In practice, however, these lists are rarely kept. It is possible that the use of LC1s was an ethnic strategy, given the predominance of Baganda in these communities (and in the leadership of the LC1s). As it turns out, however, players of all ethnic groups were equally likely to visit LC1 chairs when trying to locate others: 61 percent of Baganda compared to 57 percent of non-Baganda. These numbers indicate that Baganda were slightly better able to access LC1s, but the difference between them is not statistically significant.

To identify more systematically the set of characteristics that contribute to an individual's reachability, we employed data gathered in a short demographic survey of the subjects selected as targets in the Network game. The data include information about gender, age, religion, length of residence, and political activity. The relationship between each of these variables and the likelihood of being successfully located is given in figure 5.7.

The figure presents the marginal effect of each of the variables on the likelihood that a target will be reached, taken one at a time, as well as the estimated effects from a multivariate regression, showing the marginal effect when we control for each of the other determinants. Once we control for other factors, men were significantly (nineteen percentage points) more likely to be found than women, although the result is not significant in a bivariate specification. Religious affiliation also appears to matter for reachability. Muslims were twenty-three percentage points more likely to be reached than non-Muslims, and this finding is significant at conventional levels. Older players (older than thirty-five) and those residents who had lived in an area for longer were also easier to locate.[17] Surprisingly, we find no relationship between political activity—as measured by participation in LC1 committees—and how easily a target could be located.

Figure 5.7   Correlates of Reachability

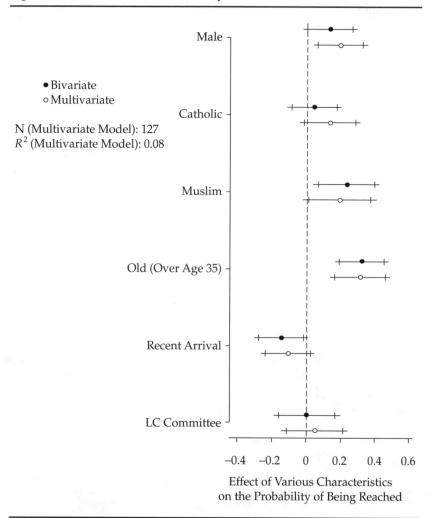

Source: Authors' calculations.
Notes: The figure reports the estimated effects of individuals' traits on the likelihood of being found in the Network game in both bivariate and multivariate specifications. Horizontal lines and ticks show 95 percent and 90 percent confidence intervals, respectively.

To examine our second observable implication, we need to know whether people who could be more easily located also behaved differently in the Dictator game. We return to data gathered in the 100-Ugandan-shilling-denomination Dictator game to examine whether men, older people, more established residents, and Muslim offerers were more generous and whether they conditioned their generosity on being seen (in non-anonymous games).[18]

Figure 5.8   Reachability and Offers

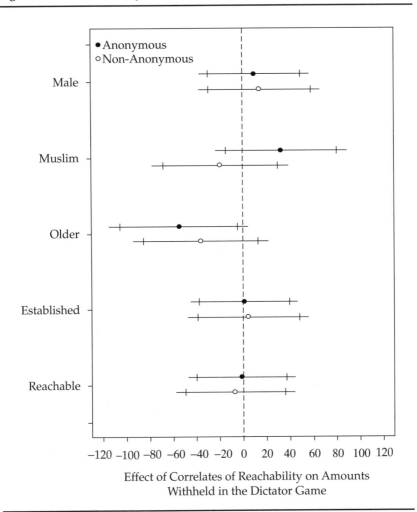

Effect of Correlates of Reachability on Amounts
Withheld in the Dictator Game

Source: Authors' calculations.
Notes: The figure reports the estimated effects of reachability traits on average offers in the 100-Ugandan-shilling-denomination Dictator game broken down by whether the offerer was anonymous. Horizontal lines and ticks show 95 percent and 90 percent confidence intervals, respectively. Individuals who can be easily located generally exhibit no tendency to keep less in the 100-Ugandan-shilling-denomination Dictator game, whether they are making their offers anonymously.

For each observable trait, figure 5.8 presents the effect of that trait on the propensity to retain money in the Dictator game as a function of whether the player's actions are anonymous. The figure also shows the effect associated with an aggregate index of reachability—an index that takes a value of one for the most reachable 50 percent of subjects and zero for the rest. If the propensity of coethnics to cooperate is a result of reachability, those individuals who are easier to locate should keep less, especially when they are seen by others in the non-anonymous games.

The data provide little support for the argument that reachability drove the behavior we observed in coethnic pairings. When observed, players who could be more easily located kept 7 Ugandan shillings less (this finding was driven particularly by older players), but they did *not* condition their play on whether they were seen any more than did non-reachable players. Further, the insensitivity of reachable people to the information that other players had about them held for both egoist and non-egoist players (results not shown). A loss of anonymity reduced how much players kept for themselves only among Muslims; in all other cases, more reachable offerers tended not to respond to the loss of anonymity, as the reachability story would have predicted.

A closer look at the data from the Network game thus suggests that ethnic cues provide a useful starting point as players seek to locate their partners. Players are indeed better able to reach coethnics (and thus, presumably, better able to sanction them for bad behavior). Understanding this, players who know that they can be seen by their partners may offer more to coethnics. But the mechanism that explains this behavior is not simply the fact that coethnics are easier to find. In general, other people who can also be located more easily do not adjust their play in the Dictator game because they fear out-of-game sanctioning. Taken together, our examination of periodicity and reachability suggests that ethnic technologies cannot account for patterns of coethnic cooperation on their own. Instead, a specifically coethnic reciprocity norm—a story of strategy selection—appears to account for the greater success of homogeneous groups in Mulago-Kyebando.

Can Reciprocity Norms Be Sustained Across Ethnic Groups?

Although coethnic reciprocity norms were strongly in evidence in binary interactions, our initial examination of the PD game with an enforcer suggests the existence of a universal norm of cooperation as well. This universal norm is apparent in strategic environments in which a third party observes play and is empowered to sanction. In such a context, the gap in cooperation between non-egoists and egoists all but disappears. Does this new strategic environment also erase the coethnic advantage in cooperation? If behavior is publicly observed and the costs of punishing coethnics and non-coethnics is rendered equal, can reciprocity norms be sustained *across* ethnic groups in addition to within them?

An affirmative answer to this question obviously has important policy implications.

To explore this question, we look again at the PD game with a third-party enforcer. This game differs from the Dictator games we have been examining insofar as there is a powerful third party who observes the play of both parties, whose role is to decide whether to enforce norms, and who disposes of a powerful technology to do so. We examined this version of PD play to see whether players still conditioned their actions on coethnicity in this context. We also investigated whether enforcement was conditioned on ethnicity, as the ethnic norms story predicts, or simply on defection, as a universal norms story would suggest.

Evidence from play in the PD game (reported in figures 5.9 and 5.10) reveals a striking finding. The presence of an enforcer eliminated the coethnic edge in cooperation. Figure 5.9 provides the basic data for the egoist subgroup. The figure illustrates (as we saw in figure 5.3) that egoists were more likely to cooperate with coethnics in the absence of an enforcer. But it also shows that this pattern disappeared when behavior was publicly observed by a third party who was empowered to sanction. Moreover, the magnitude of the enforcement effect was almost identical to that of coethnicity in games without an enforcer. The sanctioning threat provided by the enforcer appears to *substitute* for the group-specific norms (and corresponding sanctioning threats) that exist in coethnic interactions. Figure 5.10, an analogue to figure 5.3, confirms that, in the full analysis, there is no evidence for a coethnic effect in the presence of a third-party enforcer, for either egoists or non-egoists and for either ethnically or regionally defined coethnicity. Universal reciprocity norms appeared to be in operation among our subjects, and in the presence of a third party who could enforce these norms, specifically coethnic norms of cooperation became secondary.

Patterns of punishment behavior provide further evidence that universal norms may override specifically coethnic norms when behavior is publicly observed and a strong sanctioning technology is available. Figure 5.11 shows average rates of punishment conditional on a given player's defection, broken down by whether the enforcer and the defecting player were coethnics (defined using benchmark coethnicity). The figure shows that, in deciding whether to punish, enforcers responded to a strong universal norm of sanctioning when players defected, *irrespective of whether the defectors were coethnics of the enforcer*. This universal norm is powerful, accounting for an increase in rates of sanctioning of approximately fifteen percentage points when a player had defected.

One further manipulation of the information condition provides additional support for the claim that strong universal norms are in operation. Examining variation in the information made available to enforcers

Figure 5.9   The Effects of External Sanctioning on Coethnic Cooperation by Egoists

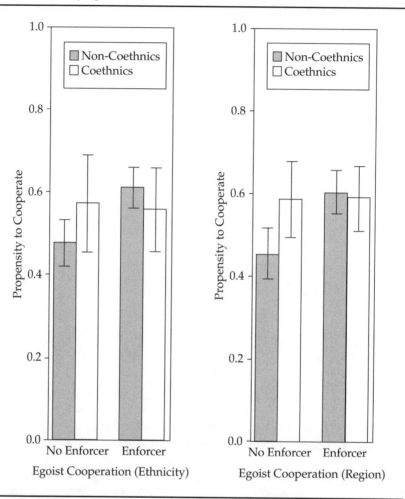

Egoist Cooperation (Ethnicity)   Egoist Cooperation (Region)

Source: Authors' calculations.
Notes: The figure reports the mean levels of cooperation by egoists in coethnic and non-coethnic pairings with and without an enforcer. The bars represent 95 percent confidence intervals. Coethnics exhibit higher rates of cooperation in the absence of an enforcer, but this coethnic advantage disappears when an enforcer is introduced.

reveals that, conditional on defection, decisions to sanction were made at similar rates even when enforcers had no information regarding the identities of the PD players. Though dominated by universal norms, there is weak evidence in figure 5.11 as well for a specifically coethnic norm: enforcers were likely to punish whenever they observed defec-

Figure 5.10   Coethnicity and Cooperation in the Prisoner's Dilemma Game with an Enforcer

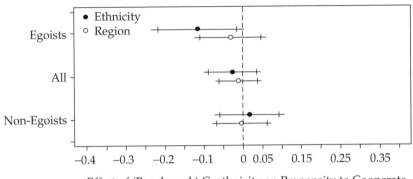

Effect of (Benchmark) Coethnicity on Propensity to Cooperate

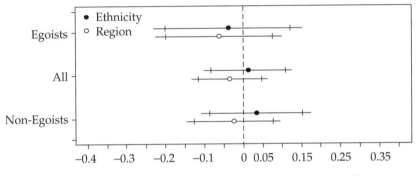

Effect of (Subjective) Coethnicity on Propensity to Cooperate

Source: Authors' calculations.
Notes: The figure reports the estimated effects of coethnicity on the propensity to cooperate in games with a third-party enforcer, broken down by player type. Horizontal lines and ticks show 95 percent and 90 percent confidence intervals, respectively. Coethnics do not cooperate at a higher rate than non-coethnics once the possibility of third-party punishment is introduced.

tion, but they were more likely to do so when playing with coethnics (although this difference is not statistically significant).

To investigate further whether punishment behavior is conditioned on ethnicity, we need to take account of both the ethnic composition of the entire trio and the unequal propensities of players from different groups to encounter trios of different types (for example, enforcers from large groups were much more likely to observe PD games played by their own coethnics than were individuals from smaller groups). We examine play among both egoist and non-egoist enforcers and present av-

Figure 5.11   Defection and Propensity to Sanction

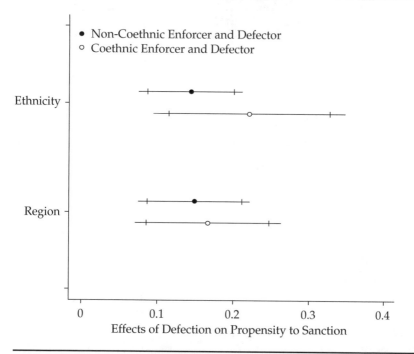

Source: Authors' calculations.
Notes: The figure reports the estimated effects of defection on the likelihood of sanctioning by enforcers, broken down by whether the enforcer and defector are coethnics (in terms of both ethnicity and region). Horizontal lines and ticks show 95 percent and 90 percent confidence intervals, respectively. Defection drives higher levels of punishment whether the enforcer and the defector are coethnics. There is weak evidence that punishment rates are especially high when they are coethnics.

erage punishment behavior across the full range of possibilities for the ethnic composition of the trio playing the game. These include games in which all three players came from different ethnic groups (heterogeneous trios); games in which the two PD players were coethnics and the enforcer was from a different group; games in which the enforcer and one of the PD players were coethnics and the second PD player was a non-coethnic; and games in which all three players came from the same ethnic group (homogeneous trios).

In a game with so many different combinations of players, there were a range of possible patterns we might have observed if ethnic norms were driving patterns of punishment. One possibility, consistent with the account given by Fearon and Laitin (1996), was that enforcers would punish coethnics who defected irrespective of whether they were paired with another coethnic, but would leave it to others to punish defecting non-coethnics. Fearon and Laitin demonstrated that such behavior which involves specifically coethnic punishment could nevertheless foster cross-ethnic cooperation. Another possibility was that enforcers would punish in-group members especially if they defected on other in-group members. Such behavior can be understood as a costly act taken to uphold specifically in-group norms. A third possibility was that players would defend coethnic norms in general, punishing players for defecting on their own coethnics, whether defectors were coethnics of the enforcer. A fourth possibility, for which Helen Bernhard, Urs Fischbacher, and Ernst Fehr (2006) found empirical support among tribespeople in Papua New Guinea, was that enforcers would punish any player who defected on a coethnic while simultaneously being lenient toward coethnics who defected. Although our data lack sufficient power to distinguish convincingly among these explanations, they do provide at least some evidence for us to weigh their face validity.

Figure 5.12 shows the propensity of enforcers to sanction a defecting PD player (player 1) as a function of the ethnic composition of the trio (P1 for player 1, P2 for player 2, and E for the enforcer). Consistent with our previous results, non-egoists were responsible for much of the punishment we observed. Egoists were simply less willing to bear costs to enforce norms. There is also some weak evidence that non-egoists conditioned their punishment behavior more strongly on the identity of the players in the trio. They appeared to punish most frequently when the PD players were coethnics (especially in the special case when the enforcer was also a fellow group member). Egoists punished less overall and conditioned their sanctioning less on the ethnic composition of the trios. However, statistical analysis—which accounts for the fact that groups were assigned to various trios with different probabilities—suggests that the estimated effects of ethnic composition on punishment, while substantively large, are statistically weak.[19]

Thus, with respect to punishment behavior, there is some evidence for the operation of both ethnic and universal norms. Where third-party sanctioning was available, however, the universal norm dominated and removed the disadvantages that non-coethnics suffered in achieving collective action.

Conclusion

We began this chapter by exploring new evidence that could support (or challenge) our interpretation of the findings in chapter 4. We sought first to confirm that coethinics are more effective at resolving collective action problems in the context of an actual public goods game. We found that they are. Moreover, in keeping with our findings in chapter 4, the

Figure 5.12   Effects of Ethnic Composition on Punishment Behavior

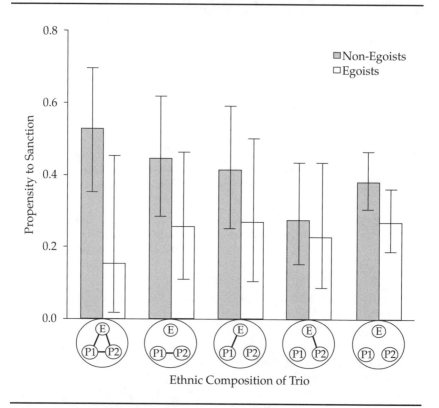

Source: Authors' calculations.
Notes: Lines connecting player labels indicate coethnicity. The figure reports the average propensity to sanction by the ethnic composition of the trio, broken down by player type. The bars represent 95 percent confidence intervals. Non-egoist enforcers are more likely to punish than egoists, and there is weak evidence that they condition their punishment on the ethnic composition of the trio. Punishment rates are highest when both players and the enforcer are coethnics.

greater propensity of coethnics to cooperate in the PD game is driven by increased levels of cooperation among egoist players in particular. Coethnicity, we found, induces egoists to cooperate at levels typical of non-egoists, thereby countering the tragedy of collective action failure that arises in the presence of self-interested players. We then looked for evidence that might confirm our tentative conclusion in chapter 4 that coethnics cooperate more successfully because they fear sanctions should they defect. Our results were strongly supportive of this story. We showed that players correctly anticipate that they will be sanctioned if they fail to cooperate and that they respond by cooperating at higher rates.

Our ambition, however, was greater than simply corroborating our finding that reciprocity norms enable coethnics to cooperate more successfully than non-coethnics. We also sought to push our analysis further by distinguishing between two rival (though related) accounts of the underlying mechanism that might explain coethnic cooperation. Specifically, we wanted to know whether reciprocity norms are universal but simply applied more frequently with coethnics—either because they are more easily found or because they engage with greater frequency—or whether reciprocity norms are specifically coethnic in structure. In this exploratory effort, much of the evidence points to the second account. Players do cooperate more if they know each other, but this does not account for the coethnic effect; indeed, it augments it. Moreover, we found no evidence that more reachable subjects (other than coethnics) also cooperate at higher levels. This suggests that the operation of specifically ethnic norms of cooperation are more important than the reachability of coethnics or the periodicity they enjoy, even if these norms are only (or partially) rendered possible by the fact that coethnics encounter one another more frequently and are more reachable.

We also found, however, that this coethnic norm coexists with another still more powerful universal norm. This universal norm becomes apparent in a different strategic context, one in which behavior is publicly observable and a third player is empowered to sanction. In this environment, the gap in cooperation between egoists and non-egoists is nearly erased, suggesting that egoist players respond to the threat of sanction with higher rates of cooperation. Enforcers, too, exhibit a tendency to punish a large proportion of subjects who defect (regardless of their ethnic group membership), far more than would be predicted if we adopted standard, self-interested models of human behavior.

Play in the PD game with an enforcer also provides insight into the conditions under which universal norms override ethnic patterns of cooperation. Although players do cooperate at higher rates with coethnics when no enforcer is present, the introduction of a powerful external enforcer activates a universal norm of cooperation that outweighs specifically ethnic considerations. The fact that heterogeneous groups do no worse than homogeneous groups in resolving collective action problems when a powerful enforcer is present suggests that reciprocity norms can be cultivated across group lines if institutions can be constructed that render actions observable and punishment possible. How this lesson might be applied to the challenge of public goods provision in diverse communities is an issue we turn to in the conclusion.

Chapter 6

Beyond the Lab

I

N THE preceding chapters, we have emphasized the importance of norms that facilitate the sanctioning of noncontributors. The results of our experimental games suggest that such norms are stronger when people are interacting with coethnics, in part because coethnics engage in repeated interactions and to be closely linked through social networks and in part because there seem to be specifically coethnic norms of cooperation. Since the likelihood that a social interaction will be with a non-coethnic increases with the diversity of the community, our experimental findings may provide an explanation for the well-documented disadvantage that ethnically heterogeneous communities around the world—and in Mulago-Kyebando—face in providing public goods.

Making this link plausible, however, requires that we address whether the behaviors we observed in our experimental games capture anything about the real world our subjects inhabit. How well do the patterns of play we observed in the laboratory map onto behaviors that affect the provision of public goods in the neighborhoods we are studying? To answer these questions, we have to step outside of the experimental lab. In this chapter, we explore a series of steps that take us from our experimental results to explaining behavior in Mulago-Kyebando and beyond. Each successive step requires ever stronger assumptions, and as such, our inferences rest on progressively weaker ground as we move farther away from the lab and, later in the chapter, farther away from our Mulago-Kyebando study area. Nonetheless, we seek to subject our results to tough tests of their internal and external validity. Our goal in doing so is not only to assess the generalizability of our findings but also to contribute to establishing new standards for evaluating the findings derived from lab experimental work and to defining a road map for future research on the impact of ethnic diversity on collective action.

In this chapter, as a first test of the validity of our experimental results, we explore in greater depth how our subjects made sense of the games we asked them to play. We then look to see whether behavior in the lab correlates with the attitudes and practices exhibited by our subjects in the community, as reported to us in our survey research.[1] We examine in particular whether individuals who cooperated more in the lab also did so in the community and whether individuals who displayed greater coethnic bias in the lab also tended to associate more with coethnics in their everyday interactions.

Next, the chapter examines data from interviews with local councilors and community members in Mulago-Kyebando to see whether their accounts of the reasons for collective action failure in their neighborhoods were consistent with our experimental finding that cooperation is hampered by difficulties in effectively sanctioning noncontributors. Evidence from our interviews suggests that, when and where collective action succeeds, it is generally among homogeneous subsets of the community or within narrow associations that have developed mechanisms for policing contributions. This is consonant with the story that emerges from our experimental games insofar as it confirms that the weakness of reciprocity norms that cross group boundaries is an impediment to the collective provision of local public goods.

Finally, we explore the generalizability of our experimental findings to communities beyond Mulago-Kyebando. In taking this step, we push our data to (and perhaps beyond) the limit of its reliability. Specifically, we generate and test predictions about the level of public goods provision we would expect to find in communities that have ethnic demographies different from Mulago-Kyebando's but are composed of similar ethnic groups. This test is difficult to pass, and while we find some support for our argument, the results are not strong.

How Our Subjects Understood the Games

A basic initial question that speaks to the validity of our findings is whether the subjects who participated in our experiments—many of whom had little formal education—understood the rules of the games. Even if they understood the rules, is it plausible that they were able to make sense of each game's subtleties and condition their behavior on the treatments we randomly assigned? Is it realistic to assume also that, despite repeated visits to our lab over three months, our subjects did not communicate with one another about the games or develop friendships that might have affected our results? In short, were our subjects playing the games we thought they were playing? We had gone to great lengths in designing our protocols to ensure that the answer to these questions was yes, and our subjects' personal reflections on the games, solicited in post-experiment interviews that we summarize here, give us confidence that the answer was indeed yes.

Comprehension

The participants taking part in our lab experiments were making unusual choices, operating in an unfamiliar environment, surrounded by strangers, and doing all this for the purposes of a research project that was foreign both in the sense that it was being run by a team of U.S.-based researchers and that it was asking participants to do something completely alien to them. We were thus very concerned about ensuring that our subjects were made to feel comfortable and understood the rules of each game they played.

We took a number of steps to address these concerns. On their arrival in the lab, our subjects attended a detailed presentation of each game by a team of enumerators.[2] Working with a computer, a digital projector, and all of the props that were used in the actual lab—the envelopes and boxes into which players would put their allocations, the headphones they would wear when they listened to the video greetings, the stacks of coins they would be given at the beginning of each round of each game—our enumerators walked the subjects through each game step by step. The projector showed the subjects what they would be seeing on the computer screen, and the enumerators demonstrated the range of strategies that could be employed in each game, highlighting both the actions that were permitted as well as those that were not. The team of enumerators responsible for instruction remained the same throughout the four experimental sessions attended by each subject, provided exactly the same set of instructions to each group of participants, and was composed of individuals able to speak the range of languages used by our subjects. While overall directions were provided in Luganda, instructions were translated for all subjects who indicated a discomfort with Luganda when they signed in for the session. To reduce confusion before each game, only the game about to be played was described. Only after all subjects finished playing that game were the rules for the next game provided.

When subjects went into the lab, they were met by a trained enumerator and seated at a computer terminal. The enumerator's first responsibility was to administer a test. Using the props for the game, the enumerator asked the subject to describe the game, to detail the range of strategies available, and to show the enumerator how he or she would indicate her offer or choice. Any subjects who were unable to pass this test returned to the main waiting area, where they received additional instructions from the presentation team.[3] Only when subjects had passed the test could they begin playing a game.

To further investigate our subjects' comprehension, we implemented a form of "back-translation" during the experiment. We hired a local university graduate who was unfamiliar with our project and the specific games we were playing and asked him to facilitate a focus group with a random sample of our subjects. His responsibility was like that of a detective: to gather the necessary information from our subjects to be able to come back and tell us the rules for each game, the strategies available to the players, what the subjects thought the games were about, and why they chose the strategies they did. After a meeting with the subjects, our facilitator was able to provide us with an accurate description of the rules, the strategies, and the choices people made for each game. It was clear from his findings that subjects generally understood the games and the decisions they were meant to make.

The most important tests of our subjects' understanding of the games came from how they played them; we were particularly alert to whether they made choices that were inconsistent with the game's instructions. Recall that, in the 500-Ugandan-shilling-denomination Dictator game, the rules require subjects to discriminate: they are not allowed to keep both coins or to give both coins to another person. Across the 3,880 rounds of this game that were played with a non-anonymous offerer, a player gave both coins to another person in only three rounds, and in only 206 rounds did a player keep both coins. In the Prisoner's Dilemma game, whose rules stipulate that players must put the 1,000-Ugandan-shilling note in one of the two boxes, a player kept the 1,000-Ugandan-shilling note in only 28 of 2,996 games. Only 7 of 300 players were coded by the enumerators as having had difficulty understanding the 500-Ugandan-shilling Dictator game and needing further instruction; just 39 and 57 (of 300) players needed additional instruction in the PD and third-party enforcement games, respectively. Our experimental setup was designed to maximize comprehension in a difficult environment, and the results of these various checks suggest that it did.[4]

Interpretation

Even if our subjects could follow the rules of the games, one might still wonder whether their behavior reflected an understanding of what the games were really about and how they differed from one another. Game theorists see analogies between these games and actual social interactions and expect that people behave in a similar way in both settings. Do subjects also see these analogies? To explore how the players made sense of the games, we conducted post-experiment debriefings with a random sample of fifty-seven of our three hundred subjects. We asked twenty-eight of them about the Dictator and third-party enforcement games and twenty-nine of them about the Prisoner's Dilemma and Lockbox games.

It is clear from their responses that our subjects understood the underlying logic of the games. They believed that each of the games had a distinct purpose, with its own parallel in their everyday lives. Many perceived (correctly) that we were interested in learning how people behave when interacting with different types of partners. That being said, our debriefings suggested that almost no one thought the games were specifically about coethnic and non-coethnic interaction. If they had harbored such thoughts, it would have represented a serious threat to the validity of our findings, but only one respondent suggested that the researchers' interest was in understanding specifically how individuals treat people of different ethnic groups.[5]

For the Dictator game, more than three-quarters described the game as being about how people share with other people, how people get along with or treat other people, or how they distribute limited resources (see table 6.1). The subjects' own words are illuminating. When asked what they thought we were trying to learn from the Dictator game, one subject volunteered that we were interested in learning "if people share what they have with persons they don't know." Another said that he thought we were trying to "find out how people behave with money when it comes to the welfare of the community." Another thought that we wanted to see "how people distribute money amongst people of different tribes, sex, and age." When asked about the rules they used to determine how to allocate the coins among themselves and the other players, our subjects were forthcoming, although not always in ways that mirrored the results we find in analyzing their behavior. For example, only 7 percent reported making their decisions based on tribe, despite the fact that our results in the non-anonymous Dictator game suggest that they often did. Nearly 50 percent described giving to those who were most needy or unable to provide for themselves (that is, the very young or very old).[6]

Subjects interpreted the Prisoner's Dilemma game as being about how people work together and whether individuals keep what they earn for themselves or share it with the group in order to earn interest (responses are summarized in table 6.2). They were conscious of the difference between the games with and without an enforcer. Subjects interpreted games without the enforcer as having the goal of finding out "whether we could work cooperatively without someone having to watch over us" or "if someone would do developmental work even if they were alone." By contrast, one subject saw the addition of the enforcer as designed to capture whether "people would change decisions in fear of the observer." Subjects believed that the role of the observer was to "act as a judge" and to "prevent one of the players from playing the wrong way." The last supposition is especially interesting since, with

Table 6.1   Post-Experiment Debriefing for the Dictator Game

	Percentage
"What were the researchers trying to learn?"	
How people share with other people	44
How people distribute limited resources	26
How people judge the fairness or trustworthiness of others	11
How people get along, treat one another	15
Don't know	4
"To whom did you give coins?"	
To people who looked needy	26
To people who looked very old or young	
(not of working age)	19
To people based on tribe	7
To people who looked nice	19
To people who looked beautiful	15
To women	7
To people who I thought would give to me	7
Randomly	15

Source: Authors' calculations.

the punishment happening ex post, the subject was describing the effects of a threat of punishment. In the words of one subject, the enforcer game was designed to measure "if people can actually punish someone else even when it's at the cost of their money."

Many subjects believed that the Lockbox game was designed to measure intelligence or ability. But nearly one-third viewed the game as a device for ascertaining whether people can work together to achieve a common task. One subject captured the purpose precisely when he described our objective as measuring "one's ability to teach others how to do something." Other subjects suggested that it was about seeing whether "people can work together in bigger companies or organizations" and whether those working together with someone "can . . . accomplish a task together."

Our findings from the post-experiment debriefings go some distance in allaying fears that our experimental methods were little more than "games" that were completely alien to the people or the setting in which they were employed. It appears that our subjects not only understood the rules of each game but also had a fairly good sense of the types of social interactions and dilemmas that the games were designed to capture.

Collusion

A final concern is that, rather than misunderstanding what we were trying to do, our subjects might have understood the games too well and

Table 6.2   The Prisoner's Dilemma Game and Third-Party Enforcement—
Post-Experiment Debriefing

	Percentage
Prisoner's Dilemma Game (Without Enforcer)	
"What were the researchers trying to learn?"	
Whether people keep money for themselves or share with the group	14
How people work together	21
Whether people would work cooperatively without someone watching over them	25
Don't know	21
Prisoner's Dilemma Game (with Enforcer)	
"What were the researchers trying to learn?"	
To see if people change their behavior when overseen	39
To see who the observer punishes	4
Don't know	10
Enforcer Game	
"What were the researchers trying to learn?"	
How people work together in a community and achieve common aims	30
Whether people will bear costs to punish others who misbehave	11
People's attitudes about saving and investment	26
Don't know	26
"Who did you punish?"	
Those who kept the money for themselves and did not put in the box for the group	41
People I didn't like	4
People I knew	4
There was no reason to punish	33

Source: Authors' calculations.

been in a position to collude with one another to try to maximize their returns. Indeed, possible discussion of the games by subjects with one another outside of the lab could have shaped their perspective on what we were trying to accomplish and affected their behavior (and thus our findings).

To investigate whether collusion was likely to have been taking place, we developed a test for whether social networks had formed among our subjects in the course of the games. After all of the games described in this book had been played, we ran a small experiment—a variant of the standard trust game. We offered half of the subjects the opportunity to earn additional money by either handing in the identification card they had been given at the beginning of the project—in which case they would be given 1,000 Ugandan shillings on the spot—or finding another subject, convincing that subject to hand over his or her identification card, and handing both identification cards in simultaneously—in which case the subject would be given three to five times as much money. Only 23 of the 130 subjects invited to earn more money by playing this game elected to do so. The vast majority chose instead just to take the 1,000 Ugandan shillings we offered up front and forgo the chance to earn more. Participation increased only slightly (from 15 to 19 percent) when we raised the stakes from 3,000 Ugandan shillings (52 total playings) to 5,000 Ugandan shillings (78 total playings). Furthermore, only 11 of the 23 subjects who elected to play (and of the 130 who had the opportunity) succeeded in finding a partner to bring in his or her card. We interpret the fact that so many subjects declined to play—leaving, in effect, so much money "on the table"—and that those who did play did so poorly as evidence that our subjects had not formed strong social ties with one another. If they had, it would have been quite easy for them to earn a significant sum of money. These findings suggest that it is unlikely that our subjects engaged in collusion during the games sessions.

Measurement Validity

Even if we believe that our subjects really did understand the games they were asked to play, we might still ask whether the behaviors they exhibited in the lab correlated with the real-life attitudes and practices that we want to use the results of the games to understand. From a methodological perspective, we can think of this as a test of measurement validity. Does play in games, which we have argued captures things like the degree to which an individual is other-regarding or driven by reciprocity considerations, track with how that same individual comports himself or herself outside of the experimental lab? The difficulty here is that we cannot observe directly how individuals behave outside of the lab. We can learn about their behavior only by asking them about it in survey questions, and surveys, like experiments, can be criticized on a number of methodological grounds. As a result, the tests presented in this section must be thought of as exploring the relationship between two different, and necessarily imperfect, measurement tools; we are not attempting to make any causal claims. Our more modest goal is simply to see whether the measures drawn from these different sources correlate. To the extent that they do, we will gain added confidence that both approaches are picking up something about the underlying characteristics of the individuals in our sample.

We begin with a very general question: are people who are more generous in the games also more active in associational life and politics? We measured observed generosity in the games as the average offer by each subject in the 100-Ugandan-shilling Dictator game when he or she had no information about the receivers, both for the cases in which the offerer was observed and those in which the offerer was not observed in making his or her offer. The latter captures pure other-regardingness, while the former combines other-regardingness and reciprocity. We computed associational activity from our subjects' responses in pre- and post-experimental questionnaires. To capture the degree to which our subjects participated in and had taken leadership roles in community groups, we computed an index of associational participation using factor analysis that combined seven questions about individual involvement in religious, cooperative, business, community development, ethnic, music or sport, and credit groups. We also created a separate index of political participation, using factor analysis to combine measures of voting behavior (across local and national elections), participation in political discussions, and attendance at community meetings. The resulting measures of associational and political participation are not highly correlated, suggesting that distinct processes may drive these two aspects of community involvement.[7]

The first two panels of figure 6.1 show correlations between associational and political participation, on the one hand, and game behavior, on the other. We see a positive correlation between generosity in the Dictator games (when subjects were seen to be generous) and participation in political and associational life. These correlations are not observed, however, when individuals were not seen to be generous, suggesting that associational and political activity may reflect adherence to reciprocity norms and not simply other-regarding preferences. This responsiveness to the loss of anonymity lends additional support to our emphasis on reciprocity norms as central to collective action in these communities.

We also investigated whether cooperation in the Prisoner's Dilemma game is associated with associational activity or political participation. For these analyses, we used a measure of the propensity of an individual to cooperate in the Prisoner's Dilemma (without an enforcer) for the cases in which individuals were seen and not seen.[8] Consistent with the generosity results, we find that individuals who cooperated in the Prisoner's Dilemma when their identities were known to their partners also participated at higher rates in political life. A similar relationship also obtains for those who cooperated even when not observed, although it is not significant at conventional levels. The correlations between game behavior and associational activity are weaker still.

Figure 6.1 also reports correlations between game behavior and a measure of generalized trust. Whereas our measures of political and

Figure 6.1 Cooperative Behavior Inside and Outside the Lab

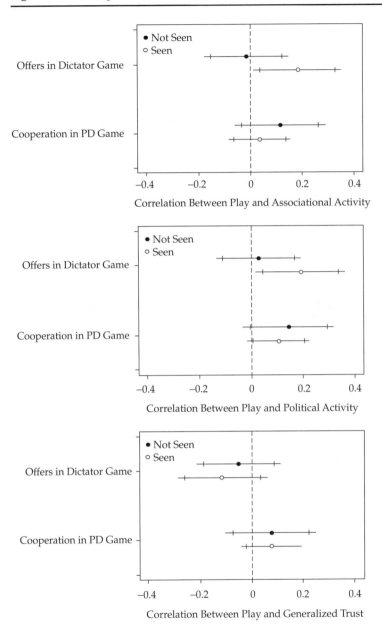

Correlation Between Play and Associational Activity

Correlation Between Play and Political Activity

Correlation Between Play and Generalized Trust

Source: Authors' calculations.
Notes: The figures report correlations between offers in the Dictator game and cooperation in the PD game (for players when not seen and when seen) and measures of associational activity, political activity, and generalized trust. Horizontal lines and ticks show 95 percent and 90 percent confidence intervals, respectively. Patterns of play when the subject was observed are more strongly correlated with associational and political activity than anonymous play; correlations between game play and attitudinal measures of trust are weak.

associational activity combine a set of behavioral measures, the trust measure is generated from a set of "attitudinal" questions, similar to those employed in many opinion surveys, in which respondents indicate the extent to which they trust different categories of people, broken down by coethnicity, co-religion, wealth, neighborhood, and education levels. These measures are aggregated, again using factor analysis, to create a measure of generalized trust. The components correlate highly (Cronbach's alpha = 0.81), but the measure is still vulnerable to the concern that self-reported trust may be subject to both reporting bias and imprecision stemming from ambiguity about what, precisely, "trust" is. (Our respondents did not ask us for a definition of trust, but we admit that we would have been hard-pressed to give a compelling answer had they done so; for a useful discussion of the difficulty of measuring trust in surveys, see Cook, Hardin, and Levi 2005.) We find that a respondent's level of generalized trust correlates positively with behavior in the Prisoner's Dilemma and negatively with behavior in the Dictator game. In neither case, however, is the correlation significantly different from zero. These weak associations might reflect the flaws of our measures, although, given the generally strong relationships exhibited between game play and behavioral measures of participation and associational activity, it is also plausible that the low correlations reflect the weakness of attitudinal measures of this form.

Next, we explore whether the coethnic bias we observed among individuals in their game behavior is associated with higher levels of coethnic friendship choice and trust and lower levels of social distance, as reported in our surveys. Although our investigations in chapter 4 produced no evidence of coethnic other-regarding preferences in the aggregate, some individuals favor coethnics at higher rates than others. Here we examined the extent to which subjects who exhibited such coethnic biases were also those who said that they were especially trusting of coethnics or who embedded themselves in networks of people who were mainly coethnics.

We measured coethnic bias by calculating the extent to which subjects favored in-group members in anonymous versions of the 100-Ugandan-shilling and 500-Ugandan-shilling Dictator games.[9] We measured an affinity for in-group members through a measure of the share of a subject's six closest friends who were coethnics. We measured within-group trust through a question about the ethnic group membership of the last person the subject had lent money to and the last person the subject had participated with in a rotating savings and credit association (ROSCA). And we measured the social distance of members of a subject's ethnic group relative to others using a version of the "Bogardus scale" of social distance.[10] The first three of these measures were based on behavioral information provided by subjects, while the fourth reflected the subjects' reporting of attitudes.

We find a positive correlation between coethnic bias and outcomes on all three behavioral measures (see figure 6.2).[11] These correlations are not significantly different from zero for the 100-Ugandan-shilling game, but in all three cases are significant at least at the 90 percent level for the 500-Ugandan-shilling game—a feature that probably reflects the greater degree of discrimination observed (by design) in these games. Again, we find that the attitudinal measure (social distance) correlates most poorly (in this case, not at all) with our measures of behavior in the experimental games.

The results of this exercise are encouraging. For key measures of subject behavior in the real world—associational activity, political participation, and the coethnic concentration of social and economic relations—we find correlations with game behavior in the expected direction. Many, but not all, of these correlations are statistically significant. Moreover, it is game play *when subjects were observed* that correlates most closely with actual levels of political and communal activity, suggesting that reciprocity norms rather than other-regardingness is central to collective action in this setting. Finally, the weakest correlations obtain for survey-based measures that asked subjects directly about their attitudes rather than about their behaviors. These results are consistent with previous work that highlights the weak associations between survey questions and game behavior (see, for example, Glaeser, Laibson, Scheinkman, and Soutter 2000).

Experimental Behavior and Everyday Life

Having drawn on experimental evidence to answer the question of why diverse communities underprovide local public goods, we now turn to everyday life in the communities from which our subjects were drawn. If the inability of diverse communities to effectively sanction noncontributors is indeed a major impediment to collective action, we should find additional evidence in support of our findings in the daily experiences of local councils in Mulago-Kyebando.

In chapters 1 and 2, we outlined the challenges of public goods provision in the urban Ugandan setting. In particular, we highlighted the central role of local councils in providing security, maintaining drainage channels to prevent flooding and disease, and ensuring that garbage is collected. Using data gathered in our household surveys in Kawempe, we showed that the common empirical relationship between ethnic diversity and the success of communities in providing these local public goods holds in urban Kampala.

We now explore the experiences of the twenty-six local council areas

Figure 6.2   Coethnic Biases Inside and Outside the Lab

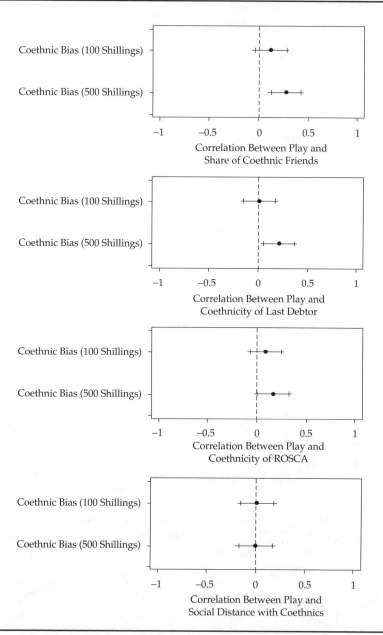

Source: Authors' calculations.
Notes: The figures report correlations between coethnic bias in the Dictator and Discrimination games (for players when not seen and when seen) and measures of coethnic social relationships. Horizontal lines and ticks show 95 percent and 90 percent confidence intervals, respectively. Patterns of coethnic bias in the 500-Ugandan-shilling game are more strongly correlated with patterns of coethnic social relationships than play in the 100-Ugandan-shilling game; correlations between game play and attitudinal measures of relative trust in coethnics are much weaker.

in Mulago-Kyebando in greater detail. Specifically, we look to see whether evidence from our interviews with local council leaders suggests that ethnic diversity does indeed impede public goods provision, and if so, whether instances of collective action success tend to be driven largely by homogeneous subsets of each community. If we find this to be the case, it will bolster our confidence that the weakness of cross-group reciprocity norms is part of what impedes the collective provision of local public goods.

Collective Action Failure

In chapter 2, we presented evidence that LC1s have great difficulty in generating contributions of time, labor, or money to support public goods provision. We also presented evidence that these difficulties are compounded by the diversity arising from in-migration. "Fifty years ago, only the Baganda were here in my area," one local council chairman told us. He added:

> There was no other tribe. I've been living here for over thirty years, and things are very different now. . . . There was a big increase in western immigrants beginning in 1996. . . . The biggest problem here today is that there is no good relationship between indigenous people and the new ones here in my zone. They don't cooperate with each other because the new ones are so proud, and they use such abusive language. Their culture doesn't cooperate with Baganda culture, and they do things that Baganda would never do.

Another council leader lamented that "you may find that the northerners oppose the fee for a project, say it is too much money when others say the fee is okay." Yet another Baganda LC1 chair told us that "the Baganda are very accommodative. Tribes from the north and the west are much less accommodative. If you go to the west or the north to visit, as I have, they might even chase you off their property." When asked why that was, he said, "Why? It's in their character."

The problem, another concurred (in an uncanny, if anecdotal, summary of the efficacy mechanism described in chapter 4), is that "you can send information to some people as messengers, but information won't be transmitted if you are sending between tribes."

Mulago-Kyebando, like the rest of Kampala, had been an area in which the Baganda were the dominant group until President Museveni came to the power in the mid-1980s. His ascendance ushered in a period of tremendous in-migration of western groups to Kampala. For many migrants, their first stop was, and continues to be, densely populated neighborhoods like Mulago-Kyebando. These accounts suggest that local leaders believe that ethnic diversity sometimes makes their jobs harder. But they tell us little about the mechanisms that might be at work. For clues, we turn from stories of collective action failure to those about success.

Successful Collective Action in Mulago-Kyebando

Despite the complaints we heard from LC1 chairs about the difficulties they encounter in securing the support and participation of community members, our investigations make clear that the communities in our study area sometimes do act to clean up garbage, clear drainage channels, and monitor the community at night (recall the summary provided in table 2.2). Closer analysis suggests that these instances of successful collective action tend to be driven by homogeneous subsets of the population in each ethnically diverse neighborhood. Of the several examples of successful public goods provision offered by our informants, very few were widespread community initiatives. Most involved only a small segment of community members.

LC1 chairpersons consistently explained that a relatively small number of volunteers were responsible for improving things in the community. "We, the committee, have one LDU [local defense unit] and one security man, and I also help with community defense, because I have experience in these things from the war," one local council chairman explained. "When there are problems, we move around at night—the three of us." Describing how garbage is collected in the council area, another told us that he and his fellow council members "converge sometimes on Saturday, we collect all the garbage from the houses and put it where it's supposed to be ready for collection. . . . The residents help us, but when we leave it up to them, we find problems." Another council chair explained that "the same group that takes care of drainage cleaning will get together for road maintenance. They come together about eight times a year for a day each time."

Mulago-Kyebando is not alone in depending on a small number of committed individuals for public goods provision. This is a pattern that has been noted in communities around the world. From the standpoint of the argument in this book, the noteworthy aspect of these small-group efforts is their largely homogeneous ethnic makeup. Take membership on the local council executive committees (typically composed of ten members, some elected and some appointed). In 74 percent of the local councils in our study area, a single ethnic group held at least half of the official positions—a striking figure given that a single ethnic group accounts for more than 50 percent of the population in fewer than half the LC1s.

Figure 6.3   Relationship Between Group Share in the Local Council and
Group Share in the Local Council Committee

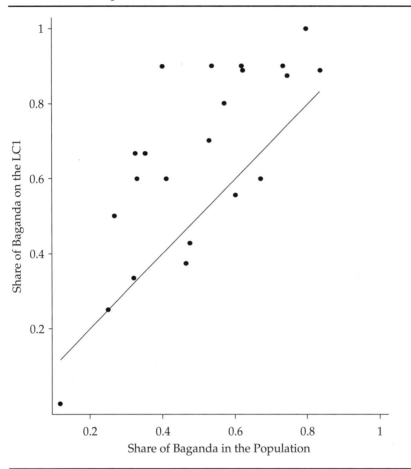

Source: Authors' calculations.
Notes: In the scatter plot of the relationship between the share of the Baganda in an LC1
and the share of Baganda on the LC committee, the forty-five-degree line indicates
proportionality. Baganda are disproportionately represented on the LC committees, even
in areas where they are not the plurality ethnic group.

Figure 6.3 plots the share of the Baganda in the local council area
against the share of the Baganda on the local council executive committee. Nearly all of the local councils exhibit dominance by the Baganda,
and in most cases the share of Baganda on the council is greater than the
share of Baganda in the population.[12]

But while the Baganda dominate in local politics, there is evidence
of in-group coordination within other ethnic groups as well. Indeed, in

Mulago-Kyebando, ethnically homogenous associations are formed for the purposes of savings, credit, and a range of other practical needs. Local council chairs spoke often about the tendency of various ethnic groups to keep to themselves and to form self-help associations only among coethnics. "People are so attached to their tribe," one told us. "They normally cooperate according to their tribe so much." Another explained that "we have some so-called groups that are organized on a tribal basis."

> For example, the Bafumbira lend to each other. They are very organized in that way. They have a society that is formalized with executive members, and if you need money and are a Bafumbira, you can go to them. If you need burial money, for example, they apply and can be lent money. They are more organized than the Baganda. The Bafumbira elect their own leaders. . . . If one of them is arrested, they try to raise money to pay his fine. For the Baganda, there is no group like this in our area.

Describing the Alur community, another council leader told us:

> This is a group of people from the northwest. They form their own association. They are mainly concerned with economic and social problems. When they get a problem, for example, losing a person, they come together; in case of a person having an economic problem, they come together. . . . They mobilize funds among themselves to solve the problem.

These are all routine collective activities. There is nothing clearly "ethnic" about them, and they do not suggest a rivalry or competition between groups. Preferences for the benefits that flow from successful collective action in these areas are common across groups. And in principle, individuals could benefit from participating in such activities independent of their ethnicity. Yet these accounts demonstrate that cooperative action that plausibly could benefit all takes place along, rather than across, ethnic lines. Moreover, building cooperation across group boundaries has not come easily to the local council chairpersons in Mulago-Kyebando. Despite an overwhelming need for successful mobilization on issues of garbage, drainage, and security, most local councils have failed in their efforts to mount community-wide responses.

Importantly, these accounts are quite consistent with the premises that motivated our study. Diversity appears to play a role in the failure of collective action in Mulago-Kyebando; ethnic homogeneity seems to be associated with instances of success. And when the ethnic homogeneity of local councils is made apparent and set up against the tremendous ethnic diversity of the communities they oversee, their failure is perhaps not so surprising. Norms of reciprocity—which operate more strongly within groups than across them—may facilitate successful collective action within groups, but the local council system is not well positioned to activate (or police) these norms in support of community-wide activities. Figuring out what this means for diverse communities, and how universal norms can be brought to bear even where ethnic norms already exist, is a topic we reserve for the conclusion.

Beyond Mulago-Kyebando

Nearing the end of this inquiry, we now know much more about the poor urban neighborhoods of Kampala than we did before. But how much power does this investigation offer us to understand the ways in which diversity shapes collective action outside of our study area? In methodological terms, this is a question of the external validity of our findings. Generalization is a risky business in experimental research. With confidence, we can say only that our subjects behaved in a particular way at a particular point in time when subjected to a particular experimental environment. We gain some additional power from the fact that our subjects were a random sample of a defined population, which gives us grounds to make statements about the ways in which diversity shapes collective action in Mulago-Kyebando. But it is natural to wonder whether our analysis tells us much about the impact of diversity on public goods in other settings.

The answer to that question is that we do not know how well these results travel. A satisfactory answer would require replicating studies of this form across different settings, a challenge we discuss in chapter 7. Short of replication, there are still some ways to push the analysis a bit further. Here we briefly discuss one such step by examining the level of public goods provision we would expect to see in communities neighboring Mulago-Kyebando given the behavior we have observed in Mulago-Kyebando.

Using our data on interactions between members of different groups in the lab, it is possible to generate predictions about levels of public goods provision in neighboring communities composed of similar ethnic groups, but with different ethnic demographies. In practice, this means taking average levels of cooperation between a person of group A and a person of group B in the lab and combining this data with population data to produce a measure of the average level of cooperation in a given area. This can be thought of as a generalization of the well-known ethnic fractionalization index. Instead of using ethnic diversity on its own to predict levels of public goods provision, this measure combines benchmark demography with estimates of how individuals from different groups actually engage with one another.[13]

Two assumptions are required to defend such a measure. First, we need to assume that outcomes in a community reflect the aggregation of a set of binary relationships rather than being driven by organizational features. This means focusing not on leadership (as many scholars of politics do) but on the nature of reciprocal relationships within a community. Second, we need to assume that the patterns of pairwise interaction are not location-specific. That is, we need to assume that the way an *A* treats a *B* in Mulago-Kyebando is the same as the way an *A* treats a *B* in other places.

Both are clearly strong assumptions. Nevertheless, in a final exploration of the external validity of our laboratory data, we used data from the 2002 population census on the ethnic composition of LC1s and a set of matrices that recorded average behavior in the lab between members of each pair of ethnic groups to compute predicted values for the level of collective action in each LC1. We focused our attention on sixty LC1s that sit just outside the borders of Mulago-Kyebando. We then checked to see whether these predicted values correlate with actual levels of community activity in support of enhanced security and garbage collection, as measured in our household survey (described in chapter 2).

This is a very difficult test to pass, and our examination of the data met with mixed results. We looked at three distinct measures: average other-regardingness (based on behavior in the anonymous Dictator game), average reciprocity (based on behavior in the non-anonymous Dictator game), and average cooperation (based on behavior in the non-anonymous Prisoner's Dilemma game). We found that our measures of other-regardingness, reciprocity, and cooperation all correlate positively with both indicators of collective action to provide public goods. However, none of these correlations was significant at conventional levels.

The weak correlations may reflect the structure of the data. Our average measures of laboratory behavior—designed to capture how individuals interact with members of a wide range of other ethnic groups—often were based on a very small number of observations, so it is likely that we measured patterns of pairwise interaction with some error. Or it may also be that the assumptions underlying this test were untenable. But at a minimum, this exploration does suggest what is possible in principle with more and better data.

Conclusion

This chapter has shown that subjects had a good understanding of the games they were playing, that how they acted in the lab corresponds well with the behavior they reported outside of the lab, and that the patterns of community life uncovered in the laboratory are quite consistent with the stories told by community leaders about the struggles they confront. But our ability to make fresh predictions regarding community-level outcomes beyond Mulago-Kyebando based on behavior in the lab is at present weak. The challenge that remains—not just for us but for all scholars engaged in micro-level research—is to find better ways to establish the generality of the social processes we uncover in a particular locale. This is an issue we return to in the conclusion.

Chapter 7

Conclusions

THE COMMUNITIES of Mulago-Kyebando sit nestled in a valley between two of Kampala's seven hills, nearly a sixty-minute drive (ninety minutes during the rainy season) from the house we rented during our four months of fieldwork in 2005. Every morning we traveled in our well-worn minivan with our mobile computer lab and thousands of coins to our research site. Potholes and pockets of traffic forced us to be creative in the routes we took. Sometimes, after passing through Kabalagala, we headed up Muyenga Hill and then wound our way down a bumpy dirt road through the Kisugu slums toward Mulago-Kyebando. On other occasions, we tried to avoid the backup at the Clock Tower in downtown Kampala by heading through Old Kampala, the seat of the Buganda kingdom, before emerging in the university district of Makerere, and then on to our field site.

These different pathways ran through an astonishingly diverse set of urban environments. Sectors of urban boom filled with shiny new offices and amenity-filled homes gave way to squalid slums where rainstorms flushed human waste onto muddy, potholed roads. The contrast between rich neighborhoods and poor neighborhoods was glaring. But we were also struck by the variation in the character of the impoverished areas we drove through. In some places, litter lined the streets, while in others almost no trash was visible. The rains made roads and walkways impassable in some areas, but flowed harmlessly through well-maintained drainage channels in others. In some neighborhoods, the fall of darkness activated community life, while in others it sent residents fleeing inside behind locked doors.

We see contrasting images of community life also in the United States where we work and live. Our kaleidoscopic commute in Kampala was preceded during the pilot phase of our project by a series of regular back-and-forth journeys between our two experimental labs at UCLA and the University of Southern California. The commute between the two took us from the tony Westside neighborhoods of Brentwood and

Bel Air to the much poorer neighborhoods of South Central Los Angeles. As in Kampala, we were struck not just by the differences in wealth but also by the very different feel of neighborhoods composed of residents at the same level of income. Like many scholars of American cities, we wondered: Why are some poor communities marked by high levels of violence and crime while others manage to police their own streets? Why are schools in some low-income neighborhoods supported by an active infrastructure of parental involvement while schools in others struggle to generate any parental interest? Why does the in-migration of new residents strengthen some poor communities but lead to a decay of services and the rapid out-migration of longtime residents in others? In the United States, as in Kampala, Uganda, the answer hinges in part on the characteristics of the community itself. The quality of public goods in a neighborhood is a function of the ability of residents to work together to confront their collective challenges, not simply a reflection of their wealth.

But what accounts for the ability of a community to work collectively to solve its problems? There are almost certainly many contributing factors. One factor that has received significant attention from scholars is ethnic diversity. The argument is that communities composed of a broad diversity of ethnic groups often have a harder time acting collectively and thus fare worse than more homogeneous neighborhoods. This argument runs against the grain of a growing embrace of multiculturalism. Yet, as uncomfortable as it may be, a large body of evidence based on studies conducted in communities around the globe backs up the claim that ethnic diversity often impedes the provision of public goods.

Rather than ignoring this evidence—or (falsely) inferring from the fact that diverse communities often face greater problems of collective action that they *inevitably* do so—we have sought to discover the logic that links ethnic diversity to poor public goods provision. Knowing the mechanism(s) that underlie this relationship not only provides a deeper understanding of an important social process but also permits us to consider interventions that might hold promise of mitigating the cooperation-undermining effects of diversity.

This is the challenge we took up in this book. In this concluding chapter, we begin by reviewing the main findings. We then focus our attention on three implications of our research. First, we discuss the implications of our work for the study of ethnicity. We ask: what have we learned about ethnicity that is relevant beyond our research site and beyond the specific connections between ethnic diversity and public goods provision? Next, we turn to the methodological implications. What does the project suggest about the potential for experimental research as a tool for understanding social processes of this form? Finally, we consider the political implications. What lessons can we draw from this research about how to foster cooperation in diverse communities?

Findings

We opened this book by observing that scholars have advanced a number of plausible explanations to account for the greater facility that ethnically homogeneous communities often have in acting collectively and providing public goods. It might be the case, for example, that people care more about the welfare of individuals from their own ethnic group than about those from other groups. This would be consistent with the observation that people often give more generously of their time and energy to charities that benefit members of their own religion, ethnic group, or community than to charities that benefit others. Indeed, research in social psychology has demonstrated that individuals commonly exhibit this sort of in-group bias, even (or at least) in cases in which the groups to which they "belong" are arbitrarily created by the experimenter. An alternative account emphasizes the ease with which members of ethnic groups work together. To the extent that coethnics share a common language and a set of common experiences, individuals may be more willing to cooperate with fellow group members because they expect the collaboration to go more smoothly. Other explanations focus on strategies: the cooperative capacity of homogeneous communities may be higher simply because everyone in an ethnic group expects other group members to cooperate and believes that noncooperation within the group should and will be punished.

Yet this list of possible explanations only scratches the surface. Other accounts have been offered, and still others might be imagined. In focusing attention on how ethnic diversity affects public goods provision, our first challenge was therefore to identify the universe of channels through which this relationship might operate. We turned to the language of game theory, using its parsimonious description of social interactions as a vehicle for identifying the set of pathways through which ethnic identities might condition behavior in a game. This exercise yielded a small number of first-order channels, which we called families of mechanisms—the *preferences* family, in which ethnicity alters the preferences that individuals have over outcomes; the *technology* family, in which ethnicity affects the toolbox of strategies available to individuals to achieve collective ends; and the *strategy selection* family, in which ethnic identities are used to condition the strategies that individuals pursue in a given social interaction. Within this set of families, we located many of the hypotheses advanced in the literature for the negative relationship between ethnic diversity and public goods provision.[1]

Armed with a set of plausible mechanisms, we then confronted the task of distinguishing among them. The central problem is that each mechanism generates the identical prediction of lower cooperation in the context of greater diversity. Discovering whether ethnic diversity impedes public goods provision through preferences, technology, or strategy selection mechanisms (or some combination of the three) required us to identify situations in which we could isolate observable implications of each mechanism. Experimental games provided a tool for doing exactly this. Inspired by the work of economists, social psychologists, and anthropologists who have used laboratory games to study altruism, trust, and cooperation, we employed a series of experimental games—some taken "off the shelf" and others invented specifically for our project—and took them to the field. We chose as our research site the urban neighborhoods of Kampala, Uganda. First, we corroborated the negative association between ethnic diversity and public goods provision in our study area. Then we set up our experimental laboratory in a rented office building and invited three hundred randomly selected subjects to participate in our games. Our hope was to use the results of the games to arbitrate among the mechanisms responsible for diversity's often pernicious consequences.

Our experiments provided support for some mechanisms and not others. These findings are summarized in table 7.1.

We found no evidence in support of any of the preferences-based mechanisms we examined. Individuals exhibited no tendency to care more about the welfare of coethnics than non-coethnics, as reflected in anonymous decisions in a Dictator game. Our survey data provide no support for the idea that ethnic groups share a set of common preferences over the types of public goods that should be provided. And the choices people made about who to work with to complete a joint task suggest that individuals do not derive greater enjoyment from working with coethnics than with members of other ethnic groups. At least in the urban neighborhoods in Kampala from which we recruited our research subjects, we can rule out the full set of preferences mechanisms advanced in the literature.

The evidence for the technology mechanisms is more mixed. We found some weak evidence that shared ethnicity facilitates the productivity of teams: coethnics performed somewhat better than non-coethnics in completing one of two joint tasks that we asked our subjects to undertake. The result is not statistically strong, but the estimated effect is nevertheless substantial. With respect to readability, coethnics were better able to guess each other's level of education. However, this may be in part driven by the fact that one group (the Baganda) was predominant in our sample and subjects may have had an easier time inferring the education of a Muganda. The evidence on beliefs about readability is much clearer: individuals expressed greater confidence in their ability to

Table 7.1 Mechanisms Linking Ethnicity to Successful Collective Action

Mechanism	Description	Finding
Preferences		
Other-Regarding Preferences	Coethnics may be more likely to take each other's welfare into account	*Not supported:* Coethnics are no more likely than non-coethnics to favor each other when allocations are made anonymously (see figures 4.3 and 4.4)
Preferences in Common	Coethnics may be more likely to care about the same outcomes	*Not supported:* Preferences over priorities for local public goods are not structured along ethnic lines (see figures 4.5 and 4.6)
Preferences over Process	Coethnics may prefer the process of working together	*Not supported:* Coethnics show no propensity to prefer working with each other on joint tasks (see table 4.1)
Technology		
Efficacy	Coethnics may be able to function together more efficiently	*Weakly supported:* Coethnic pairs are better able to complete some joint tasks (solving a puzzle but not opening a lockbox) than non-coethnic pairs (see tables 4.3 and 4.4)
Readability	Coethnics may be better able to (or believe they are better able to) gauge each other's characteristics	*Supported:* Weak evidence that coethnics can better infer each other's education levels and strong evidence that they believe they can (see figure 4.8)
Periodicity	Coethnics may engage each other with greater frequency	*Supported:* Subjects' friends, neighbors, and acquaintances are more likely to be coethnics (see figure 4.9)
Reachability	Coethnics may be more able to track each other down	*Weakly supported:* Coethnics are better able to track each other down (see table 4.5)
Strategy Selection		
Reciprocity	Coethnics may be more likely to punish each other for failing to cooperate	*Supported:* Coethnics are more likely to favor each other and cooperate if (and only if) they are seen to do so (see figures 4.11, 4.12, and 4.13)

Source: Authors' compilation.

infer unobservable characteristics of coethnics than of non-coethnics. This confidence in knowing who one is dealing with could plausibly affect decisions to cooperate, even if this confidence is sometimes misplaced. We also examined two technology mechanisms that could affect collective action by supporting the ability of groups to sustain reciprocity norms: periodicity and reachability. On periodicity, we found that individuals were substantially more likely to know coethnics (and by inference, to encounter them in the future), an attribute that could render a strategy of reciprocation more beneficial. On reachability, our Network game yielded evidence that individuals were better able to locate coethnics even when they did not know them (a result that is consistent across ethnic groups). Because our sample size for this game was fairly small, the estimated effects, though substantively large, are statistically weak. Nevertheless, the evidence on reachability and on periodicity could support an argument that coethnics are better able to maintain reciprocity norms.

Turning to mechanisms of strategy selection, the experiments revealed that individuals favored coethnics and cooperated at higher rates with coethnics when they were seen to do so, but they showed no such coethnic bias when their behavior was not observed. Our interpretation of this finding is that individuals expect that, when engaging with coethnics, their noncooperative actions are more likely to be met with future sanctions. This interpretation is supported by evidence that individuals sanction others (even at a cost to themselves) for failing to act cooperatively and that the anticipation of such sanctioning does lead to higher levels of cooperation in a public goods game.

In our introductory chapter, we noted that multiple mechanisms may simultaneously be in operation, and this is indeed what we found. Moreover, there are various ways in which these seemingly distinct mechanisms may interact with each other. This issue is especially germane for interpreting our findings with respect to periodicity and reachability, on the one hand, and strategy selection, on the other. It is possible that the evidence in support of the strategy selection mechanism does not simply reflect the fact that coethnics employ different strategies than non-coethnics, but that different strategies are available to them owing to greater periodicity and reachability. Thus, one might argue that it is simply because of these technological advantages that reciprocity norms can be sustained among coethnics but not (or more weakly) among non-coethnics. Alternatively, it could be that even after accounting for these technological advantages, coethnics still manage to coordinate on more cooperative strategies than non-coethnics. Our evidence in chapter 5 supports the latter of these two hypotheses. Periodicity appears to facilitate reciprocity norms specifically for coethnics, but not generally. In addition, the reachability of a given individual does not account for the extent to which he or she practices reciprocity.

Thus, our evidence suggests that the positive impact of ethnic homogeneity on collective action stems from the fact that ethnic groups employ strategies that induce others to act more cooperatively. For those who have studied the evolution of cooperation (for example, Axelrod 1984), this story is familiar. But our evidence points to a different account than the one emphasized by scholars of repeated games. We did not find that reciprocity norms operate in the same way across all individuals or that those individuals who respond to the threat of sanction also take actions to sustain reciprocity by maintaining a system of sanctioning for norm violation. Instead, we found that many players cooperate even when sanctioning is not possible and that reciprocity norms affect the behavior of a subset of individuals who, absent the social connections provided by ethnicity, would be least likely to cooperate. We call these individuals "egoists," and we showed that their tendency to look out only for their own interests is altered when they interact with coethnics. When playing with fellow group members, our evidence suggests, such players expect cooperative behavior to be reciprocated and noncooperative behavior to be punished.

An important additional finding is that this coethnic reciprocity norm exists alongside a powerful universal norm. This universal norm is in evidence in a different strategic context, one in which the choices individuals make are publicly observed by a third party who is empowered to sanction them in the event that they behave uncooperatively.[2] Egoists expect to be sanctioned if they do not cooperate (whether the third party is a coethnic) and respond with higher rates of cooperation. Enforcers act in line with these expectations, paying real costs to sanction when players defect. This universal reciprocity norm dominates coethnic norms in this strategic environment. In the presence of an external enforcer who makes the universal norm salient, the coethnic advantage in cooperation is erased.

The implication is that, while coethnic strategies of cooperation appear useful for sustaining cooperation among individuals when behavior is not widely observed and when there may be real differences in the ability of individuals to impose sanctions, universal reciprocity norms can override ethnic norms in a more institutionalized setting. But this setting is one that has three distinct components—greater transparency, a designated monitor, and a powerful technology for sanctioning—and further research is needed to identify which of these components matters most. Nevertheless, this is a promising result for those interested in determining how the negative impact of diversity on cooperation might be mitigated. We return to its implications in the final section of the conclusion.

Our confidence that the findings of our experimental games can account for the greater success we observed among more homogeneous communities in Kampala in achieving collective ends derives in part from the research strategy we employed. The selection of our research site was guided by our focus on causal mechanisms. Combining high levels of ethnic diversity and low levels of public goods provision, the neighborhoods of Mulago-Kyebando offered a good environment in which to explore the relative power of different explanations. By working with a representative sample of community residents, we were in a position to test whether the patterns of play we observed among our subjects in the laboratory would mirror the behavior patterns and outcomes observed in Mulago-Kyebando more broadly. And the experiments were designed explicitly to get around the thorny inferential problems that previous studies had confronted. While evidence that ethnic diversity impedes cooperation in Kampala provided the basis for our work, the experimental games allowed us to go much further, isolating distinct mechanisms from one another by testing the unique predictions associated with the preferences, technology, and strategy selection accounts of the effects of coethnicity. Additional evidence, drawn from survey work, focus groups, and extended interviews with community leaders, reinforces the explanation we offer for Mulago-Kyebando's failure to provide public goods.

Implications for Scholarship on Ethnicity

The argument we advance in these pages may account for the lack of social cooperation in Kampala's diverse urban slums, but does it have broader explanatory power? Setting aside the question of public goods provision per se, has this exercise provided us with more general insight into the power of ethnic identities in shaping political and social outcomes?

Undoubtedly, the direct generalizability of our experimental findings beyond Mulago-Kyebando is limited. The caveats we noted in chapter 1 regarding the anonymous, low-stakes nature of our games still apply. Nonetheless, the families of mechanisms we describe and investigate are quite general, and the methodologies we have developed can be fruitfully applied in other contexts and to other questions. Our approach has provided one set of answers to a specific puzzle that is of great relevance to the people living in our research site. We hope that extensions of this approach to other sites and other contexts will allow for an assessment of the generalizability of the patterns we have uncovered and the illumination of other puzzles.

The scope for such applications is broad. Shared ethnicity is called upon to enable groups to act collectively in arenas that go far beyond those examined in this book. It is used to facilitate recruitment in civil wars—hence the tendency for such conflicts to be described explicitly in ethnic terms (the Hutu against the Tutsi during Rwanda's genocide; the Tamils fighting for autonomy from the Sinhalese in Sri Lanka; the Uighurs challenging the hegemony of the Han in China). Shared ethnicity is also widely used for political mobilization—hence discussions of public spending that emphasize the ethnic ties that link political leaders to their constituents (as in the civil service jobs reserved for members of the Kalenjin tribe in President Daniel arap Moi's Kenya or the infrastructure investments promised by President Evo Morales to indigenous groups in Bolivia). Depictions of political parties, coalitions, and social movements also often underscore their ethnic character: the Uganda People's Congress is "known" to be the party of two closely related northern groups, the Teso and Langi; the Inkatha Freedom Party is understood as the political wing of the Zulu in South Africa; the United Party for National Development in Zambia is viewed as the Tonga party; and the Bharatiya Janata Part in India is recognized as the party of Hindu nationalists. Yet, while ethnicity figures centrally in the descriptions we read of many political activities, precisely *why* ethnic identities are central to these outcomes is often unclear.

Take as an illustration the problem of determining why political coalitions are often formed along ethnic lines. In one classic account, Robert Bates (1983, 164) proposes that the boundaries delineated by ethnic group membership represent an attractive foundation for the mobilization of political interests since "ethnic groups are, in short, a form of minimum-winning coalition, large enough to secure benefits in the competition for spoils, but also small enough to maximize the per capita value of these benefits." But why organize along ethnic lines as opposed to along some other cleavage, such as class, sector, or age? Bates suggests rival explanations, and these can be examined within the framework we provide. Plausibly, for example, technological features of ethnic groups (such as shared language or access to networks) reduce the costs to political entrepreneurs of organizing along ethnic lines. Alternatively, shared preferences among coethnics—perhaps resulting from the fact that administrative boundaries often coincide with the geographic segregation of ethnic groups—may account for these patterns of coalition formation. Strategy selection accounts are also possible. Generating a minimum winning coalition could, for example, be a matter of coordination: even in the absence of preferences or technology mechanisms, ethnicity could provide a focal point around which to coordinate.[3]

The research agenda that explores why ethnicity is so often the cleavage around which political violence is organized provides another illustration. In many accounts (Posen 1993; Fearon 1994), it is assumed that the population is divided along ethnic lines, that people know on which side they and others belong, and that the fact of membership in an ethnic group is enough to generate collective action. Ethnic groups are treated as already mobilized, unitary actors (Fearon 2006). But a complete account for why violence takes place along ethnic lines requires an answer to the prior question of how (and of course when) ethnicity facilitates mobilization for violence in the first place. Donald Horowitz (1985) has contributed a great deal to addressing this question. He argues that conflicts among ethnic groups are more likely to turn violent than those among other groups because group members are linked to one another as metaphorical family members. Yet embedded in his argument is a series of distinct claims that could, in principle, be separated and tested using the framework we have described. One part of the claim is that the distinctive feature of ethnic groups that facilitates mobilization for interethnic violence is a set of affective ties that bind group members to one another. In our language, this reflects other-regarding preferences. However, Horowitz draws on many other notions of what it might mean to be connected as family, including aspects that reflect technological and strategy selection considerations. He argues that "to call ethnicity a kinlike affiliation is thus to call into play the panoply of rights and obligations, the unspoken understandings, and the mutual aspiration for well-being that are so characteristic of family life in most of Asia and Africa" (Horowitz 1985, 64). It may be that all of these features matter, or perhaps some do and others do not. The approach offered in this book could be used to separate out the impact of these different aspects of ethnicity in a way that might better account for variation in the mobilization capacity of different groups.

Thus, the question of how ethnic identity works as a tool for mobilizing collective action is clearly not unique to the literature on the provision of local public goods. Concepts such as culture, kinship ties, or trust underlie many explanations of ethnic collective action, but these notions are often too general to be helpful for analysis. If we seek to understand why people think of themselves in ethnic terms and act in particular ways as a consequence, we need an approach, like the one provided here, that allows us to unpack these arguments.

Thus far, our discussion has proceeded as if it makes sense to think about isolating a single way or set of ways in which "ethnicity" works. Yet once we begin to break down general concepts of "culture" and "kinship," we arrive at the conclusion that ethnicity may work in different ways for different groups and in different contexts. Moreover, the mechanisms examined here and the ways in which they operate may not be particular to "ethnic" groups per se.[4] Ultimately, the question becomes one of conditions. What determines the salience of different mechanisms for different types of social groups? A frontier of research in ethnic politics involves understanding not just the diversity of the mechanisms through which ethnicity shapes behavior but also the conditions that make particular mechanisms more or less salient.

There are two additional ways in which this research agenda can be broadened. The first is by examining how the relationship between ethnic identity and behavior may vary with reference to specific ethnic groups within a given polity. Does the story we tell about coethnicity apply to all ethnic groups, or is it particular to a subset? At least in the data from Mulago-Kyebando, many of the effects we examined operate across multiple ethnic groups. Even so, we are cognizant of the fact that ethnic groups may have distinct beliefs, norms, and practices (some of which may evolve and change over time, as may the group boundaries) and that patterns of ethnic cooperation may be driven by different mechanisms, depending on the group.[5] Some ethnic groups may actively inculcate beliefs about the importance of sharing what one has with other group members. Other groups may draw on existing social structures to enforce reciprocal obligations through the threat of social sanction. Still others may develop particular cultural practices, traditions, and skills that imbue group members with technological advantages when it comes to resolving collective action problems.

Classical anthropology offers some support for these ideas. Ethnographers have long sought to capture the distinctive cultural practices of a range of different, largely tribal societies. Some of what they find suggests the commonality of social structures and practices across groups, but much of what they report points to apparent differences in culture. How can we begin to think more systematically about the conditions under which the power of ethnic identity operates through these different channels? Our results in chapter 3 suggest one avenue worth pursuing.

Work on ethnic politics has tended to assume that individuals can readily identify the ethnic background of the people with whom they interact. Kanchan Chandra (2004) suggests that one of the major factors that distinguishes ethnic from non-ethnic identities is that the former are more readily "visible." But our findings on ethnic identifiability suggest that treating visibility as part of a definition of ethnicity may be problematic in practice. Some groups that are broadly recognized as ethnic groups are more identifiable than others, and groups vary considerably in their ability to identify their own coethnics. Moreover, these differences in the identifiability of groups may have substantive implications for the operation of different mechanisms linking ethnicity to cooperation. If, for example, the mechanism driving the formation of ethnic coalitions in distributive politics is the ability of ethnic groups to better police the boundaries of their membership (Fearon 1999), then the likelihood that patronage coalitions will be constructed along ethnic lines should depend on the degree to which group membership is "visible" (and also "sticky," or difficult to change). The argument that coethnics achieve higher levels of cooperation because they have norms that facilitate the sanctioning of noncontributors (Miguel and Gugerty 2005) also depends on the ability of group members to distinguish coethnics from non-coethnics. To the extent that identifiability varies in systematic and observable ways across groups, so should the likelihood of collective action or cooperation through these mechanisms. Furthermore, because the costs and benefits of gathering information about the ethnic identities of others vary across groups, patterns of identifiability provide us with some leverage in generating predictions about the possibility that coethnic cooperation will be observed and the likelihood that it will operate through different types of mechanisms.

To make concrete the implication that differences in identifiability have for the probability of mobilization and the likelihood that particular mechanisms are at work, consider the civil wars in the north of Mali (1990 to 1995) and the south of Senegal (1982 to the present). These two conflicts have much in common. Both involve bids for separation by movements dominated by members of minority groups: the Tuaregs and Maures in Mali and the Diola in the Casamance region of Senegal. However, differences in the identifiability of the parties to each conflict relate to differences in how group members have been mobilized and how violence has been carried out.

In Mali, the ready identifiability of the Tuaregs and Maures as the "whites" led to ethnicity being used to pressure members of these groups, including intellectuals living in the capital, to join the rebel movements. It also allowed "black" sedentary groups and the Malian army to take quick reprisals against Tuareg and Maure civilians. The result was a rapid polarization of camps and the descent of the separatist struggle into communal violence. In Senegal, by contrast, a ready association of individuals with ethnic groups was more difficult. There the mobilization of partisans and the targeting of reprisals was more challenging and the intensity of the violence was much lower (Humphreys and ag Mohamed 2005). The contrasting degree of ethnic identifiability corresponds to a sharp difference in the form of group mobilization and the scope of violence in each case—a difference that would be hard to account for if we simply assumed that all ethnic groups are equally identifiable.

Of course, some mechanisms do not depend on assumptions about identifiability. Coethnic cooperation may be facilitated by a shared set of preferences, making it possible to solicit contributions more easily in homogeneous environments regardless of whether individuals can distinguish in-group members from out-group members. The same goes for a technology mechanism that emphasizes the reservoir of common cultural material (language, experience, understandings about modes of interaction) that makes it easier for group members to communicate and work together. Coethnics can realize these technological advantages even if information about in-group and out-group membership is imperfect. For other questions of interest, the ability to identify strangers also may be irrelevant, as when, for example, interactions take place between people who know each other, or technologies, such as identity cards, with information on group membership obviate the need to identify others in the manner described here.

The second area of inquiry relates to the impact of context on the operation of distinct mechanisms linking ethnic identities to individual behavior. Our research focused on community-level outcomes and on what one might call "micro-politics." We intentionally constructed an experimental environment that employed dyadic and triadic interactions among community members to capture the dynamics of local public goods provision in an urban community. The collective action problems faced by a small, urban neighborhood are nicely encapsulated in the micro-level interactions captured by our games, which test directly whether people cooperate to achieve collective ends in small-stakes interactions. At this level, a micro-level approach is perhaps most defensible.

But what does this approach tell us about how ethnicity matters at other levels of analysis? Is it the case, for example, that ethnic coalitions form in national politics because of reciprocity norms that operate at a micro level to prevent defection to other political groups?

It is not immediately clear that an analysis of how ethnicity conditions individual choices (the sort of data about which we are able to make inferences from our experimental games) makes sense as a strategy for understanding the formation of ethnic coalitions in national politics, the mobilization of ethnic interests for war, and so on. As we move from local public goods provision to other macro-level outcomes, a mapping of binary interactions onto social outcomes becomes potentially more problematic. Lars-Erik Cederman and Luc Girardin (2007) emphasize that the use of measures of ethnic fractionalization as a proxy for the degree of ethnic grievances rests on the notion that we can learn something about the likelihood of violence from the frequency of the interaction of non-coethnics in binary pairings.[6] They point out that violence is typically organized by political entrepreneurs rather than being the result of a bottom-up process and that ethnic conflict is often related to group status concerns rather than hostilities among individuals. They stress that the state figures centrally in most accounts of ethnic violence, as marginalized groups evaluate their position relative to the ethnic group in power. All of this suggests a very different empirical strategy for investigating the link between ethnicity and violence—one rooted in measuring the relative status of groups rather than in the probability that individuals from different ethnic groups will interact with one another in a context where the state's role is minimal.

This does not mean, however, that there is nothing to learn from patterns of micro-level interaction if we seek to understand the formation of coalitions, the mobilization of groups, the distribution of patronage, patterns of corruption, and other macro-level outcomes. Indeed, many of these processes can be broken down into a set of component pieces in which individuals are actively making choices—choices that may be shaped in predictable and measurable ways by their ethnic identities. Cederman and Girardin (2007) focus their explanation on group status concerns, but they assume away the collective action problem that ethnic groups confront. If intergroup ethnic inequalities increase the likelihood of ethnic conflict, this must operate in part through the impact of such status concerns on individual decisions about whether to take risks to participate in violence. Corrupt practices that favor coethnics, perhaps reflected in the aggregate distribution of jobs and patronage, are the result of interactions between politicians and their constituents. In these interactions, other-regarding preferences or the threat of sanction could plausibly be the mechanisms conditioning a politician's choice to favor a coethnic or prioritize funding to a region populated by coethnics. Individual choices are at the core of many of the aggregate processes we observe, even in arenas beyond local community mobilization. By breaking down these outcomes into their component pieces, one can identify the underlying logic that conditions interaction among coethnics and non-coethnics.

Methodological Implications: Experiments and the Study of Ethnicity

Beyond the substantive issues raised by our findings, our approach highlights the power and some of the limitations of experimental methods for uncovering the causal mechanisms driving political and social outcomes. The particular strategy we employed—the use of laboratory games in the field—is now common in the tool kit of academic economists, but political scientists have so far shown comparatively little interest in the use of behavioral games, particularly in the field of comparative politics.

We have benefited from the control that the experimental approach has afforded us to isolate different mechanisms. By most accounts, the greatest advantage of experiments is their ability to identify *causal* effects. By randomly assigning subjects to treatment or control groups, investigators can ensure that the only systematic difference between subjects in these two groups (at least in expectation) is the treatment itself. In our research, we benefited from this feature in a number of specific tests—for example, in estimating the impact of a loss of anonymity on decisions about how to distribute benefits, or the effect of the introduction of an enforcer on decisions to cooperate in a Prisoner's Dilemma. Furthermore, our experimental setup put us in a position to examine these effects for both coethnic and non-coethnic pairs.

We could not, however, exploit the benefits of randomization for our central treatment of interest: coethnicity. In each game, we could control whether a player's partner was drawn from the pool of coethnic partners, but not whether a given partner would be a coethnic. Assigning identities at random was beyond our reach. While at some level this point is obvious, it also signals a serious limitation that we face in the study of ethnicity.[7] Of course, we gain from the randomization in other ways—for example, we could be sure that the encounters we observed between players were not driven by selection effects. Moreover, while we could not rely on the randomization to ensure that there were no other confounds, we could "control" for such potential confounds in the usual manner—and as we reported in chapter 4, controlling for these confounds did not change our core findings. Finally, even in the absence of controls, in any given setting one can still interpret the effect of the random assignment as the "total" effect of engaging with an individual from the pool of coethnics, where this total includes the effect of any covariates, such as wealth or education.

Beyond these difficulties, the most common objection we hear to the use of experimental games emphasizes issues of external validity. There exists an immediate skepticism about how much can be gleaned from behavior in a simulated laboratory setting to make sense of real-world outcomes. The separate external validity question (discussed earlier as well as in chapter 6) of whether we can generalize what we have learned about how ethnicity works in Mulago-Kyebando to other contexts is not a critique of experimental methods, inasmuch as it can be asked of any micro-level study, regardless of the methodology it employs. Much more pressing, we believe, are questions that speak to the challenges associated with mapping the estimated effects from a laboratory setting (in our case, of the strength of various mechanisms through which ethnicity might condition behavior) to the social dilemmas that people encounter in the real world.

Three challenges strike us as particularly important. First, for a question such as why ethnic diversity impedes cooperation, it is difficult to maintain the claim implicit in many laboratory studies that the quantity of interest is universal to humans. Instead, we expect that patterns of ethnic interaction are likely to be acutely context-dependent. This means taking the setting seriously and thinking about the population for which reliable inferences can be drawn, concerns that have not yet seemed to resonate in the community of lab experimentalists.

A second challenge is that, by using laboratory games, we assume the existence of a set of individual-level behaviors—such as the degree of coethnic favoritism—that are stable and measurable. We also assume that what we observe about these behaviors in one game tells us something about the general propensity of individuals to exhibit a specific trait across games. This assumption is common to non-experimental approaches as well—for example, in accounts that explain ethnic violence in terms of observed ethnic hatreds or voting behavior in terms of social distance—but it is one that lays bare a tension in the design of experimental games. On the one hand, while simple laboratory games permit us to identify a set of "primitives" (underlying patterns of individual behavior) in a population, we then must make an inferential leap from these primitives to real-world behavior. Alternatively, we can ask people to participate in games that far more closely approximate the real-world challenges they face, although the complexity of these games makes it far more difficult to identify the specific mechanisms at work.

Third, any estimate of how ethnicity conditions behavior in the laboratory reflects other features of the controlled environment in which the games are carried out. The advantage of using the laboratory is that the experimenter can control the environment sufficiently to get a precise measure of a particular parameter. The disadvantage, however, is that experimental data may tell us something about how ethnicity works in a specific context unrelated to the real settings of interest. In practice, for example, in our experiments we set the level of ethnic salience to zero in the sense that ethnicity was not referred to in any of the game descriptions (even our enumerators did not know that we were interested in ethnicity) and each interaction involved relatively low stakes (at least when compared to the high stakes of ethnic politicking associated with distributive conflict in Uganda). Thus, based on the results from our games, we cannot know for sure how ethnicity shapes people's actions in a setting in which ethnic identities are explicitly made salient.

We believe that we have introduced a set of innovations in this project that address some of these concerns. Perhaps most important, we took the laboratory to the field and carefully chose the site of our experiments on the basis of a demonstrated relationship between ethnic diversity and public goods provision. In addition, departing from much of the work in experimental economics, we selected our subjects through random sampling of the population of the area we were studying to ensure that the patterns we observed in the lab would be as representative as possible of the behaviors and interactions we might discover in the community at large. The representativeness of our sample also helps us deflect the sorts of criticisms (justifiably) directed at studies that make

general claims on the basis of games played by university undergraduates or self-selected participants from the population.

Finally, we utilized a set of experimental protocols that mirror (insofar as one can in the laboratory) the real-world interactions associated
with the local provision of public goods. In some instances, we pulled
these games off the shelf—for example, using Prisoner's Dilemma
games to simulate situations in which collective action is required to
produce social welfare–improving outcomes. In picking games, we
erred generally on the side of simple games that would allow us to identify underlying features of individual behavior (that is, the extent of
other-regardingness or the degree of coethnic favoritism). In other cases,
however, we designed more complex games (the Network, Puzzle, and
Lockbox games) to capture characteristics of ethnic interaction not easily
measured through computer-mediated interactions. The fact that our
subjects recognized everyday parallels to the games they were playing
in the laboratory (as reported in chapter 6) adds to our confidence in the
external validity of our findings. All of these design features provided a
basis for expecting that the results generated in the lab would contain
broader lessons. But if experimental games are to gain broader currency
in political science, scholars will have to dedicate more attention to trying to actually *demonstrate* external validity.

In this book, we pursued two main avenues to test how well our experimental results spoke to the impact of ethnicity diversity on cooperation in Mulago-Kyebando. First, we looked for correlations between
play in the laboratory games and the real-world behaviors they were
meant to represent. We looked for these correlations in chapter 6 by
comparing observed behavior in the laboratory with survey responses
about trust, participation, cooperation, and interethnic social distance.
In some cases we found correlations; in others we did not. Part of the
difficulty of this exercise stems from the fact that both experiments and
surveys are imperfect strategies for uncovering actual beliefs and behavior. Tellingly, the coethnic biases we observed in our experimental
games (when subjects were not primed to ethnicity) correlate more
strongly with behavioral measures than with self-reported attitudes, a
possible result if responses to these attitudinal questions more readily
reflect social desirability biases.

A second strategy asked a great deal more of our laboratory-generated
data by exploring its power to help us predict outcomes in places other
than those where the games were played. To push our data in this way,
we used our measures of the reciprocal relationships among ethnic
groups in Mulago-Kyebando to predict how different ethnic configura-
tions in neighboring communities might perform with respect to public
goods provision. The basic intuition underlying this exercise was simple: if games teach us anything about the cooperative capacity of com-

munities with different ethnic demographies, then the patterns we observe in the laboratory should provide some predictions about public goods outcomes in real-world communities. Here, we found few supportive results. This step involved some heroic assumptions, and as we saw in chapter 6, it was a tough test to pass. But it is a strategy that has the potential to make a compelling case for the broader insights that can be generated through experimental research.

Although our evidence on external validity was mixed, we believe that finding ways to demonstrate a correspondence between how subjects interact in the laboratory and how they behave in their communities is important if we are to make a stronger case for the utility of this approach for understanding political processes. Some research is already moving in this direction, showing, for example, that patterns of trusting behavior in the lab correlate highly with financial decisions made in the context of a micro-finance group (Karlan 2005).

Even with these steps, those who are skeptical about experimental games may remain unconvinced, believing that laboratory environments are simply too far removed from the actual contexts in which people interact. The challenge, then, is to pioneer new approaches to experimentation that leave behind the artificiality of the lab while retaining the experimental control that permits the identification of causal effects. The growing popularity of field experiments in political science and economics represents a step in this direction. With respect to the questions we deal with in the present study, a possible approach might involve nongovernmental organizations (NGOs) working with community groups on joint projects such as housing construction or agriculture. The "groups" could be formed in such a way as to ensure that individuals are randomly allocated to homogeneous or heterogeneous groups, and the level of information available to individuals about the inputs of others on their team could be varied. Although this design would not enable us to distinguish all the causal stories we have discussed in this book (and still does not resolve the problem that ethnicity cannot be randomly assigned), it does demonstrate how the logic of experimental games can be taken from the laboratory and brought closer to the field. Research designs in which the control that is so valued in the laboratory is harnessed in the context of real-world interactions are potentially powerful ways of making the case for the external validity of experimental approaches.

The final methodological issue we highlight relates to analysis rather than design. A striking conclusion in this book is that the reciprocity norms made salient by shared ethnic ties condition the behavior *only* of a subset of the population—the "egoists"—whose noncooperation most undermines the potential for collective action. The power of ethnic identity, at least in Mulago-Kyebando, is in how it shapes the incentives for cooperation faced by a certain type of person. By analyzing our data separately for different types, we could uncover patterns that would have been obscured in an aggregate analysis.

The idea that the world is composed of different types of people challenges an assumption underlying prominent models of human behavior in the social sciences—namely, that individuals invariably act to maximize their material gains. Experiments in behavioral economics have demonstrated repeatedly that many individuals exhibit remarkably high levels of altruism, often passing on material gains when keeping them would be costless, or displaying behavior indicative of inequality-aversion or strong fairness norms. As we noted in chapter 4, the consensus in the behavioral literature is that the world is composed of a diversity of types, some of whom closely approximate the rational, self-interested individual while many do not. But this evidence on the diversity of human motivations has failed, as of yet, to shape much recent work in political science.

In practice, making operational the idea of distinct types presents a number of problems. These problems are similar to those we face when analyzing ethnic groups. We do not, for example, believe that there really is a discrete collection of types, given by nature, or that types necessarily correspond to permanent attributes of individuals. Rather, the question is how best to generate clusters of individuals (or, in a more continuous approach, to identify dimensions of difference) based on their attributes or behavioral patterns for the purpose of analysis. If such an exercise is to be of more value than simply a labeling of subjects, the clustering should predict patterns of behavior beyond the data used to generate the clusters. But how to do this is a subject of contentious debate.

Our approach has been to draw distinctions between types based on a measure of preferences. Our working hypothesis was that patterns of play in the Dictator game, which illuminate the extent to which one is other-regarding, reflect the underlying structure of one's utility function. The coding decisions we made—separating individuals into two discrete types, egoists and non-egoists—were clearly an extreme simplification, yet they proved powerful in practice. Our taxonomy predicted patterns of play across games (egoists in the Dictator game were less likely to cooperate in the PD game; non-egoists were more likely to engage in costly punishment), thereby adding plausibility to our definition of types on the basis of preferences. Yet some behavioral economists have resisted defining types in terms of preferences, instead suggesting that they be defined in terms of patterns of behavior—specifically, the strategies selected—within the context of a single game. Evolutionary processes then determine the distribution of behavioral patterns within specific structures of interaction (Bowles and Gintis 2004b). Such an interpretation is closer to the data—in practice, we only ever observe behavior, not preferences. But if we do not attempt to make inferences about preferences, we are left unable to make predictions across settings, which ultimately is our ambition as social scientists.

Political Implications

This book began with the premise that ethnic diversity often undermines the ability of communities to act collectively. As a result, diverse communities can fare worse in terms of the public goods and services that people typically desire. We accepted this as a starting point because the basic empirical result appears to be robust across contexts, and because we were able to replicate it in an examination of urban neighborhoods in Uganda that we undertook before beginning our experimental work. In addition, we found that the very same result could be replicated in the lab, as reflected in the higher rates of cooperation among coethnics in Prisoner's Dilemma games.

The power of this empirical finding might lead us to conclude that ethnically heterogeneous communities should be discouraged or somehow made more homogeneous. If homogeneity indeed fosters cooperation, we might be tempted to take this line even further and propose that diversity should be avoided in environments (such as the workplace) where the success of teams depends on everyone pitching in.

Drawing the conclusion that segregation is an optimal policy solution, however, would be a mistake. There are returns to diversity that this book does not begin to discuss; we focus only on a single issue: how diversity affects collective action. Scott Page (2007) has recently documented the many advantages of diverse groups, showing how teams with a wide range of perspectives typically outperform brilliant individuals or groups of like-minded people. Will Kymlicka (1995) and others also provide normative arguments in support of multiculturalism. We do not claim to weigh the costs and benefits of diversity, but rather focus attention on the mechanisms associated with one of diversity's negative effects. In doing so, our hope is that a better understanding of the causal process linking diversity to poor public goods provision will enable the design of more appropriate interventions for those who wish to improve outcomes in diverse societies.

Our core finding about how ethnicity works in Mulago-Kyebando suggests some strategies for mitigating the cooperation-reducing effects of social diversity. Recall that, across all games, non-egoists cooperated at very high rates, both with coethnics and with non-coethnics. Cooperation among egoists, however, was higher only when they were paired with coethnics and when their behavior could be observed. When at risk of being sanctioned by in-group members for acts of noncooperation,

egoists began to act more like non-egoists, leading to greater cooperation among coethnics. Our results also suggest, however, that when
third parties are able to monitor and punish noncooperation (even at a
cost to themselves, as in the PD game with a third-party enforcer), universal norms of reciprocity predominate and the coethnic advantage in
cooperation is erased. Taken together, these findings point to the utility
of developing institutions that might facilitate monitoring, sanctioning,
and the cultivation of reputations for cooperative behavior (Habyarimana et al. 2008). Transparency rests at the core of these strategies. But
transparency must be embedded in institutional arrangements that provide a technology for norm enforcement across groups, because in diverse societies ethnic ties alone will not be sufficient to police the behavior of those types disinclined to cooperate.

The government of Uganda is already experimenting with institutional arrangements that aim to enhance collective action to combat corruption by facilitating the flow of information to community members,
making it easier for people to identify transgressions and bring social
sanctions to bear. Reinikka and Svensson (2005), for example, describe a
newspaper campaign launched by the government to address the mas-
sive leakage of funds from a large education grant program. Estimates
from a public expenditure tracking survey suggested that less than 20
percent of the central government funds ever reached most local schools
(Reinikka and Svensson 2004). In response, the government began to
publish data on monthly transfers of capitation grants to districts in national newspapers (and their local language editions). The goal of facilitating citizen enforcement was achieved: head teachers in schools closer
to a newspaper outlet were more knowledgeable about the rules governing the grant program, claimed a significantly larger part of their en-
titlement, and experienced better testing outcomes at their schools. The
authors attribute these stunning results to "client power": citizens were
in a far better position to identify and sanction the transgressions of
local government officials. A parallel study, also in Uganda, demonstrates that a community-based monitoring intervention (a citizen report card) led to dramatic increases in local health system performance:
average utilization of services was higher, infant weights increased, and
the death rates of children under five dropped significantly (Bjorkman
and Svensson 2007). The authors show that the observed improvements
in health quality can be linked directly to efforts by the health unit staff
to better serve the interests of the community.

Even where it is not possible to foster institutional structures that facilitate monitoring and sanctioning in diverse communities, the power
of ethnic ties can still be harnessed to promote activities that improve social welfare. Consider the strategy pursued by one of the LC1 chairmen
in Mulago-Kyebando, as described by one of our interviewers:

Before the LC system was put into place [in 1986], there were clashes between the Bafumbira and the Batoro, to the point that there was an actual
residential boundary between the two groups within his zone. In 1992,
when he became chair, he attempted to find the cause of these conflicts
and resolve them. He found that very small disputes between individuals
blew up and very quickly became conflicts between the two groups. His
strategy: "If a Mufumbira causes a problem or starts a fight with a Mutoro,
he is punished right away within his own community by the elders/opin-
ion leaders within his tribe. The punishments vary according to the crime—
[they] are often fines. Punishment [is] kept within the zone—no police or
other outside authorities [are] involved." By 1993 the intergroup conflicts
had almost entirely disappeared. He is very proud of this.

This approach is reminiscent of the in-group policing strategy theo-
rized by Fearon and Laitin (1996). In their account, ethnic ties (on their
own) can be used to generate peaceful and cooperative equilibria. Transgressions by members of one group are ignored by members of other
groups because they correctly anticipate that the ethnic brethren of the
culprits will identify and punish them. Fearon and Laitin demonstrate
the existence of such a mechanism in societies as diverse as premodern
Europe, the Ottoman Empire, and British-ruled Nigeria, and we saw it
at work in Uganda. Yet this approach is perhaps more fragile than one
that involves the construction of transparent institutions that facilitate
interethnic cooperation. Strategies of in-group policing may reify ethnic
differences. Moreover, the same in-group practices that permit sanctioning can be captured by ethnic entrepreneurs who are intent on promoting violence between groups.

Our proposals for mitigating the corrosive effects of ethnic diversity
follow from our findings about how ethnicity works in Mulago-
Kyebando. Yet, as we have emphasized repeatedly, the mechanisms
linking ethnic identities to cooperation may be different in different contexts. For example, while we find weak evidence that cooperation in
urban Kampala is impeded by technological constraints, this mechanism might turn out to be more important in other communities. Such a
finding would have clear policy implications. Strategies that promote
the acquisition of a shared language or that shift the structure of contributions to collective activities from labor to money would be essential if
one wanted to facilitate higher levels of cooperation among diverse
groups. If, instead, we found that individuals exhibit altruism only toward members of their own ethnic group, it might be necessary to advo-
cate investments in nation-building strategies in which educational institutions are employed to promote greater attachment to national
(rather than tribal) identities. Edward Miguel (2004), for example, has
shown that there is no negative relationship between community diversity and public goods provision in northern Tanzania (even though such

a relationship does exist just across the border in Kenya, among the same ethnic groups). He attributes this difference to the nation-building efforts of the Tanzanian government after independence. A finding that ethnic groups exhibit starkly different preferences with respect to which public goods should be provided suggests a different policy approach: decentralization, in which funding streams are segregated by group, could be a welfare-improving approach.

In short, a focus on identifying mechanisms is not simply of academic interest. Policymakers committed to improving social outcomes in diverse societies must also be careful to understand how ethnicity works before imagining strategies to combat the negative effects of diversity.

Final Thoughts

Our results suggest that coethnics cooperate more effectively because they follow reciprocity norms that stipulate cooperation with coethnics and sanctioning should a coethnic fail to cooperate. For some, the association between ethnic heterogeneity and adverse social outcomes with which we began this book may seem disturbing, implying as it might a rationale for promoting greater homogeneity. But our results suggest that a deeper analysis does not support this view. Based on a careful analysis of Kampala's urban neighborhoods we call into question explanations that suggest that the adverse effects of heterogeneity spring from some fundamental feature of human relations. We find no evidence in Kampala that these inefficiencies reflect any deep incompatibilities or attitudes between members of different ethnic groups. Rather, they appear to reflect patterns of norm enforcement that can be sustained both within and across groups. This finding gives us grounds to believe that there are workable solutions in which transparency embedded in effective formal institutions can substitute for or complement the informal enforcement that comes from close ethnic ties and so resolve the dilemmas of collective action in diverse communities.

Appendix A:
Sampling Procedure

1. Sampling Strategy

One of the key innovations in our experimental design was our effort to bring ordinary people from Mulago-Kyebando into an environment in which we could maintain experimental control. Given the questions we sought to answer, a sample of university students (even in Uganda) would not have provided us with the data we needed to understand how ethnic diversity undermines public goods provision. The only sampling strategy that could deliver reliable answers was one that generated a representative sample of people from a highly diverse community with poor public goods.

The most common way to generate a representative sample is to randomly select study participants from the population of interest. To obtain a random sample from any given population, one needs an accurate sampling frame. The sampling frame must satisfy two important criteria. First, it must define the actors relevant to the study. In our case, the relevant actor was an adult—someone who could provide labor, material, or cash contributions to help deliver the public goods we discuss in this book. Second, given a definition of the appropriate unit of analysis, the sampling frame must include the entire universe of relevant actors. This means that the sampling frame must exhaustively list all the adults in the community.

However, as described briefly in chapter 3, to answer the question that motivates this book, we needed a more nuanced sampling strategy. In general, random sampling is desirable if one wants to determine average behavior, such as smoking or firm productivity, within a given population of individuals or firms. If the objective is to learn something about the behavior of particular groups within a population, however, then a random sample is not always the best sampling strategy. To see this, assume that we have a population of 10,000 individuals, 9,500 of whom are of type A and 500 of whom are of type B. Suppose we want to know something about smoking in each group. A 1 percent sample, which is a typical proportion used in national surveys, implies drawing 100 individuals from this community. A random sample would draw on average 95 type As and 5 type Bs. Although this would be a representative sample for the entire community and would generate reliable estimates of mean behavior in the community, it would not allow the researcher to make reliable claims about the behavior of type Bs. With only five observations, it is not possible to generate a precise measure of type B behavior.

Given the objectives of this hypothetical study, it made sense to abandon random sampling in order to increase the number of type Bs in the drawn sample. One way to do this would be to increase the size of the drawn sample to 120, of which 30 would be type Bs and 90 would be type As. With 30 observations, a researcher would have a large enough sample of type Bs to make reliable statements about group B behavior. To generate 30 type Bs, one would have to oversample type Bs. That is, the probability of being selected into the study would differ for type As and type Bs.

Imagine that Mulago-Kyebando was composed of only those two groups, type As and type Bs, instead of the full range of ethnic groups we described in chapter 3. Because our interest is in the impact of coethnicity on social behavior, we need to understand the nature of dyadic interactions between groups (type A with type As, type B with type Bs, type A with type Bs, type B with type As), not just average behavior within groups. Assuming random matching of subjects, as we did in the study, a random sample (or equal probability of selection for both types) of only five type Bs would have produced a minuscule share of B-B interactions. Given our focus on individual behavior as conditioned by a partner's identity, there was an even greater imperative to sample considerably more type Bs so as to generate a sufficient number of B-B interactions. Returning to the real demographics of Mulago-Kyebando, the challenge was even more daunting. Nearly twenty different ethnic groups inhabit the study area, and some of these groups are so small that generating the suitable sample sizes to properly characterize ingroup behavior would have involved identifying these households explicitly.

To make this sampling problem more tractable, we elected to reduce the number of effective groups to four. In practice, this meant reorienting the sampling strategy to generate reasonable numbers for these four groups. Even with this more modest goal, however, we confronted the challenge that Baganda account for nearly half of the Mulago-Kyebando population, while the next three largest groups together account for only about 20 percent.

Table A.A1 lists the LC2s in our study area and the distribution of

Table A.A1   Distribution of Target Groups in the Study Area

Zone	Bafumbira	Banyankole	Baganda	Bakiga
Mulago I	8.0%	7.5%	31.4%	3.6%
Mulago II	8.5	8.0	54.1	3.4
Mulago III	8.4	7.5	44.4	4.0
Kyebando	3.3	6.2	59.6	3.0

Source: Authors' calculations based on official census data (Uganda Bureau of Statistics 2002).

critical groups in each zone that shaped our sampling strategy. Within each LC2, there were six to eight LC1s. Of the twenty-six possible LC1s we could sample from, eight either had a share of Baganda that was too high or a share of the other groups that was too low if we were to ensure a sufficient number of coethnic pairings. Of the remaining eighteen, we assigned a sampling weight that was proportional to the share of the smaller groups in the LC1. This implies that we drew more subjects from LC1s with a large share of the three small groups. In our example, this means that the probability of *any* individual being selected was higher in areas where the proportion of group Bs was high.

Having established the desired sample size for each community, we then randomly drew subjects in each of the eighteen LC1s. Drawing a random sample requires a listing of all the relevant actors in the LC1. Obtaining such lists in the communities that we were working in was problematic. Although a number of LC1s did have such lists (derived primarily from voting registers), many did not have lists that, from our perspective, reliably enumerated all eligible residents, either because the lists had been generated for voting purposes and the biases of community leaders excluded particular individuals or because of bureaucratic inefficiencies.

Given the unreliability of community lists, we decided to use point sampling, a method in which particular points within a community are selected at random and then a set of guidelines is used to sample households around that point. Figure A.A1 shows the compass that was used to guide the selection of points in these communities.

Sampling in each LC1 proceeded as follows. A team of enumerators went to one of the target LC1s with the compass. When they arrived at the geographic center of the LC1 (using LC1 maps), they identified a visible landmark. By pointing the compass at this landmark, they determined the location of each of the eight points on the compass within the community. The enumerators could then partition the area and mark off each of the points. At each of the specified points, they identified and recorded another landmark. Once the enumerators arrived at a point,

Figure A.A1   Point Sampling Compass

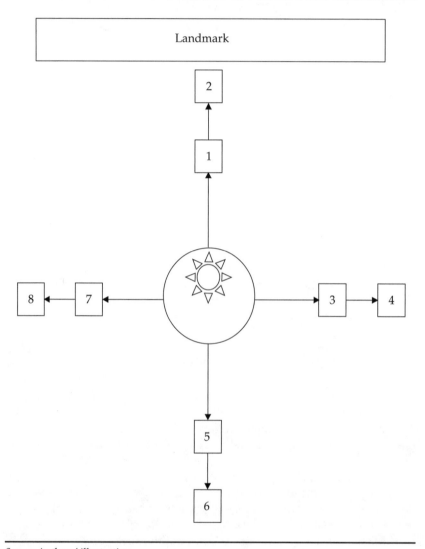

Source: Authors' illustration.

they were given a set of guidelines that informed the selection of house-holds around the point. For even-numbered points, the enumerators picked the first house to their left and sampled that house. If a member of this household declined to participate, then the enumerators were in-structed to go to the first alternative house on the right. The use of clear landmarks at each of the sampling points allowed the team to potentially regenerate the same sample. The number of households per point was determined by the size of the desired sample from a particular LC1.[1]

Once a household had been selected, the enumerators would introduce themselves politely and explain the purpose of the study and how subjects were being selected. The enumerator would also tell the respondent that selection of an eligible member from the household would be done at random. After obtaining consent from the respondent, a coin was flipped to determine whether a female or male would be drawn from that household. Depending on the outcome of the coin flip, a full list of all eligible individuals of the relevant gender was then written down. Using a set of cards with the numbers corresponding to each individual on the list, the respondent was asked to draw a card. The individual corresponding to the drawn card was asked to report to the Mulago-Kyebando community study office as soon as possible. The name of the selected person was recorded by the enumerator, and a pink ticket with the individual's name written in ink was left behind (to be shown when the person arrived at the study office).

As one might expect, not every sampled household was willing to participate. Moreover, not all of those selected eventually showed up at the study office to take part in the study. For reliability purposes, it is important to establish that the biases associated with nonresponse (refusal to participate or not showing up conditional on being selected) do not generate samples that look very different from the population in Mulago-Kyebando. To assess these potential biases, the enumerators recorded information about the material of the roof, floor, and window type for every household they visited. They also recorded whether the respondent agreed to participate or declined. Using these data, we can establish the direction of the bias introduced by nonresponse. The set of households that were visited are divided into three categories: eventual sample, willing no-shows, and refusals. In table A.A2, we explore the extent to which nonresponse is problematic.

Virtually all of the households sampled had an iron roof. In addition, a large proportion of households had concrete floors. This was true across all three samples, with close to 90 percent of households having a concrete floor. Wealthier households—whose members were probably too busy to come to our office—were more likely to decline. The share of declining households with a concrete floor was significantly higher than the eventual samples or the willing-no-show samples. In addition, the share with glass windows was higher than our subject sample. The differences, however, are not statistically significant at conventional levels.

We have no reason to believe that the nonresponse patterns we observed are a cause for concern for the results of our analysis. Most of the refusals from wealthy households came from individuals living in upper-middle class LC1s on the edge of our study area, where the public goods we discuss in this book are generally privately provided.

Table A.A2   Sampling Characteristics

Sample	Overall	Eventual Sample	Willing No-Shows	Refusals
Roof (1 = iron sheets)	1.00	1.00	1.00	1.00
	(0.00)	(0.00)	(0.00)	(0.00)
Floor (1 = concrete)	0.87	0.86	0.88	0.96
	(0.02)	(0.02)	(0.04)	(0.04)
Windows (1 = glass)	0.40	0.39	0.40	0.52
	(0.03)	(0.03)	(0.06)	(0.11)
Share of men in the sample	0.42	0.42	0.39	
	(0.03)	(0.03)	(0.06)	
Observations with data	383	287	73	23
Observations missing	15	13	1	1

Source: Authors' calculations.

Finally, we examined the gender distribution of our eventual sample. Given the sampling protocol we outlined, we would have expected to draw a sample with a more even distribution of men. As it turned out, only 42 percent of our subjects were men. The actual proportion in the population of Mulago-Kyebando is 48 percent, according to the Uganda Bureau of Statistics. Although some of the nonresponse may account for this, it appears that there was a slight sampling bias toward the selection of individuals who were at home. Since formal employment rates are typically skewed toward males, it is likely that violations in our sampling protocol accounted for the slight gender imbalance.

2. Sample Characteristics

In the previous section, we described the sampling procedure we used to generate the sample of subjects in this study. In this section, we briefly describe our sample in terms of their socioeconomic characteristics. Table A.A3 shows selected sample means. Only 44 percent of the subjects who played the games were male.[2] Looking at the gender composition in each of the egoism categories reveals slightly higher percentages of males among the egoists. The difference in proportions across the two groups, however, is not statistically significant.

The average age of our subjects, among both egoists and non-egoists, was twenty-eight. Sixty-four percent of our sample had completed primary schooling. This is a considerably higher share than the national average, and it reflected the urban nature of our sample. Egoists had a higher proportion of primary school graduates, with 70 percent compared to 60 percent for the non-egoist category. This difference is significant only at the 90 percent level.[3] Our subjects exhibited a very high de-

Table A.A3   Socioeconomic Status: Selected Means

	Overall Sample	Egoists	Non-Egoists	Difference
Gender (1 = male)	0.44	0.41	0.49	0.085
	(0.03)	(0.04)	(0.05)	[0.142]
Age (years)	28.41	28.41	28.40	–0.006
	(0.62)	(0.79)	(0.99)	[0.996]
More than primary school	0.64	0.60	0.70	0.097
	(0.03)	(0.04)	(0.04)	[0.078]
Go to place of worship at least	0.71	0.71	0.71	0.001
once a week	(0.03)	(0.03)	(0.04)	[0.987]
Catholic	0.35	0.36	0.33	–0.032
	(0.03)	(0.04)	(0.04)	[0.564]
Protestant	0.35	0.32	0.40	0.076
	(0.03)	(0.03)	(0.04)	[0.173]
Evangelical	0.16	0.18	0.14	–0.044
	(0.02)	(0.03)	(0.03)	[0.296]
Muslim	0.11	0.11	0.12	0.011
	(0.02)	(0.02)	(0.03)	[0.768]
Proportion mixed parentage	0.28	0.33	0.21	–0.114
	(0.03)	(0.04)	(0.04)	[0.036]
Married	0.36	0.36	0.35	–0.01
	(0.03)	(0.04)	(0.04)	[0.17]
Married to coethnic	0.53	0.56	0.48	–0.083
	(0.05)	(0.06)	(0.08)	[0.889]
Own the house they live in	0.28	0.25	0.33	0.078
	(0.03)	(0.03)	(0.04)	[0.144]
Asset index	0.02	0.08	–0.07	–0.142
	(0.05)	(0.06)	(0.09)	[0.184]
Number of observations	306	182	124	

Source: Authors' calculations.
Notes: Standard errors are in parentheses; *p*-values are in square brackets. Age and asset index are continuous variables. All other variables are measured as binary variables with the indicated category taking the value 1, and 0 otherwise.

gree of religiosity: more than two-thirds of our sample attended a place of worship at least once a week, and a little over 91 percent went to a place of worship at least once a month. This is comparable to recent survey evidence from the World Values Survey (2001), in which about 87 percent of Ugandans attended a place of worship at least once a month. There were no differences in religiosity across the egoist categories. The distribution of our sample by religious denomination accorded well with the distribution in the population as a whole: 35 percent of our sample were Roman Catholic, 35 percent were Protestant, 16 percent were evangelical, and 11 percent were Muslim.[4] There was no significant difference in the proportion belonging to each religious denomination across the egoists and non-egoists. A little over one-third of the sample were married. Of those who were married, about half were married to a coethnic. There was no difference between egoists and non-egoists in marriage rates or the share married to a coethnic.

Less than one-third of our sample owned the dwelling they were living in. This reflects the transitory nature of migration in these areas. A slightly higher proportion of egoists owned their dwelling, but the difference is not statistically significant. Finally, we used an asset index as a measure of wealth. The index used responses on the type of floors, walls, roof, and windows of the subjects' dwellings. We used principal components to estimate a wealth index for each subject. As table A.A3 shows, the two groups were of the same wealth level. While the average wealth index for egoists was negative, the difference between the two groups is not significant.

3. Attrition

One feature that distinguishes this study within the realm of experimental studies is that we had the subjects come to the lab on four different occasions. During the first session, subjects were registered and photographs of them were taken. The first set of games was played in the second session (the Dictator, Prisoner's Dilemma, and Lockbox games). In the third session, subjects played the back end of the Dictator game and the Voting and Enforcer games. Finally, in the fourth session, subjects played the Identification and Puzzle games.

A research design with repeat visits is generally associated with very high levels of attrition. Given that attrition is typically nonrandom, attrition would have been fatal to our results, since our research design relied on a comparison of play across different games. To forestall attrition, we took special care in organizing a team of enumerators who went around to subjects' homes or called those who had cell phones on the day before they were due in the lab to remind them or to reschedule. In addition, the payoffs and entertainment value associated with the games were a powerful incentive for subjects to make return visits.

Overall, attendance rates were very high. As table A.A4 shows, just over 90 percent of subjects attended all of the games sessions. About 5.6 percent of subjects missed one session, and 4 percent missed more than one session.

What was the nature of attrition in our sample? There were basically two kinds: random attrition in which the process determining who did not show up was unrelated to behavior in the games, and attrition that was systematically related to behavior in the games. Researchers are much more concerned about the latter kind of attrition. For example, if subjects who had more or less education, or who were more or less

Table A.A4   Distribution of Attrition

Number of Sessions Missed	Frequency	Percentage
0	271	90.03
1	17	5.65
2	6	1.99
3	7	2.33
Total	301	100.00

Source: Authors' calculations.

likely to reciprocate, were more or less likely to attend sessions, then our results would be biased, particularly in the later games in which these subjects would be absent. In general, it is very difficult to gauge the impact of attrition because there are many potential behavioral characteristics that we do not observe and therefore cannot compare. What we can say here, however, is that our attrition rates were very low.

Across all three games sessions, we had a minimum and maximum attendance of 93 percent and 97 percent of registered subjects, respectively. Attrition was concentrated among a small number of individuals (thirteen) who missed more than one session. These individuals accounted for two-thirds of all absences. The fourth session had the highest level of attrition, at 6.6 percent.

We turn next to a determination of whether attrition is likely to have affected our interpretation of the results. In table A.A5, we examine whether there were differences in observable characteristics between attendees and "attriters." On the whole, the short answer is no. Attendees and attriters looked very similar across a broad range of covariates that we might expect to have affected comprehension and behavior in the games. Only along the wealth and political participation measures did attriters look different. Using the asset index, attriters appeared to be poorer than attendees. In the second session, the difference is significant at the 95 percent level of confidence. However, they were more likely (insignificant) to be living in houses that were owned by a household member. In addition, attriters in the second session were less likely to be involved in political activity. This difference is also significant at the 95 percent level of confidence. In the third and fourth sessions, these differences were no longer significant, suggesting that they were driven by a handful of absentee subjects in the second session. What is also clear from the table is that egoists were less likely to be absent than non-egoists. The share of egoists in the attriters was considerably lower than the share in the registered population (or among attendees). The difference in the distribution of egoists was statistically significant at the 95 percent level of confidence in the third session, but insignificant in the fourth session.[5]

Table A.A5   Correlates of Attrition

	Session 2		Session 3		Session 4	
	Attendees	Attriters	Attendees	Attriters	Attendees	Attriters
Number (Percentage registered)	291 [96.7]	10 [3.3]	284 [94.4]	17 [5.6]	278 [93.4]	23 [6.6]
Characteristics						
Proportion male	0.43 (0.03)	0.40 (0.16)	0.43 (0.03)	0.41 (0.12)	0.42 (0.03)	0.48 (0.11)
Age (years)	27.21 (0.56)	26.20 (2.08)	27.18 (0.57)	27.24 (1.57)	27.12 (0.57)	27.96 (1.72)
Proportion more than primary schooling	0.64 (0.03)	0.60 (0.16)	0.64 (0.03)	0.65 (0.12)	0.64 (0.03)	0.65 (0.10)
Proportion own dwelling	0.27 (0.03)	0.40 (0.16)	0.27 (0.03)	0.29 (0.11)	0.27 (0.03)	0.26 (0.09)
Asset index	-0.01 (0.05)	-0.68 (0.27)	-0.02 (0.05)	-0.17 (0.25)	-0.03 (0.05)	-0.03 (0.23)
Political participation index	0.01 (0.06)	-0.44 (0.20)	0.01 (0.06)	-0.26 (0.19)	0.00 (0.05)	0.26 (0.27)
Associational participation index	0.01 (0.05)	0.58 (0.71)	0.01 (0.05)	0.18 (0.38)	0.02 (0.05)	-0.26 (0.51)
Share egoists	0.40 (0.03)	—	0.41 (0.03)	0.11 (0.11)	0.41 (0.03)	0.25 (0.11)

Source: Authors' calculations.

Appendix B:
Main Statistical Results

Table A.B1 (Figure 4.3)   **Effect of Coethnicity on Average Offers in the 100-Ugandan-Shilling Dictator Game with an Anonymous Offerer**

	Benchmark Coethnicity		Subjective Coethnicity	
	Ethnicity	Region	Ethnicity	Region
Egoists	−17.71	−8.33	2.90	−0.32
	(10.40)[12.71]	(9.16)[9.98]	(16.81)	(15.71)
Number of observations	362	486	358	463
Non-egoists	−9.07	−9.40	−12.39	−5.52
	(11.77)[9.95]	(9.52)[8.32]	(15.49)	(14.83)
Number of observations	609	661	596	634

Source: Author's calculations.
Notes: The cells report average treatment effects on the treated (ATT) using exact matching to average over the treatment effects obtained for offerers for each ethnic or regional group. Standard errors in parentheses are calculated using weighted OLS regression (with weights to account for different assignment probabilities across groups), and disturbance terms are clustered for each player across all of his or her games. Standard errors in brackets are heteroskedastic-consistent standard errors that assume independence across all observations.

Table A.B2 (Figure 4.4)   **Effect of Coethnicity on the Probability of Discrimination in the 500-Ugandan-Shilling Dictator Game with an Anonymous Offerer**

	Benchmark Coethnicity		Subjective Coethnicity	
	Ethnicity	Region	Ethnicity	Region
In-group member	−0.03	0.06	0.08	0.08
	(0.10)[0.06]	(0.08)[0.05]	(0.15)	(0.14)
Number of observations	222	354	122	160

Source: Authors' calculations.
Notes: Discrimination game analysis is limited to games in which players play with exactly one in-group member and one out-group member and discrimination is observed. The cells report average treatment effects on the treated (ATT) using exact matching to average over the treatment effects obtained for offerers for each ethnic or regional group. Standard errors in parentheses are calculated using weighted OLS regression (with weights to account for different assignment probabilities across groups), and disturbance terms are clustered for each player across all of his or her games. Standard errors in brackets are heteroskedastic-consistent standard errors that assume independence across all observations.

Table A.B3 (Figures 4.3 and 4.4) Variation in Policy Preferences Across Ethnic Groups

	First Priority for Public Goods Provision			How Public Goods Are to Be Provided		
	Drainage	Garbage Collection	Security	Preference for Fee-Based Garbage Collection over Free but Lower-Quality Provision	It is Better Not to Have to Pay Anything or Volunteer for Patrols, Even if That Means Security is Low	It is Better to Have Well-Maintained Drainage Channels, Even if We Have to Make Contributions of Money or Labor
Banyankole	-0.10	0.23	-0.13	0.08	-0.36	0.15
	(0.10)	(0.13)	(0.12)	(0.18)	(0.19)	(0.16)
Bagisu	-0.20	0.00	0.20	-0.07	0.38	-0.01
	(0.19)	(0.23)	(0.22)	(0.33)	(0.34)	(0.29)
Bakiga	0.05	0.10	-0.15	0.12	0.17	-0.45
	(0.13)	(0.15)	(0.15)	(0.23)	(0.25)	(0.22)
Banyarwanda	-0.09	0.05	0.05	-0.21	0.25	-0.23
	(0.14)	(0.17)	(0.17)	(0.23)	(0.24)	(0.21)
Basoga	0.10	-0.10	0.00	0.34	0.13	0.15
	(0.14)	(0.17)	(0.16)	(0.29)	(0.32)	(0.26)
Batoro	-0.00	0.10	-0.10	0.10	0.26	0.08
	(0.14)	(0.17)	(0.16)	(0.23)	(0.23)	(0.20)
Banyoro	-0.00	0.20	-0.20	-0.11	0.28	-0.09
	(0.19)	(0.23)	(0.22)	(0.28)	(0.29)	(0.25)
Iteso	0.13	0.10	-0.23	0.36	-0.04	0.28
	(0.17)	(0.21)	(0.20)	(0.33)	(0.34)	(0.29)
Bafumbira	0.34	-0.13	-0.22	0.05	0.05	-0.16
	(0.13)	(0.16)	(0.15)	(0.23)	(0.24)	(0.21)
Constant	0.20	0.40	0.40	3.21	1.62	3.29
	(0.04)	(0.05)	(0.05)	(0.08)	(0.08)	(0.07)
Number of observations	185	185	185	238	236	235
Adjusted R-squared	0.01	-0.01	-0.01	-0.02	0.00	0.00
F-statistic	1.29	0.71	0.75	0.49	1.11	1.04
p-values	(0.25)	(0.70)	(0.67)	(0.88)	(0.35)	(0.41)

Source: Authors' calculations.

Table A.B4 (Figure 4.8)   Effect of Coethnicity on Success and Confidence in the Education-Guessing Game

	Coethnicity	Co-Region
Effect on the probability that . . .		
Player 1 guesses correctly	0.03	0.01
	(0.01)[0.01]	(0.01)[0.01]
Player 2 is correctly guessed	0.01	0.01
	(0.01)[0.01]	(0.01)[0.01]
Effect on the belief that . . .		
Player 1 guesses correctly	0.01	0.01
	(0.01)[0.01]	(0.01)[0.01]
Player 2 is correctly guessed	0.06	0.03
	(0.02)[0.01]	(0.01)[0.01]

Source: Authors' calculations.
Notes: The cells report average treatment effects on the treated (ATT) using exact matching to average over the treatment effects obtained for offerers for each ethnic or regional group. Standard errors in parentheses are calculated using weighted OLS regression (with weights to account for different assignment probabilities across groups), and disturbance terms are clustered for each player across all of his or her games. Standard errors in brackets are heteroskedastic-consistent standard errors that assume independence across all observations.

Table A.B5 (Figure 4.9)   Coethnicity and Frequencies of Interaction

	Coethnicity	Co-Region
Effect on the probability that . . .		
Subject knows partner	0.03	0.02
	(0.01)[0.01]	(0.00)[0.00]
Subject is known by partner	0.03	0.03
	(0.01)[0.01]	(0.01)[0.01]

Source: Authors' calculations.
Notes: The cells report average treatment effects on the treated (ATT) using exact matching to average over the treatment effects obtained for offerers for each ethnic or regional group. Standard errors in parentheses are calculated using weighted OLS regression (with weights to account for different assignment probabilities across groups), and disturbance terms are clustered for each player across all of his or her games. Standard errors in brackets are heteroskedastic-consistent standard errors but assume independence across all observations.

Table A.B6 (Figure 4.11)   **Effect of Coethnicity on Average Offers in the 100-Ugandan-Shilling Dictator Game When Offerers Are Seen**

	Benchmark Coethnicity		Subjective Coethnicity	
	Ethnicity	Region	Ethnicity	Region
Egoist	25.95	18.65	44.42	27.50
	(12.18)[13.26]	(10.01)[10.68]	(25.35)	(17.53)
Number of observations	343	422	339	415
Non-egoist	−14.82	−6.04	−26.36	−7.27
	(11.05)[11.80]	(10.40)[10.03]	(22.56)	(19.73)
Number of observations	400	511	395	492

Source: Authors' calculations.
Notes: The cells report average treatment effects on the treated (ATT) using exact matching to average over the treatment effects obtained for offerers for each ethnic or regional group. Standard errors in parentheses are calculated using weighted OLS regression (with weights to account for different assignment probabilities across groups), and disturbance terms are clustered for each player across all of his or her games. Standard errors in brackets are heteroskedastic-consistent standard errors that assume independence across all observations.

Table A.B7 (Figure 4.12)   **Effect of Coethnicity on the Probability of Discrimination in the 500-Ugandan-Shilling Dictator Game When Offerers Are Seen**

	Benchmark Identity		Subjective Identity	
	Ethnicity	Region	Ethnicity	Region
In-group member	0.12	0.14	0.28	0.24
	(0.07)[0.05]	(0.06)[0.04]	(0.13)	(0.11)
Number of observations	406	608	188	272

Source: Authors' calculations.
Notes: Discrimination game analysis is limited to games in which players play with exactly one in-group member and one out-group member and discrimination is observed. The cells report average treatment effects on the treated (ATT) using exact matching to average over the treatment effects obtained for offerers for each ethnic or regional group. Standard errors in parentheses are calculated using weighted OLS regression (with weights to account for different assignment probabilities across groups), and disturbance terms are clustered for each player across all of his or her games. Standard errors in brackets are heteroskedastic-consistent standard errors that assume independence across all observations.

Table A.B8 (Figure 4.13)   The Importance of Being Seen Coethnicity

	100-Ugandan-Shilling Game (Egoists Only)		500-Ugandan-Shilling Game	
	Benchmark Coethnicity	Subjective Coethnicity	Benchmark Coethnicity	Subjective Coethnicity
Coethnicity				
Offerer is seen	−6.96	−9.08	−0.08	−0.08
	(8.04)	(12.09)	(0.06)	(0.09)
In-group member	−17.22	4.71	−0.03	0.08
	(10.40)	(17.05)	(0.10)	(0.16)
Seen and in-group member	42.43	41.24	0.15	0.19
	(14.50)	(30.34)	(0.12)	(0.21)
Number of observations	797	892	628	310
Co-Region				
Offerer is seen	−8.23	−11.33	−0.04	−0.08
	(7.54)	(11.03)	(0.05)	(0.08)
In-group member	−7.72	0.49	0.06	0.08
	(9.16)	(15.63)	(0.08)	(0.14)
Seen and in-group member	27.09	29.21	0.08	0.16
	(13.45)	(23.73)	(0.09)	(0.18)
Number of observations	916	892	962	432

Source: Authors' calculations.
Notes: Robust standard errors in parentheses. The columns report coefficients from an OLS regression with weights to take account of different assignment probabilities for different groups. Disturbance terms are clustered for each player across all of his or her games.

Table A.B9 (Figure 5.2)   Cooperation in the Prisoner's Dilemma Game

	(1) Non-Egoist (standard error)	(2) Egoist (standard error)	(3) Total (standard error)	(4) Difference (standard error)
Likelihood of cooperation with no enforcer	0.61 n = 584	0.50 n = 382	0.56 n = 969	0.11 (.03)
Likelihood of cooperation with an enforcer	0.64 n = 791	0.60 n = 497	0.62 n = 1293	0.04 (0.03)
Difference	0.03 (0.03)	0.10 (0.03)	0.06 (0.02)	0.07 (0.05)

Source: Authors' calculations.
Notes: Result of a probit (dprobit) model. Marginal coefficient estimates are reported (at mean values for the explanatory variables). Disturbance terms are clustered for each player across all of his or her games.

Table A.B10 (Figure 5.3)   Coethnicity and Cooperation in the Prisoner's Dilemma Game

	(1) Non-Egoist (standard error)	(2) Egoist (standard error)	(3) Total (standard error)	(4) Difference (standard error)
Likelihood of Cooperation	0.61	0.50	0.56	0.11
	n = 584	n = 382	n = 966	(0.04)
Marginal Effect of Benchmark Coethnicity	0.00 (0.05)[0.05]	0.11 (0.08)[0.08]	0.04 (0.04)[0.04]	0.11 (0.09)
Marginal Effect of Subjective Coethnicity	0.15 (0.09)	0.30 (0.13)	0.21 (0.07)	0.14 (0.15)
Marginal Effect of Benchmark Co-Region	0.01 (0.04)[0.04]	0.15 (0.06)[0.06]	0.06 (0.04)[0.04]	0.14 (0.07)
Marginal Effect of Subjective Co-Region	0.07 (0.08)	0.27 (0.11)	0.14 (0.06)	0.20 (0.13)

Source: Authors' calculations.
Notes: The cells report average treatment effects on the treated (ATT) using exact matching to average over the treatment effects obtained for offerers for each ethnic or regional group. Standard errors in parentheses are calculated using weighted OLS regression (with weights to account for different assignment probabilities across groups), and disturbance terms are clustered for each player across all of his or her games. Standard errors in brackets are heteroskedastic-consistent standard errors that assume independence across all observations.

Table A.B11 (Figure 5.4)   Punishment Behavior by Type and Player Action

	Egoist			Non-Egoist		
	Front-End Player Cooperates (*n*)	Front-End Player Defects (*n*)	Difference (standard error)	Front-End Player Cooperates (*n*)	Front-End Player Defects (*n*)	Difference (standard error)
Likelihood of punishment	0.14 (358)	0.26 (228)	0.11 (0.04)	0.21 (506)	0.38 (364)	0.17 (0.04)

Source: Authors' calculations.
Notes: Result of a probit (dprobit) model. Marginal coefficient estimates are reported (at mean values for the explanatory variables). Disturbance terms are clustered for each player across all of his or her games.

Table A.B12 (Figure 5.6)   Periodicity and Offers

	Coethnic Pairings		Non-Coethnic Pairings	
	(1) Egoist (standard error)	(2) Non-Egoist (standard error)	(3) Egoist (standard error)	(4) Non-Egoist (standard error)
Effect of being seen when player does not know partner	27.47 (14.84)	−10.60 (12.23)	−7.90 (7.60)	2.02 (8.92)
Effect of being seen when player does know partner	118.75 (30.94)	−24.70 (30.41)	−22.36 (23.72)	−0.74 (27.55)
Difference	91.28 (33.85)	−14.09 (32.12)	−14.46 (25.43)	−2.76 (28.68)

Source: Authors' calculations.
Notes: Result of an OLS regression. Disturbance terms are clustered for each player across all of his or her games.

Table A.B13 (Figure 5.7)   Correlates of Reachability

	Marginal Effect on Success Rates (Bivariate Relationship)	Marginal Effect on Success Rates (Multivariate Relationship)
Male	0.13 (0.08)	0.19 (0.08)
Catholic	0.04 (0.08)	0.13 (0.09)
Muslim	0.23 (0.10)	0.19 (0.11)
Old (subject is older than 35)	0.32 (0.08)	0.31 (0.09)
Recent arrival	−0.15 (0.08)	−0.11 (0.08)
LC Committee	0.003 (0.10)	−0.05 (0.10)
Observations	148	127
R-squared		0.18

Source: Authors' calculations.
Notes: Reports OLS regression results, with standard errors in parentheses.

Table A.B14 (Figure 5.8)   Reachability and Offers

	Male	Muslim	Older	Established	Reachable
Effect of being (male, Muslim, etc.) on amount withheld in anonymous dictator game	10.19 (23.89)	32.38 (28.52)	−54.72 (30.47)	0.73 (23.40)	−1.47 (23.48)
Effect of being (male, Muslim, etc.) on amount withheld in non-anonymous dictator game	14.46 (26.45)	−19.17 (29.84)	−36.01 (29.77)	4.47 (26.35)	−7.04 (26.01)
Difference (standard error)	4.28 (21.54)	−51.55 (27.65)	18.71 (22.22)	3.74 (21.72)	−5.57 (21.23)

Source: Authors' calculations.
Notes: Rows 1 and 2 report average offers with the number of observations in parentheses. Row 3 reports OLS regression results with standard errors in parentheses; disturbance terms are clustered across each player for all of his or her games.

Table A.B15 (Figure 5.9)   The Effects of External Sanctioning on Coethnic Cooperation by Egoists

	Ethnicity			Region		
	Non-Coethnic (n)	Coethnic (n)	Difference (standard error)	Non-Coethnic (n)	Coethnic (n)	Difference (standard error)
Level of cooperation without an enforcer	0.47 (308)	0.58 (73)	0.11 (0.08)[0.08]	0.45 (262)	0.59 (119)	0.15 (0.06)[0.06]
Level of cooperation with an enforcer	0.61 (395)	0.56 (100)	−0.11 (0.06)[0.06]	0.61 (333)	0.59 (162)	−0.03 (0.05)[0.05]

Source: Authors' calculations.
Notes: Differences are average treatment effects on the treated (ATT) using exact matching to average over the treatment effects obtained for offerers for each ethnic or regional group. Standard errors in parentheses are calculated using weighted OLS regression (with weights to account for different assignment probabilities across groups), and disturbance terms are clustered for each player across all of his or her games. Standard errors in brackets are heteroskedastic-consistent standard errors that assume independence across all observations.

Table A.B16 (Figure 5.10)   **Coethnicity and Cooperation in the Prisoner's Dilemma Game with an Enforcer**

	(1) Non-Egoist (standard error)	(2) Egoist (standard error)	(3) Total (standard error)	(4) Difference (standard error)
Marginal effect of benchmark coethnicity with an enforcer	0.02 (0.05)[0.05]	−0.11 (0.06)[0.06]	−0.03 (0.04)[0.04]	−0.13 (0.08)
Marginal effect of subjective coethnicity with an enforcer	0.03 (0.07)	−0.04 (0.09)	0.01 (0.06)	−0.08 (0.12)
Marginal effect of benchmark co-region with an enforcer	0.00 (0.04)[0.04]	−0.03 (0.05)[0.05]	−0.01 (0.03)[0.03]	−0.03 (0.06)
Marginal effect of subjective co-region with an enforcer	−0.03 (0.06)	−0.06 (0.08)	−0.04 (0.05)	−0.04 (0.10)

Source: Authors' calculations.
Notes: The cells report average treatment effects on the treated (ATT) using exact matching to average over the treatment effects obtained for offerers for each ethnic or regional group. Standard errors in parentheses are calculated using weighted OLS regression (with weights to account for different assignment probabilities across groups), and disturbance terms are clustered for each player across all of his or her games. Standard errors in brackets are heteroskedastic-consistent standard errors that assume independence across all observations.

Table A.B17 (Figure 5.11)   **Defection and Propensity to Sanction**

	Ethnicity		Region	
	Non-Coethnic Enforcer and Defector (standard error)	Coethnic Enforcer and Defector (standard error)	Non-Coethnic Enforcer and Defector (standard error)	Coethnic Enforcer and Defector (standard error)
Effect of defection on likelihood of sanction	0.14 (0.03)[0.03]	0.22 (0.06)[0.06]	0.15 (0.04)[0.03]	0.17 (0.05)[0.04]

Source: Authors' calculations.
Notes: The cells report average treatment effects on the treated (ATT) using exact matching to average over the treatment effects obtained for offerers for each ethnic or regional group. Standard errors in parentheses are calculated using weighted OLS regression (with weights to account for different assignment probabilities across groups), and disturbance terms are clustered for each player across all of his or her games. Standard errors in brackets are heteroskedastic-consistent standard errors that assume independence across all observations.

Table A.B18 (Figure 5.12)   Effects of Ethnic Composition on Punishment Behavior

	Frequency with Which Player Is Punished Conditional upon Defection (All Players Seen)		
	Non-Egoist (n)	Egoist (n)	Difference (standard error)
Trio homogeneous	0.53 (36)	0.15 (13)	−0.37 (0.14)
Players 2 and 3 share ethnicity	0.45 (38)	0.26 (27)	−0.19 (0.14)
Enforcer and player 2 share ethnicity	0.42 (36)	0.27 (22)	−0.14 (0.13)
Enforcer and player 3 share ethnicity	0.28 (43)	0.23 (26)	−0.05 (0.11)
Trio heterogeneous	0.39 (153)	0.27 (110)	−0.11 (0.06)

Source: Authors' calculations.
Notes: The averages shown are calculated using the sample of games in which there was positive information on all three players. Column 3 reports results of an OLS regression. Disturbance terms are clustered for each player across all of his or her games. Standard errors in parentheses.

Appendix C:
Images of the Field Site, Experimental Games, and Research Team

The office building in Mulago where the experiments were conducted.
Source: Jacobia Dahm

A view of Mulago and Kyebando from our office balcony.
Source: Jacobia Dahm

Subjects waiting to be registered for participation in the games.
Source: Authors' photograph.

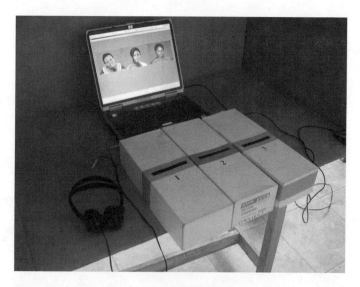

The basic setup of the computer for the Dictator game. The screen shows information for all three players.
Source: Authors' photograph.

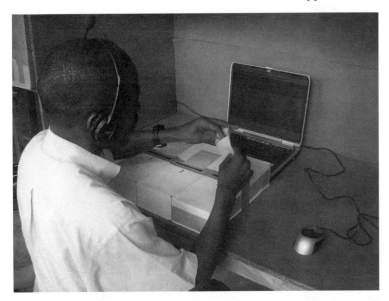

Livingstone Ntensibe demonstrates how an offerer puts coins into an envelope to send to a receiver.
Source: Authors' photograph.

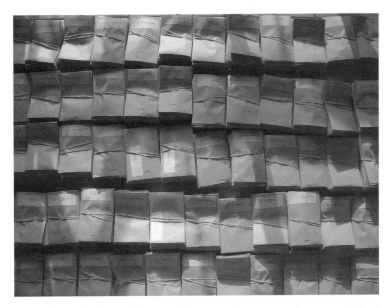

The envelopes containing offers made by one player to another are weighed and then sorted in preparation to be returned to the receivers.
Source: Jacobia Dahm

Winfred Naziwa providing instruction to Brenda Nakkazi about how to play the Prisoner's Dilemma game. Two images are visible on the screen, identifying both of the participating players. One of the two boxes is for the player, and the other is for the group. A 1,000-Ugandan-shilling envelope is provided to the player with a single envelope. She must decide whether to put the envelope in the box for herself or for the group.
Source: Authors' photograph.

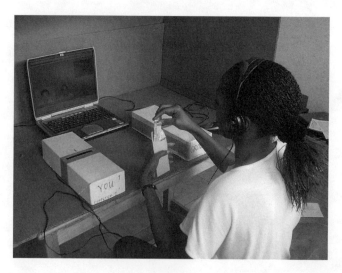

Brenda demonstrates how to put the 1,000-Ugandan-shilling note in an envelope before placing it in the box. Note that the screen for this version of the Prisoner's Dilemma game includes an image in the upper-right-hand corner that identifies the third-party enforcer.
Source: Authors' photograph.

Two of our enumerators, Douglas Musunga and Winfred, demonstrate how to play the Lockbox game. Douglas is trying to teach Winfred how to open the padlock on the chest. Six thousand Ugandan shillings are locked inside the chest. *Source:* Authors' photograph.

Ruth Nagawa and Alex Odwong demonstrate the setup of the Puzzle game. Each player has half of the puzzle inside his or her box. *Source:* Authors' photograph.

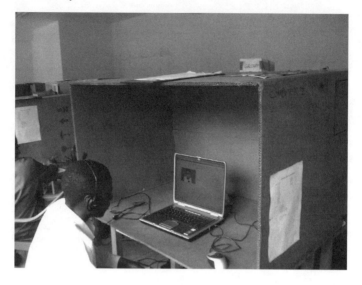

A subject views an image in the identification exercise before being asked to guess the partner's ethnic group and level of education.
Source: Authors' photograph.

The team of researchers, research assistants, and enumerators who implemented the Mulago-Kyebando Community Study.
Source: Authors' photograph.

Notes

Chapter 1

1. Uganda has a hierarchical administrative structure of local councils (LCs). The capital, Kampala, is partitioned into five divisions (LC3s), which are divided in turn into parishes (LC2s) and zones (LC1s).
2. Interviews with Chairmen Ssalongo and Kashaija took place on July 18, 2005, and July 11, 2005, respectively.
3. Technically, a public good is "non-excludable"—it can be consumed by everyone irrespective of whether they contributed to providing it—and "non-rival"—one person's consumption of the good does not diminish the ability of others to consume it as well. For the obstacles to public goods provision that are of interest to us here, non-excludability is the more important aspect.
4. This informal description of the collective action problem actually describes a family of distinct strategic situations enumerated by game theorists. To see this, assume that each of two players is less happy with both not contributing than with both contributing. Then, if each individual prefers not to contribute no matter what the other does, the problem is a Prisoner's Dilemma; if each would rather contribute if and only if the other contributes, then the problem is an Assurance game; if each would rather contribute if and only if the other does *not* contribute, then the problem is a Chicken game. The classic discussion of the dilemma of public goods provision is provided by Mancur Olson (1965).
5. Okten and Osili's (2004) finding is confirmed by Jeffrey Nugent and Shailender Swaminathan (2006), who used similar data from Indonesia and reached the same conclusion about the impact of diversity on contributions to village health posts.
6. Chandra (2004), Okten and Osili (2004), Alesina and LaFerrara (2005), and Bowles and Gintis (2004a) are exceptions in that they lay out a number of possible mechanisms.
7. The description we use here is that of a game in normal or strategic form. Games in extensive form use more primitives; those in characteristic function form use fewer.
8. See, for example, Horowitz (1985), who took his cue from a rich tradition in

201

social psychology that emphasizes how a sense of belonging to a particular group, no matter how arbitrary the definition of group, leads individuals to demonstrate an in-group bias, even if it comes at a cost to their own welfare (Tajfel et al. 1971).

9. Robert Bates (1973) pointed out that a salient feature of ethnic groups is that they are often geographically concentrated. This, he suggested, can induce a commonality of interests over outcomes that have a geographic component, such as the location of public investments. In a model of educational choices, Edward Miguel (1999) proposed that individuals have preferences over the *type* of education they receive (for example, the language of instruction or the language in which parent-teacher meetings are conducted) that is correlated across coethnics. This can lead to an unwillingness to invest in education in more heterogeneous communities simply because the public good that is produced is of lower value to some individuals than others.

10. Note that, strictly speaking, other-regarding preferences and preferences over process formally can be treated as special cases of a commonality of preferences over "outcomes" broadly defined. Because other-regarding preferences and preferences over process have received special attention in the literature, we treat them separately here.

11. Strikingly, in one recent study of what is known as the "disease threat" model of intergroup attitudes, scholars found that women displayed lower propensities to cooperate with out-group members in periods when they were vulnerable, specifically during their first trimester of pregnancy (Navarrete, Fessler, and Eng 2007).

12. Karl Deutsch's (1966) conceptualization of ethnic groups as "communities of communication" whose cohesiveness is a function of how quickly and effectively they can transmit complicated messages captured exactly this notion. In the economics literature, this mechanism would be described in terms of variation in "transaction costs."

13. A recent paper by Enrico Spolaore and Romain Wacziarg (2009) employed a variant of the technology mechanism in accounting for income differences across countries. The authors used genetic distance between populations as a proxy for the ease with which new technologies can diffuse across borders. In particular, they suggested that the horizontal diffusion of development may be impeded by language and other cultural differences.

14. A literature in economics on "statistical discrimination" has explored how observable markers (such as ethnic identities) might be used by economic actors as a shortcut for assessing unobservable characteristics, such as trustworthiness or competence (Foster and Rosenzweig 1993; Fafchamps 2003). Here we take the additional step of suggesting that the ability to engage in such discrimination may itself depend on group membership.

15. In Habyarimana et al. (2007), we use the term "findability" instead of "reachability." Reachability, a concept developed in network theory, better captures the general nature of the mechanism we discuss, which emphasizes the ability of individuals to link to each other, whether or not they can physically locate one another. For a discussion of ethnic networks as information conduits, see Platteau (1994) and Landa (1994). For a discussion of

the role of networks in sanctioning, see Bernstein (1992), Richman (2006), Kandori (1992), Greif (1993, 1994), and Fafchamps (2003). Many of the insights about the importance of networks for the enforcement of contracts in environments with no sovereign authority build on work by Mark Granovetter (1985), who described the "embeddedness" of business relations in a social context.

16. For an account of how cooperation can be sustained in networks even when repeated interactions are rare, see Kandori (1992).

17. Our approach is very similar to the idea of a "group heuristic" by which "people facing a group situation assume, by default (that is, when no salient clue indicating otherwise is available), that social interactions that take place in the group involve generalized exchange, and, thus … behave in a way that minimizes the risk of developing a bad reputation among the members of their group" (Yamagishi and Mifune 2008, 8).

18. This behavior is generally referred to as a type of *reciprocity*. The logic here shows how reciprocity can work even in a single, or "one-shot," encounter. Reciprocity also can induce cooperative behavior when interactions are sustained. Specifically, it is possible that a group of people can support cooperation by playing strategies in which each cooperates as long as the others do too. But should one fail to cooperate, that individual will be punished by being excluded from future group benefits as the other players stop cooperating (Axelrod 1984). This "tit-for-tat" solution to the collective action problem may be selected in some groups but not in others. In some cases, each player might expect that all other players are playing tit-for-tat and will play that way in response; in other cases, each player might expect that no one will cooperate under any circumstances and so no one does. Like the one-shot example, this strategy selection mechanism has a self-fulfilling aspect to it: individuals cooperate because they expect that certain types will also cooperate with them.

19. Evolutionary models of reciprocity include, for example, Gintis (2000) and Bowles and Gintis (2004b). A rich literature in economics offers a range of theoretical models advancing the mechanisms that drive reciprocal behavior (see, for example, Rabin 1993; Fehr and Schmidt 1999; Bolton and Ockenfels 2000).

20. Note that these experiments have a feature that might surprise many. In both cases, the core study required no random assignment of subjects to treatment and control groups. While randomization is often central to experiments, the key experimental feature is control, not randomization. This point is made particularly clearly by David Cox and Nancy Reid, who noted that "the word experiment is used in a quite precise sense to mean an investigation where the system under study is under the control of the investigator. This means that the individuals or materials investigated, the nature of the treatments or manipulations under study, and the measurement procedures used are all selected, in their important features at least, by the investigator" (2001, 1).

21. A point we return to is that what we can control is the probability that any given interaction is with a coethnic or a non-coethnic; we cannot, of course, vary whether any given interacting partner is a coethnic or not.

22. Public goods provision at the LC1 level is the focus of our analysis because LC1s, which can be thought of as local communities or neighborhoods, are the principal units in which the public goods that we treat in this study are generated (or not).
23. The data come from a sample of 594 informants interviewed at randomly selected sites in Kawempe. Further details of the survey are provided in chapter 2.
24. Regression results (not shown) confirm the statistical significance of the relationship (p-value 0.07).
25. A fuller discussion of Kampala's administrative structure is provided in chapter 2.
26. We describe our sampling procedures in chapter 3.
27. Jean-Philippe Platteau and Tomasz Strzalecki (2004), for example, studied two communities in Senegal in which expectations regarding cross-group collective action outcomes differed markedly—a difference the authors attributed to the contrasting histories of group conflict in the two settings.

Chapter 2

1. For a parallel example of an investigation into the impact of community characteristics on neighborhood collective action outcomes, see Sampson, Raudenbush, and Earls (1997).
2. Enumerators were asked to indicate their degree of confidence in each respondent's familiarity with the community characteristics about which he or she was asked. Enumerators reported being "confident" or "very confident" in the respondent's local knowledge 97 percent of the time. The results reported here exclude responses in which enumerators were not confident in a respondent's answers.
3. The survey was conducted by the Economic Policy Research Centre with financial and technical assistance from the World Bank.
4. Each enumeration area contains approximately 200 to 250 households and corresponds roughly to an LC1.
5. Satisfaction with public goods provision is, admittedly, an imperfect measure of the quality of local goods since communities may vary in their standards of what constitutes "satisfactory" public goods provision. An alternative is to use data on per capita spending on local public goods (see, for example, Alesina, Bagir, and Easterly 1999; Poterba 1997). The problem with this approach, however, is that the disbursed funds may not actually translate into public goods delivery on the ground. A study by Ritva Reinikka and Jakob Svensson (2004), which found that schools in Uganda received an average of just 13 percent of the grant funds allocated to them by the central government, illustrates the extent of the problem.
6. The link between poverty and low public goods provision is a major theme of the 2004 World Development Report (World Bank 2004).
7. The national police also play a role in local crime prevention, at least formally. However, they are notoriously unreliable. "The [local defense units]

were stopped and now we have to use the police," one local council chairman explained to us. "But the police are very irregular. They are not reliable. When you call the police, you need to motivate them. You need to give them cigarettes or a bribe of 20,000 [Ugandan shillings] or they won't come back." The chairman of another local council agreed: "We almost never see patrols trying to protect us. Mostly when the police come to this area, they are coming to go drink in the bars. They come here to drink and leave after one hour." Given this unreliability, the preponderant share of public security—to the extent that it is provided at all—is provided by the local councils.

8. Those who cannot afford to pay for the water have been known to pierce the pipes or steal from the taps at night.

9. Short of blockading streets and collecting tolls—as the most aggressive child pothole fillers sometimes do—road maintenance is less amenable to a fee-for-service arrangement, as the vast majority of motorists simply drive past without paying. However, the opportunity costs for the children who engage in pothole filling are so low that they can usually earn enough from the occasional contributions to make the undertaking worthwhile.

10. As noted in chapter 1, these twenty-six LC1s are located in Kawempe in the adjacent parishes (LC2s) of Mulago I, Mulago II, Mulago III, and Kyebando, which we thus refer to collectively as Mulago-Kyebando. We are indebted to Claire Adida, Alex Scacco, Liz Carlson, Dan Young, and Bernd Beber for their excellent contribution to this part of the project.

11. We exclude wealthier LC1s because residents reported that collective action was not necessary to improve the level of public goods provision in these locations. In the Doctors zone and the Hospital zone, most public services were provided directly by Mulago Hospital. In National Housing, Owen Road, Tufnel, and Upper Mawanda, residents were significantly wealthier than the residents of the rest of Mulago-Kyebando; consequently, most paid for garbage pickup and employed private security guards. Drainage was not an issue in these LC1s because they were located at the top of a hill.

Chapter 3

1. For an illuminating discussion of how populations are categorized in national censuses, see Kertzer and Arel (2002).

2. Note that this treatment is consistent with ethnic or racial "nominalism": a benchmark demography may be no more than a statement about how the theorist likes to categorize people and is not a statement about what or who people "really are." Theorists make these categorizations all the time, sometimes in ways that sit uncomfortably with the self-perceptions of their subjects. Thus, a theorist might classify people as being in group X if the national census records them as members of group X, or perhaps if they self-identify as members of group X, or if perhaps their DNA contains a particular sequence of code. Such statements allow a theorist to construct a

"benchmark" ethnic demography, and of course, there may be as many benchmark demographies for a given population as there are classification rules.

3. Some do argue, however, that the use of *any* such categories reifies the boundaries between the citizens of a country (see Kertzer and Arel 2002). For this reason, questions about ethnic identity were removed from Uganda's censuses in 1969 and in 1980.

4. Andrew Mwenda (2006), for example, emphasizes the "strong sense of grievance among the Baganda and Basoga political and bureaucratic elite, and also among their business community that they do not get as many jobs and private sector contracts as Banyankole."

5. James Fearon and David Laitin (1996) demonstrate how rare ethnic conflict actually is across Africa, within the universe of potential conflicts among ethnic groups.

6. Although commonly used, this index has been shown to have a number of flaws. Daniel Posner (2004b) enumerates a number of facets of ethnic demography that ELF fails to adequately capture, including different distributions in the size of ethnic groups (many of which, when summarized in ELF, produce the same value), the spatial distribution of groups, and the depth of divisions among different ethnic groups.

7. Donna Bahry and Rick Wilson's (2006) study of fairness norms in Russian republics provides a rare but important counterexample to the tradition of employing nonrandom samples.

8. Random sampling was conducted using a random compass. Teams entered each LC1 at a central point and chose random directions and a random walking period. At the designated stopping time, they selected the closest house and created a roster of household members over eighteen years old. Stratifying by gender, a household member was then selected at random and invited to participate in the games. Household members were invited whether or not they were present at the time of the selection. (In cases where household members were not present, their names and ages were recorded, and these were confirmed upon registration.) More than 75 percent of those we selected agreed to participate in the study. This is a high rate given that prospective subjects were made aware that full participation would entail attendance at four separate experimental sessions spread out over several weeks. Of those who chose to enter the study, more than 95 percent attended all four sessions. Additional details about our sampling strategy, nonparticipation, and attrition are provided in appendix A. In addition to the 300 sampled subjects, we invited local council chairpersons to participate in a subset of our games, notably the Dictator game and the Prisoner's Dilemma game. Seventeen LC chairs elected to participate. Although we report results with these plays included, our substantive results are robust to the exclusion of these plays.

9. Many other notions of correct identification could be considered; indeed, one could use a correspondence between a guess and any other classification rule (such as the typical guess of a population).

10. Note that two groups may not be highly distinct for a given individual yet that person may find *individual members* of those groups highly identifiable.

11. In measuring processes of subjective identification, we take our lead from a number of studies that have explored how people classify others into ethnic categories in an effort to better understand prejudice; see Allport and Kramer (1946), Secord (1959), Lent (1970), Blascovich et al. (1997), and Harris (2002). However, while these studies shed light on how people classify others, they are not as useful for generating measures of subjective demographies because neither the sample of subjects that are being categorized nor the sample of individuals asked to do the categorization is representative of any larger population.

12. See Isaacs (1975) and Chandra (2004) for discussions of the information contained in a name. In Fershtman and Gneezy (2001), names are employed as the sole marker of ethnic group affiliation in experiments that seek to uncover patterns of inter- and intra-ethnic interaction. Charness and Gneezy (2003) measure the more general impact of names on behavior in Dictator and Ultimatum games.

13. Subjects also were asked to guess the level of education of each of their partners. Results from this aspect of the identification exercise are discussed in chapter 4.

14. To preserve the integrity of our experimental design—that is, not to tip off our subjects to the fact that we were studying ethnicity in the experimental games—this exercise was conducted after all other game sessions were completed. We can thus be confident that players were not primed to our particular interest in ethnicity as they played the core games that will be described in chapters 4 and 5.

15. If players could gain no additional information from the video images, an optimal guessing strategy would be for all subjects to guess Baganda all of the time. The result, however, would be an aggregate subjective demography quite different from the aggregate benchmark demography.

16. "Munyankole" is the singular form of "Banyankole." In general in Bantu languages, a single member of a group is referred to using a "mu" prefix and multiple members are referred to using a "ba" prefix.

17. Thus, if guessers, confronted with no information at all, were to guess Baganda *all the time*, they would be correct 100 percent of the time whenever they saw Baganda, but still be correct only 44 percent of the time overall.

18. This is the average treatment effect on the treated, and it can be calculated by matching observations either for each individual or at the group level.

19. Finally, we can also calculate the coethnic effect for a viewer controlling for the ethnic group of the individual being viewed. This is done by matching treatment and control observations at either the viewer's individual level or group level and entering fixed effects for each ethnic group being viewed (and clustering over all the guesses of each player). Doing this, we find that coethnicity increases the likelihood of correct identification by eight percentage points, an effect that is also significant at the 99 percent level.

20. Although we use the terms "error of exclusion" and "error of inclusion," others have referred to these misclassifications as Type I and Type II errors, respectively.

21. Although, in principle, a group of any size may make few errors, if subjective demographies accurately reflect the benchmark demography, then the *scope* for large errors is maximized for groups with 50 percent of the population ($p = 0.5$). Such a group could in principle always be getting it wrong, committing errors of exclusion or errors of inclusion 50 percent of the time each. A group with size $p < 0.5$, however, can only get it wrong (and maintain a correspondence between the subjective and benchmark distributions) $2p$ of the time. Similarly, a group size $p > 0.5$ can only get it wrong $2(1 - p)$ of the time.

22. Although Francesco Caselli and John Coleman (2006) base a theoretical model of ethnic conflict on a similar notion of distinctness, we know of no attempts to measure distinctness in this way empirically.

23. It is of interest to note that this definition of distinctness is equivalent to the *determinant* of the 2×2 matrix P in which each cell entry, p_{ij}, denotes the probability with which a row type is classified as a column type given that it is classified among some column type. In this case, the determinant is given by $p_{11}p_{22} - p_{12}p_{21} = p_{11}p_{22} - (1 - p_{11})(1 - p_{22}) = p_{11} + p_{22} - 1$. Thus, the distinctness measure is a natural measure of the extent to which this matrix diverges from the identity matrix.

Chapter 4

1. As noted earlier, we were able to randomly determine whether an individual encountered a coethnic or a non-coethnic partner, but this was not equivalent to randomly determining whether a given partner was a coethnic or not. To illustrate: if it were the case that in our sample all coethnics were wealthy and non-coethnics were poor, then we could randomly determine whether an individual encountered a wealthy coethnic or a poor non-coethnic, but we could not vary the coethnicity of a partner while keeping wealth constant.

2. Information treatments are now a common part of research in experimental economics. Iris Bohnet and Bruno Frey (1999) demonstrated how decreasing social distance (by increasing the amount of information people have about their partners) affects play in Dictator games. Rick Wilson and Catherine Eckel (2006) controlled the information available about playing partners to test whether attractive subjects receive a "beauty premium" in a trust game, and Gary Charness and Uri Gneezy (2003) introduced family names as an informational treatment. We see our PIB as a natural extension of this work, allowing for the introduction of multiple levels of information and the creation of common knowledge.

3. See Crawford and Haller (1990) for evidence of coordination deriving from repeated interaction.

4. The only exceptions were the Lockbox and Network games. In the former, one of the aims was to study a selection process; in the latter, our relatively small sample size required that we abandon random matching to ensure a sufficient number of coethnic pairings. Yet even in this case, our matching strategy used no information on individual attributes and was random conditional on group and date of play.

5. We created this subjective measure for each level of information that the first player had about the second.

6. In some models, a player's type is defined over behavioral patterns (Bowles and Gintis 2004b); in others, types are distinguished by their preferences (Güth and Kliemt 1998; Ostrom 2000). We focus on preferences here because our aim is to generate inferences across different games based on a single definition of types.

7. Subjects played an average of six rounds of the Discrimination game.

8. We examined two alternative coding rules for egoists. In the first, we calculated the average offer made by an individual in an anonymous Dictator game where the individual was given ten 100-Ugandan-shilling coins and asked how much she wished to keep and how much she wished to give to each of two other players. In the second, we produced residuals from a regression of offers in the 100-Ugandan-shilling version of the Dictator game on fixed effects for the receivers and the amount of information available to the offerer. We averaged these residuals for each player as a measure of their baseline willingness to give money away. Both of these measures correlate highly with our measure of egoism extracted from the Discrimination game. The first correlates at 0.45, and the second at 0.70. All of the results we present in this chapter are robust to the use of these alternative measures of egoism.

9. Note that this research examines arbitrary groups; it is less well established whether such favoritism also exists among non-arbitrary groups, which is the question we examine here.

10. The online appendix provides a transcript of the exact proctors' instructions and protocols for this and all other experimental games. Available at: https://www.russellsage.org/publications/CoethnicityAppendix.

11. Some aspects of the games we employed differed from those commonly reported in the literature. Although it naturally would be desirable to be able to compare the results of our games with those reported by other researchers, this goal was secondary to designing games that would permit us to make the clearest tests possible of the competing explanations we were studying. A large literature confirms that the results of experimental games are highly dependent on seemingly small game parameters, including the pro- or anti-social nature of the proctor's instructions and whether players think their behaviors are anonymous (see, for example, Hoffman, McCabe, and Smith 1996; Haley and Fessler 2005). However, because we are interested in comparing variation in patterns of play *across subjects and across pairings*, whatever biases our game designs might have entailed were constant across them and thus should not undermine our ability to make the inferences we seek to make.

12. So that the actions of offerers would approximate a direct transfer to the maximum extent possible, we did not open the envelopes but instead calculated the value of the contents by weighing them.

13. See chapter 6 for a description of various checks we instituted to ensure that our subjects understood the games they were playing.

14. To take account of this difference in assignment probabilities across groups, we calculate the average treatment effect on the treated by examining the

effect of coethnicity for each group and then averaging these effects across groups with weights to reflect the share of the treated observations in each group.

15. Because the Discrimination game was played with two partners for each offerer, we stacked the data and coded a dependent variable that captured whether a given receiver was favored. In stacking the data this way, we doubled the number of observations in our regressions. In our analyses, however, we clustered standard errors across all games for a given player. Our results are also robust to treating each game as a single game.

16. Here, and in all results reported in chapters 4 and 5, average treatment effects are estimated by using exact matching to average over the treatment effects obtained for offerers for each ethnic or regional group. Averaging over differences between treated and untreated subjects within groups ensures that the results are not confounded by "main" effects that could result from the fact that treatment assignment probabilities varied across groups. We calculated standard errors using weighted ordinary least squares (OLS) regression (with weights to account for different assignment probabilities across groups) and clustered disturbance terms for each player across all of his or her games. The tables in appendix B report both these standard errors and heteroskedasticity-consistent standard errors that assumed independence across all observations. In addition, the findings reported here are robust to the inclusion of a battery of controls for age, education, income, gender, and other characteristics (which, by design, were uncorrelated with the experimental treatment).

17. Tables containing all results described in the figures presented in chapters 4 and 5 are provided in appendix B.

18. It bears mention that egoists played somewhat differently than non-egoists. They gave approximately 100 Ugandan shillings less to each partner than did non-egoists (results not shown). This is a substantively large difference, and one that is significant at the 99 percent level. It serves to demonstrate that, although our definition of egoists is based on play in the Discrimination game, the categorization strongly predicted how subjects would play in other games as well. It lends support to the notion that the categorization captured something general about players rather than simply behavior in one particular game.

19. This restriction is similar to examining only the behavior of egoists, except that we included all games in which non-egoists also made discriminatory choices. Because this game is designed specifically to measure patterns of discrimination, we did not include games in which subjects gave both coins away or, violating the rules, kept both or gave both to another person. In the subjective coethnicity analysis, we coded a player as believing that he or she was facing one coethnic partner and one non-coethnic partner if the difference in his or her estimated belief that each of the two partners was a coethnic exceeded 0.5.

20. In this sense, unlike the other results described here, our exploration of this particular mechanism is not experimental.

21. Although we confirmed empirically that there was considerable diversity in attitudes toward these issues, we emphasize that the issues were se-

lected for their general salience and thus may not necessarily represent the most ethnically divisive issues in Mulago-Kyebando. In this sense, our surveys explored whether preferences over *salient* issues were structured along ethnic lines rather than the somewhat more obvious, and perhaps more trivial, question of whether preferences over *ethnically contentious* issues were structured along ethnic lines.

22. The figures report the relative likelihood that each ethnic group would rank a given issue as a priority, as compared to the ranking by the Baganda.

23. Typically there were six subjects divided in this way, although because of variations in scheduling, sometimes five or fewer participated at one time.

24. We note that while this evidence speaks against the idea that players selected more efficient partners, it is still possible that players *believed* they were selecting more efficient partners.

25. This was accomplished with our subjects by asking player 1 to stand on a balcony out of reach of the lockbox and talk to player 2 through an open window (see Appendix C for a photograph).

26. Because there were uneven numbers of subjects at some of our sessions, seven subjects played the role of player 1 twice. Our results are robust to the exclusion of these pairings.

27. Most of the technology games we used involved substantial face-to-face interaction, and our subjects were thus able to obtain additional information about the identities of their partners from cues beyond those provided in our computer-based experimental games. We therefore assume that players had greater opportunities to figure out the coethnic or non-coethnic status of the person they were playing with, and we limit our analyses of these games to benchmark demographies.

28. Since language is likely to be important in this context, we also looked at the success rates of pairings of players who shared the same primary language. We found that sharing a primary language did not matter. Not surprisingly, the difference that did appear to matter—and to matter critically—was whether the pair spoke *any* common language. When they did not, success rates tumbled to 25 percent. While this may be considered an ethnic effect, it is one that is relevant for only a very small share (7 percent) of the random pairings in our sample.

29. The data do suggest, however, that success rates were related to the educational characteristics of the players. Pairs containing players who both had more than a primary school education completed the task successfully 79 percent of the time, as compared with a 45 percent success rate for pairs with little education. These results suggest that the game was sufficiently difficult that the education effect trumped whatever productivity gains might have been realized from membership in the same ethnic group. Indeed, we find some evidence that, among pairs with high education, shared language group membership significantly raised success rates.

30. The puzzle depicted in figure 4.7 was "easy."

31. In this table, weights are used to reflect matchings of treatment and control observations that are based on both ethnicity and whether a game was hard or easy. If game type is ignored and the process is modeled as a linear relation with fixed effects for each ethnic group, then the effect is weaker

and not statistically significant, as we reported previously (Habyarimana et al. 2007).

32. These certainty reports were incentivized by tying a claim of extreme certainty to a gamble. Subjects who claimed to be extremely certain bet their winnings on their claim. Apart from this incentive, claims of certainty could be validated to some extent by examining the relation between certainty and the actual correctness of guesses. The resulting correlation is 0.2, which has an associated t-statistic of 26.

33. The distinction here can be confusing. To illustrate, we ask the reader to imagine that there were only two groups, A and B, comprising two-thirds and one-third of the subjects, respectively. Say, in addition, that partners were randomly matched and asked to guess each other's education levels; thus, four in nine encounters would have involved an A group coethnic pairing, one in nine a B group coethnic pairing, and so four-fifths of coethnic pairings involve A group players. Say that in fact everyone could perfectly guess the education levels of people in group A but that no one could guess the education levels of people in group B. For A players, the effect of a coethnic matching would have been to increase accuracy by 100 percent; for B players, the effect would be to reduce it by 100 percent. The average treatment effect would be $(4/5) \times 100 - (1/5) \times 100 = +60$, and so coethnicity would increase the accuracy of a guess by 60 points on average. However, for either A types or B types, whether they were correctly guessed would be independent of the ethnicity of the viewer, and so the effect of coethnicity on the probability that a given person would be guessed correctly would be zero.

34. Note that we did not ask our subjects directly whether they believed they were more likely to be correct when guessing the education of coethnics. We inferred this from the data we collected about their certainty about each guess and from what we knew about the ethnic background of the person whose educational attainment they were guessing.

35. For this analysis, we drew on pairings in a subset of our games (the Dictator game and the Prisoner's Dilemma game, which we discuss in chapter 5).

36. This implies, for example, that the effect was not driven by one dominant group whose members were more likely to be known. Since members of a given group were more likely to be known by a coethnic than by a non-coethnic, the effect of coethnicity obtained across all sizable groups.

37. Moreover, it is possible that the likelihood of knowing someone is itself a function of successful collective action, such that past coethnic cooperation creates more frequent interaction among coethnics. Given our non-experimental approach to the issue of periodicity, we cannot rule out this possibility.

38. Runners who managed to find their targets were debriefed extensively when they came back to the laboratory to be paid. We also debriefed a random sample of forty of the unsuccessful runners. Results of these debriefings are explored in chapter 5.

39. We surmise that some runners simply pocketed the 5,000 Ugandan shillings we gave them for transport money and never tried to find their targets.

40. This is the result reported in Habyarimana et al. (2007).

41. There are at least three potential reasons why coethnics performed better in the Network game. First, any tendency of coethnics to live in geographically concentrated areas (within Mulago-Kyebando's highly diverse LC1s) would have shortened the network distance between two individuals from the same group. Second, kinship relations within an ethnic group may have contributed to a more effective flow of information within that group. Third, the shared ethnicity of the runner and the target may have given the runner access to a shared language that facilitated the extraction of relevant information about the target.

42. Note, however, that strategy selection mechanisms may be in operation even if players are not attempting to play "in equilibrium." All that is required is that players condition their strategies on coethnicity. How "efficient" they are in their choices is beside the point.

43. In practice, both pieces of information were provided together since payments were given to receivers as they viewed the public information box for the corresponding game.

44. For another recent study (in the U.S. context) in which changes in behavior induced by public information are interpreted as evidence of norm enforcement, see Gerber, Green, and Larimer (2008).

45. Offers in this version of the game were slightly lower than in the anonymous-offerer Dictator game, but these differences are not statistically significant.

46. Yamagishi and Mifune (2008) reported similar findings in a sample of 155 Japanese students classified into one of two minimal groups. Players in the common-knowledge condition (both offerer and receiver knew each other's in-group or out-group status) made systematically more generous allocations to in-group members, whereas players in the unilateral-knowledge condition (only the offerer knew the within-group or cross-group nature of the pairing) did not discriminate. Yamagishi and Mifune do not, however, explore differences between egoist and non-egoist players.

47. These results are also robust to the inclusion of a battery of controls for age, education, income, gender, and other characteristics that, by design, are uncorrelated with the experimental treatment in expectation.

Chapter 5

1. Implicitly, we assume that the private return on a dollar invested is –25 percent. The game we describe is strategically equivalent to any game in which the return is negative, but greater than –50 percent.

2. Here we outline a number of plausible and prominent explanations that are consistent with the greater success of coethnics in resolving PDs. This is not, however, an exhaustive set of mechanisms. Depending on how one understands the preferences of the players (egoistic versus non-egoistic) and the structure of the game (simultaneous versus sequential, one-shot versus repeated), other solutions to this game exist.

3. PD games were played with the same set of subjects who participated in

the games described in chapter 4. The sampling strategy used to select sub-jects, the randomized nature of pairings, and a number of basic protocols regarding instruction, checks for comprehension, and the manner in which pairings were revealed on the screen were all identical. Full details are pro-vided in the online appendix, available at https://www.russellsage.org/publications/CoethnicityAppendix.

4. We initially labeled the "group" box the "bank" box. After finding that sub-jects mistakenly believed that the game was about their patterns of saving (and their trust in the banking system), we changed the name to "group." We made this change after only a day and a half of play (out of ten days). We find no difference in cooperation rates across these two periods.

5. Subjects were actually paid at the end of the experimental session, but earnings from each round were calculated separately.

6. As with all coethnic effects described in this book, these average treatment effects were estimated by using exact matching to average over the treat-ment effects obtained for offerers for each ethnic or regional group. Averag-ing over differences between treated and untreated subjects within groups ensures that the results are not confounded by the "main" effects that could result from the fact that treatment assignment probabilities varied across groups. Standard errors were calculated using weighted OLS regression (with weights to account for different assignment probabilities across groups) and disturbance terms were clustered for each player across all of his or her games. The tables in appendix B report both these standard er-rors and an alternative estimate of heteroskedasticity-consistent standard errors that assume independence across all observations.

7. This basic finding is in keeping with a large literature, including studies by Marilynn Brewer and Roderick Kramer (1986), Arjaan Wit and Henk Wilke (1992), and Lorenz Goette, David Huffman, and Stephan Meier (2006). Bradley Ruffle and Richard Sosis (2006) have found that even kibbutz members, who are socialized to be universal cooperators, discriminate be-tween fellow kibbutz members and outsiders (city dwellers) in a PD game.

8. Coethnic cooperation among egoists in the PD game was consistent with what we observed in the Dictator game insofar as the players had informa-tion about one another (as in the non-anonymous Dictator game). Unlike in that game, however, they did not actually observe one another's actions, since we reported PD results to players in the aggregate and not game by game, as we did in the Dictator game.

9. The introduction of an enforcer—as with the informational treatments—was assigned randomly to pairings. Although we discuss games with an enforcer as if they were separate games, subjects played a series of ten PD games in total, some of which included an enforcer, some which did not, and across which levels of information (from none to full information videos) varied at random.

10. These were games with information on both the players and the enforcer.

11. In principle, there is no reason that punishment should be observed only in response to defection. In fact, evidence from subject populations around the world indicates that punishment for cooperative behavior is quite com-mon (Herrmann, Thöni, and Gächter 2008; see also Fehr and Gächter 2000, 2002).

12. Moreover, sanctioning did not appear to be supported in this game by second-order threats of out-of-game sanction: we observed no difference in sanctioning rates between enforcers who were seen and enforcers who were not seen.

13. One should keep in mind that, in contrast to our analyses of coethnicity, defection was not experimentally manipulated.

14. These observations of punishment in response to cooperation, although they could in principle have been driven by spite or negative other-regarding preferences, could also signal failures of our subjects to understand the game or mistakes in the execution of punishment.

15. Note that, as with coethnicity, we can randomly determine whether an individual encounters someone they know or someone they can track down. However, we have not randomly determined whether a subject knows a *given* player. For this reason, readers should be conscious of the fact that whether a player knows a partner could in principle reflect other features, such as shared interests or affinities.

16. In the words of the respondent: "I knew the name of that person, and I knew her tribe was Munyankole, coming from western Uganda. I went from household to household, asking where maybe her fellow tribemates were staying. So wherever I find them, or a household speaking her language, I would ask."

17. One might have expected the opposite relationship with respect to migrants, insofar as recent migrants are often distinguishable by their manner of dress. Our seemingly low cutoff for age is a result of the skewed age distribution. Slightly more than half of Uganda's population is under the age of fifteen. Moreover, the age distribution of our sample was centered at twenty-six, with only one-quarter of the subjects older than thirty-five.

18. We did not examine the Discrimination game since our measure of reachability was determined by the characteristics of one player only and thus could not help in determining which player the offerer should have favored in the 500-Ugandan-shilling game.

19. If we restrict our analysis of punishment behavior to those games in which PD players actually played (as opposed to games in which they were absent but their behavior was reported to the enforcer as "did not contribute"), the evidence that enforcers conditioned on ethnicity is stronger (see Habyarimana et al. 2007). In cases where one PD player did not show up to participate, we still presented his or her action in those games to an enforcer, indicating that the player who did not show up did not cooperate. The analysis of enforcement decisions in this chapter makes use of this additional data.

Chapter 6

1. We recognize that the comparison of survey data with behavior in the experimental games is not a strict test of the validity of the latter, since a survey is itself subject to bias and measurement error.

2. The complete text of the proctors' instructions for all games is provided in the online appendix, available at https://www.russellsage.org/publications/CoethnicityAppendix.

3. A record was kept of all subjects who required additional instruction.

4. Even so, we tested to make sure that our results were not affected by mis-comprehension. The results of all of the games presented in chapters 3, 4, and 5 are robust to the exclusion of games in which the rules were violated and to the inclusion of controls for players who had difficulty understanding the games.

5. Until they participated in the identification exercise during the final experimental session, it would have been difficult for subjects to find out the narrow purpose of the project. Our enumerators were not even aware of our particular interest in coethnic effects. The fact that the debriefings were conducted *after* the identification game suggested that, even subsequent to participating in a task that was explicitly about ethnicity, our subjects were not aware of the project's particular focus on ethnic effects.

6. By design, the individual characteristics of the receivers were unrelated to the experimental treatment, although they could be correlated with membership in a particular ethnic group. Our results survive the inclusion of controls for the age and educational achievement of the receiver.

7. Both measures are, however, somewhat noisy. The components entering the two measures yield Cronbach's alpha scores of 0.5 and 0.55, respectively.

8. Note that although these players were "seen" in the PD games, players did not learn directly what actions were taken by the other player.

9. We measured coethnicity here using the benchmark measure described in chapter 3.

10. We asked about respondents' attitudes to having members of different groups as close kin by marriage, as a neighbor, and as a fellow member of a community group. We then used these measures to create distance scales for in-group members and for out-group members; the measure used in figure 6.2 uses the in-group distance scale controlling for out-group distance.

11. These correlations are generally weaker if we calculate coethnic bias using information on both other-regarding preferences and reciprocity (for example, when there is information on the offerer as well as the receiver).

12. The Baganda occupy more than their share of executive committee posts partly because they entered the council system years ago, at a time when their group made up a far larger share of the local population. Indeed, the average tenure of an LC chairperson in Mulago-Kyebando is nearly ten years.

13. To see this formally, assume there are m groups in an LC1, let p_i denote the relative size of group i, and let p denote the vector $(p_i)_{i=1, 2, \ldots, k}$. Let a_{jk} denote average offers made by individuals in group j to individuals in group k, and let the $m \times m$ matrix A denote the collection of such behaviors. The *average* altruism arising in random encounters in a community given its demography can then be written as: $y = p'Ap$. When the typical measure of ethno-linguistic fragmentation (ELF) is used to explain variation in public goods provision, it is the equivalent of assuming that the A matrix is an identity matrix, I. With that assumption, we can write: $ELF = 1 - p'Ip$.

Chapter 7

1. The specific mechanisms we have examined here are not exhaustive. They represent the set of plausible explanations that have been offered to account

for the specific relationship between diversity and public goods provision. Applied to other contexts and other questions, new mechanisms can be imagined and tested against those we have evaluated. Indeed, once we start down the path of unearthing the micro-foundations of social outcomes, the story inevitably becomes more complex. Other complexities arise when we consider the interaction of different mechanisms. We have examined some of these but expect that future research could go considerably further in this direction.

2. The third party may also sanction players who behave cooperatively, and we find that occasionally they do.

3. Such an account is consistent with the description given by Fearon (1999) and Laitin (1998).

4. As Kanchan Chandra has pointed out in comments on this work provided at the First Annual CESS-NYU Experimental Political Science Convention at New York University (February 8, 2008), our research does not rest on an explicit definition of ethnicity. Rather, we implicitly employ an ostensive definition. In Uganda there is common understanding of what the ethnic categories are (even if, as we saw in chapter 3, individuals have difficulties placing each other into those categories). Thus, we can proceed in our analysis using Uganda's ethnic group categories. But this does not provide a basis for inference to other ethnic categories in other settings unless there is reason to believe that what makes a group an ethnic group in Uganda has some correspondence to what makes a group an ethnic group elsewhere.

5. For example, our Ugandan colleagues were often surprised that we found no evidence for differential other-regardingness among particular pairs of ethnic groups in the sample. Conscious of the historical enmity between the Baganda, the dominant ethnic group in central Uganda, and northern ethnic groups, which dominated the country's politics for the first twenty-five years of independence, we too might have anticipated a "taste for discrimination" across members of these two communities. But we found no evidence in our data that northern ethnic groups favor their own or are more likely to do so when faced with the choice of how to allocate money between a coethnic and a Muganda (and vice versa). While this result often puzzled our Ugandan colleagues, it also pointed to the importance of context. The arena of contention defined in our experiments may have affected the way northerners and the Baganda viewed one another.

6. Fearon, Kasara, and Laitin (2007) disagree.

7. This problem also arises for non-experimental studies that seek to identify the causal effects of coethnicity; on "Dorn's question," see Sekhon (2008).

Appendix A

1. In a number of cases, more than one household was sampled per point. In those cases, guidelines defining selection of the second and third houses were provided to each enumerator: if house 1 is the nearest household on the right, then house 2 is X number of paces on the left and house 3 is Z number of paces on the right. X and Z were determined by the density of the LC1.

2. Note that this share of male participants is slightly higher than reported in

the discussion of household sampling. This number reflects the inclusion of seventeen local council chairs who participated in a subset of the games alongside the sampled players.

3. The median age in the full sample and both subsamples was twenty-five.

4. The World Values Survey (2001) indicates 36 percent Catholic, 45 percent Protestant, 17 percent Muslim, and only 1 percent evangelical. The difference in this distribution and ours likely comes from the coding of many individuals who belonged to evangelical faiths as Protestants in the World Values Survey.

5. "Egoist" is defined by observing play in games during the second session. Since session 2 attriters did not play the games, this measure is undefined.

References

Alesina, Alberto, Reza Baqir, and William Easterly. 1999. "Public Goods and Ethnic Divisions." *Quarterly Journal of Economics* 114(November): 1243–84.

Alesina, Alberto, and Eliana LaFerrara. 2005. "Ethnic Diversity and Economic Performance." *Journal of Economic Literature* 63(September): 762–800.

Allport, Gordon, and Bernard Kramer. 1946. "Some Roots of Prejudice." *Journal of Psychology* 22: 9–39.

Andreoni, James. 1990. "Impure Altruism and Donations to Public Goods: A Theory of Warm-Glow Giving." *Economic Journal* 100(June): 464–77.

Andreoni, James, and Ragan Petrie. 2008. "Beauty, Gender, and Stereotypes: Evidence from Laboratory Experiments." *Journal of Economic Psychology* 29: 73–93.

Andreoni, James, and Lise Vesterund. 2001. "Which Is the Fairer Sex? Gender Differences in Altruism." *Quarterly Journal of Economics* 116(February): 293–12.

Axelrod, Robert. 1984. *The Evolution of Cooperation.* New York: Basic Books.

Bacharach, Michael, and Diego Gambetta. 2001. "Trust in Signs." In *Trust in Society*, edited by Karen S. Cook. New York: Russell Sage Foundation.

Bahry, Donna, and Rick Wilson. 2006. "Confusion or Fairness in the Field? Rejections in the Ultimatum Game Under the Strategy Method." *Journal of Economic Behavior and Organization* 60(May): 37–54.

Baland, Jean-Marie, Pranab Bardhan, Sanghamitra Das, Dilip Mookherjee, and Rinki Sarkar. 2006. "Inequality, Collective Action, and the Environment: Evidence from Firewood Collection in Nepal." In *Inequality, Collective Action, and Environmental Sustainability*, edited by Jean-Marie Baland, Pranab Bardhan and Samuel Bowles. New York and Princeton, N.J.: Russell Sage Foundation and Princeton University Press.

Banerjee, Abhijit, Lakshmi Iyer, and Rohini Somanathan. 2005. "History, Social Divisions, and Public Goods in Rural India." *Journal of the European Economic Association* 3(April–May): 639–47.

Banerjee, Abhijit, and Rohini Somanathan. 2004. "The Political Economy of Public Goods: Some Evidence from India." Discussion Papers in Economics 04-17. Kolkata: Indian Statistical Institute (June).

Bardhan, Pranab. 2000. "Irrigation and Cooperation: An Empirical Analysis of

Forty-Eight Irrigation Communities in South India." *Economic Development and Cultural Change* 48(4): 847–65.

Bates, Robert. 1973. *Ethnicity in Contemporary Africa*. Syracuse, N.Y.: Program in East African Studies.

———. 1983. "Modernization, Ethnic Competition, and the Rationality of Politics in Contemporary Africa." In *State Versus Ethnic Claims: African Policy Dilemmas*, edited by Donald Rothchild and Victor Olorunsola. Boulder, Colo.: Westview Press.

Becker, Gary. 1957. *The Economics of Discrimination*. Chicago: University of Chicago Press.

Bernhard, Helen, Urs Fischbacher, and Ernst Fehr. 2006. "Parochial Altruism in Humans." *Nature* 442(August): 912–15.

Bernstein, Lisa. 1992. "Opting Out of the Legal System: Extralegal Contractual Regulations in the Diamond Industry." *Journal of Legal Studies* 21(1): 115–57.

Besley, Timothy, Stephen Coate, and Glenn Loury. 1993. "The Economics of Rotating Savings and Credit Associations." *American Economic Review* 83(September): 792–810.

Bjorkman, Martina, and Jakob Svensson. 2007. "Power to the People: Evidence from a Randomized Field Experiment of a Community-Based Monitoring Project in Uganda." Working paper 6344. Washington D.C.: Center for Economic Policy Research.

Blascovich, Jim, Natalie Wyer, Laura Swart, and Jeffrey Kibler. 1997. "Racism and Racial Categorization." *Journal of Personality and Social Psychology* 72(6): 1364–72.

Bohnet, Iris, and Bruno Frey. 1999. "Social Distance and Other-Regarding Behavior in Dictator Games: Comment." *American Economic Review* 89(March): 335–39.

Bohnet, Iris, and Fiona Greig. 2008. "Is There Reciprocity in a Reciprocal-Exchange Economy? Evidence of Gendered Norms from a Slum in Nairobi, Kenya." *Economic Inquiry* 46(January): 77–83.

Bolton, Gary E., and Axel Ockenfels. 2000. "A Theory of Equity, Reciprocity, and Competition." *American Economic Review* 90(1): 166–93.

Bowles, Samuel, and Herbert Gintis. 2004a. "Persistent Parochialism: Trust and Exclusion in Ethnic Networks." *Journal of Economic Behavior and Organizations* 55(September): 1–23.

———. 2004b. "The Evolution of Strong Reciprocity: Cooperation in Heterogeneous Populations." *Theoretical Population Biology* 65(February): 17–28.

Brewer, Marilynn B., and Roderick M. Kramer. 1986. "Choice Behavior in Social Dilemmas: Effect of Social Identity, Group Size, and Decision Framing." *Journal of Personality and Social Psychology* 50(3): 542–49.

Burns, Justine. 2003. "Insider-Outsider Distinctions in South Africa: The Impact of Race on the Behavior of High School Students." Unpublished paper, University of Cape Town.

Camerer, Colin F. 2003. *Behavioral Game Theory: Experiments in Strategic Interaction*. Princeton, N.J.: Princeton University Press.

Camerer, Colin, George Loewenstein, and Matthew Rabin. 2004. *Advances in Behavioral Economics*. Princeton, N.J.: Princeton University Press.

Cardenas, Juan Camilo, and Jeffrey Carpenter. 2008. "Experimental Development Economics: Lessons from Field Labs in the Developing World." *Journal of Development Economics* 44(3): 337–64.

Carpenter, Jeffrey, Stephen Burks, and Eric Verhoegen. 2005. "Comparing Students to Workers: The Effects of Social Framing on Behavior in Distribution Games." In *Field Experiments in Economics,* edited by Jeffrey Carpenter, Glenn Harrison, and John List. Stamford, Conn.: JAI Press.

Carpenter, Jeffrey, Amrita Daniere, and Lois Takahashi. 2004. "Cooperation, Trust, and Social Capital in Southeast Asian Urban Slums." *Journal of Economic Behavior and Organization* 55(December): 533–51.

Carpenter, Jeffrey, and Erika Seki. 2005. "Do Social Preferences Increase Productivity? Field Experimental Evidence from Fishermen in Toyama Bay." Discussion paper 1697. Bonn: Institute for the Study of Labor (IZA).

Casella, Alessandra, and James Rauch. 2002. "Anonymous Market and Group Ties in International Trade." *Journal of International Economics* 58(1): 19–47.

Caselli, Francesco, and John Coleman. 2006. "On the Theory of Ethnic Conflict." Unpublished paper, London School of Economics.

Cederman, Lars-Erik, and Luc Girardin. 2007. "Beyond Fractionalization: Mapping Ethnicity onto Nationalist Insurgencies." *American Political Science Review* 101(February): 173–85.

Chandra, Kanchan. 2004. *Why Ethnic Parties Succeed: Patronage and Ethnic Headcounts in India.* New York: Cambridge University Press.

Charness, Gary, and Uri Gneezy. 2003. "What's in a Name? Anonymity and Social Distance in Dictator and Ultimatum Games." Unpublished paper, University of California, Santa Barbara.

Colman, Andrew M. 1995. *Game Theory and Its Applications in the Social and Biological Sciences.* London: Routledge.

Cook, Karen S., Russell Hardin, and Margaret Levi. 2005. *Cooperation Without Trust?* New York: Russell Sage Foundation.

Cox, David, and Nancy Reid. 2000. *The Theory of the Design of Experiments.* Monographs on Statistics and Applied Probability 86. Boca Raton, Fla.: Chapman & Hall/CRC.

Crawford, Vincent P., and Hans Haller. 1990. "Learning How to Cooperate: Optimal Play in Repeated Coordination Games." *Econometrica* 58(May): 571–95.

Davis, Douglas D., and Charles A. Holt. 1993. *Experimental Economics.* Princeton, N.J.: Princeton University Press.

Dayton-Johnson, Jeffrey. 2000. "Determinants of Collective Action on the Local Commons: A Model with Evidence from Mexico." *Journal of Development Economics* 62(1): 181–208.

Deutsch, Karl. 1966. *Nationalism and Social Communication.* Cambridge, Mass.: MIT Press.

Eckel, Catherine C., and Philip J. Grossman. 1996. "The Relative Price of Fairness: Gender Differences in a Punishment Game." *Journal of Economic Behavior and Organization* 30(2): 143–58.

———. 1998. "Are Women Less Selfish Than Men? Evidence from Dictator Experiments." *Economic Journal* 108(May): 726–35.

———. 2001. "Chivalry and Solidarity in Ultimatum Games." *Economic Inquiry* 39(2): 171–88.

Fafchamps, Marcel. 2003. "Ethnicity and Networks in African Trade." *Contribu-*

tions to Economic Analysis and Policy 2(1): Article 14. Available at: http://www.bepress.com/bejeap/contributions/vol2/iss1/art14/ (accessed May 10, 2008).

Fafchamps, Marcel, and Bart Minten. 2002. "Returns to Social Network Capital Among Traders." *Oxford Economic Papers* 54(April): 173–206.

Fearon, James D. 1994. "Domestic Political Audiences and the Escalation of International Disputes." *American Political Science Review* 88(September): 577–92.

———. 1999. "Why Ethnic Politics and 'Pork' Tend to Go Together." Unpublished paper, Stanford University, Stanford, Calif.

———. 2006. "Ethnic Mobilization and Ethnic Violence." In *Oxford Handbook of Political Economy*, edited by Barry R. Weingast and Donald Wittman. Oxford: Oxford University Press.

Fearon, James D., Macartan Humphreys, and Jeremy Weinstein. 2009. "Can Development Aid Contribute to Social Cohesion After Civil War? Evidence from a Field Experiment in Post-Conflict Liberia." *American Economic Review, Papers and Proceedings* 99(2): 287–91.

Fearon, James D., Kimuli Kasara, and David Laitin. 2007. "Ethnic Minority Rule and Civil War Onset." *American Political Science Review* 101(February): 187–93.

Fearon, James D., and David D. Laitin. 1996. "Explaining Interethnic Cooperation." *American Political Science Review* 90(4): 715–35.

Fehr, Ernst, and Urs Fischbacher. 2004. "Third-Party Punishment and Social Norms." *Evolution and Human Behavior* 25(March): 63–87.

Fehr, Ernst, and Simon Gächter. 2000. "Cooperation and Punishment in Public Goods Experiments." *American Economic Review* 90(4): 980–94.

———. 2002. "Altruistic Punishment in Humans." *Nature* 415(6868): 137–40.

Fehr, Ernst, and Klaus M. Schmidt. 1999. "A Theory of Fairness, Competition, and Cooperation." *Quarterly Journal of Economics* 114(3): 817–68.

Ferraro, Paul J., and Ronald G. Cummings. 2007. "Cultural Diversity, Discrimination, and Economic Outcomes: An Experimental Analysis." *Economic Inquiry* 45(2): 217–32.

Fershtman, Chaim, and Uri Gneezy. 2001. "Discrimination in a Segmented Society: An Experimental Approach." *Quarterly Journal of Economics* 116(February): 351–77.

Foster, Andre, and Mark Rosenzweig. 1993. "Information, Learning, and Wage Rates in Low-Income Rural Areas." *Journal of Human Resources* 28(4): 759–90.

Frolich, Norman, Joe A. Oppenheimer, and Oran R. Young. 1971. *Political Leadership and Collective Goods*. Princeton, N.J.: Princeton University Press.

Gambetta, Diego, and Heather Hamill. 2005. *Streetwise: How Taxi Drivers Establish Their Customers' Trustworthiness*. New York: Russell Sage Foundation.

Gerber, Alan S., Donald P. Green, and Christopher W. Larimer. 2008. "Social Pressure and Voter Turnout: Evidence from a Large-Scale Field Experiment." *American Political Science Review* 102(1): 33–48.

Ghosh, Parikshit, and Debraj Ray. 1996. "Cooperation in Community Interaction Without Information Flows." *Review of Economic Studies* 63(3): 491–519.

Gil-White, Francisco. 2004. "Ultimatum Game with an Ethnicity Manipulation: Results from Kohvdiin Bulgan Sum, Mongolia." In *Foundations of Human Sociality: Economic Experiments and Ethnographic Evidence from Fifteen Small-Scale Societies*, edited by Joseph Henrich et al. New York: Oxford University Press.

Gintis, Herbert. 2000. "Strong Reciprocity and Human Sociality." Working paper 2000-02. University of Massachusetts–Amherst, Department of Economics.

Glaeser, Edward L., David I. Laibson, José A. Scheinkman, and Christine L. Soutter. 2000. "Measuring Trust." *Quarterly Journal of Economics* 115(3): 811–46.

Goette, Lorenz, David Huffman, and Stephan Meier. 2006. "The Impact of Group Membership on Cooperation and Norm Enforcement: Evidence Using Random Assignment to Real Social Groups." Working paper 06-7. Boston: Federal Reserve Bank.

Goldin, Claudia, and Lawrence Katz. 1999. "Human Capital and Social Capital: The Rise of Secondary School in America, 1910–1940." *Journal of Interdisciplinary History* 29(4): 683–723.

Golooba-Mutebi, Frederick. 2003. "Devolution and Outsourcing of Municipal Services in Kampala City, Uganda: An Early Assessment." *Public Administration and Development* 23(December): 405–18.

Granovetter, Mark. 1985. "Economic Action and Social Structure: The Problem of Embeddedness." *American Journal of Sociology* 91(3): 481–510.

Green, Elliott D. 2008. "Understanding the Limits to Ethnic Change: Lessons from Uganda's 'Lost Counties.'" *Perspectives on Politics* 6(September): 473–85.

Greif, Avner. 1993. "Contract Enforceability and Economic Institutions in Early Trade: The Maghribi Traders' Coalition." *American Economic Review* 83(June): 525–48.

———. 1994. "Cultural Beliefs and the Organization of Society: A Historical and Theoretical Reflection on Collectivist and Individualist Societies." *Journal of Political Economy* 102(5): 912–50.

Güth, Werner, and Hartmut Kliemt. 1998. "The Indirect Evolutionary Approach: Bridging the Gap Between Rationality and Adaptation." *Rationality and Society* 10(August): 377–99.

Habyarimana, James, Macartan Humphreys, Daniel Posner, and Jeremy Weinstein. 2007. "Why Does Ethnic Diversity Undermine Public Goods Provision?" *American Political Science Review* 101(November): 709–25.

———. 2008. "Is Ethnic Conflict Inevitable? Better Institutions, Not Partition." *Foreign Affairs* 87(4, July–August): 138–41.

Haley, Kevin, and Daniel Fessler. 2005. "Nobody's Watching? Subtle Cues Affect Generosity in an Anonymous Economic Game." *Evolution and Human Behavior* 26(May): 245–56.

Harbaugh, William, Kate Krause, and Steven G. Liday. 2003. "Bargaining by Children." Unpublished paper, University of Oregon, Eugene.

Harris, David. 2002. "In the Eye of the Beholder: Observed Race and Observer Characteristics." Research Report 02-522. Ann Arbor: University of Michigan, Population Studies Center.

Henrich, Joseph, Robert Boyd, Samuel Bowles, Colin Camerer, Ernst Fehr, and Herbert Gintis. 2004. *Foundations of Human Sociality: Economic Experiments and Ethnographic Evidence from Fifteen Small-Scale Societies.* New York: Oxford University Press.

Herrmann, Benedikt, Christian Thöni, and Simon Gächter. 2008. "Antisocial Punishment Across Societies." *Science* 319(March 7): 1362–67.

Hoffman, Elizabeth, Kevin McCabe, and Vernon L. Smith. 1996. "Social Distance and Other-Regarding Behavior in Dictator Games." *American Economic Review* 86(June): 653–60.

Horowitz, Donald. 1985. *Ethnic Groups in Conflict*. Berkeley: University of California Press.

Humphreys, Macartan, and Habaye ag Mohamed. 2005. "Senegal and Mali: A Comparative Study of Rebellions in West Africa." In *Understanding Civil War: Evidence and Analysis*, edited by Paul Collier and Nicholas Sambanis. Washington: World Bank.

Isaacs, Harold. 1975. "Idols of the Tribe." In *Ethnicity: Theory and Experience*, edited by Nathan Glazer and Daniel P. Moynihan. Cambridge, Mass.: Harvard University Press.

Kahneman, Daniel, Jack Knetsch, and Richard Thaler. 1986. "Fairness as a Constraint on Profit-Seeking: Entitlements in the Market." *American Economic Review* 76(September): 728–41.

Kandori, Michihiro. 1992. "Social Norms and Community Enforcement." *Review of Economic Studies* 59(January): 63–80.

Karlan, Dean. 2005. "Using Experimental Economics to Measure Social Capital and Predict Financial Decisions." *American Economic Review* 95(December): 1688–99.

Kasfir, Nelson. 1998. "'No-Party Democracy' in Uganda." *Journal of Democracy* 13(4, April): 49–63.

Kertzer, David I., and Dominique Arel. 2002. *Census and Identity: The Politics of Race, Ethnicity, and Language in National Censuses*. New York: Cambridge University Press.

Khwaja, Asim. 2008. "Can Good Projects Succeed in Bad Communities? Collective Action in the Himalayas." Unpublished paper, Harvard University, Cambridge, Mass.

Kymlicka, Will. 1995. *Multicultural Citizenship*. Oxford: Oxford University Press.

Laitin, David D. 1998. *Identity in Formation: The Russian-Speaking Populations in the Near Abroad*. Ithaca, N.Y.: Cornell University Press.

Landa, Janet Tai. 1994. *Trust, Ethnicity, and Identity: Beyond the New Institutional Economics of Ethnic Trading Networks, Contract Law, and Gift-Exchange*. Ann Arbor: University of Michigan Press.

Ledyard, John. 1995. "Public Goods: A Survey of Experimental Research." In *The Handbook of Experimental Economics*, edited by John H. Kagel and Alvin E. Roth. Princeton, N.J.: Princeton University Press.

Lent, Richard. 1970. "Binocular Resolution and Perception of Race in the United States." *British Journal of Psychology* 61(4): 521–33.

Li, Xin Sherry. 2005. "Ethnic Diversity, Social Identities, and Tax Compliance: Evidence from the European and World Values Surveys." Unpublished paper, University of Michigan, Ann Arbor.

Marlowe, Frank W., J. Colette Berbesque, Abigail Barr, Clark Barrett, Alexander Bolyanatz, Juan Camilo Cardenas, Jean Ensminger, Michael Gurven, Edwins Gwako, Joseph Henrich, Natalie Henrich, Carolyn Lesorogol, Richard McElreath, and David Tracer. 2008. "More 'Altruistic' Punishment in Larger Societies." *Proceedings of the Royal Society* 275(1634): 587–90.

Mayhew, David. 1975. *Congress: The Electoral Connection*. New Haven, Conn.: Yale University Press.

Miguel, Edward. 1999. "Ethnic Diversity, Mobility, and School Funding: Theory and Evidence from Kenya." Unpublished paper, Harvard University, Cambridge, Mass.

———. 2004. "Tribe or Nation? Nation Building and Public Goods in Kenya Versus Tanzania." *World Politics* 56(April): 327–62.

Miguel, Edward, and Mary Kay Gugerty. 2005. "Ethnic Diversity, Social Sanctions, and Public Goods in Kenya." *Journal of Public Economics* 89(December): 2325–68.

Milgram, Stanley. 1974. *Obedience to Authority: An Experimental View.* New York: Harper & Row.

Murnighan, J. Keith, John Oesch, and Madan M. Pillutla. 2001. "Player Types and Self-Impression Management in Dictatorship Games: Two Experiments." *Games and Economic Behavior* 37(2): 388–414.

Mwenda, Andrew. 2006. "What Museveni, Besigye Need to Do Before 2011." *Sunday Monitor*, March 5–11. Available at: http://www.monitor.co.ug/artman/publish/oped/What_Museveni_Besigye_need_to_do_before_2011_printer.shtml

Navarrete, Carlos David, Daniel Fessler, and Serena J. Eng. 2007. "Elevated Ethnocentrism in the First Trimester of Pregnancy." *Evolution and Human Behavior* 28(1): 60–65.

Nugent, Jeffrey, and Shailender Swaminathan. 2006. "Voluntary Contributions to Informal Activities Producing Public Goods: Can These Be Induced by Government and Other Formal Sector Agents?" In *Linking the Formal and Informal Economy,* edited by Basudb Guha-Khasnobis et al. Oxford: Oxford Scholarship Online Monographs.

Okten, Cagla, and Una Okonkwo Osili. 2004. "Contributions in Heterogeneous Communities: Evidence from Indonesia." *Journal of Population Economics* 17(December): 603–26.

Olson, Mancur. 1965. *The Logic of Collective Action: Public Goods and the Theory of Groups.* Cambridge, Mass.: Harvard University Press.

Onyach-Olaa, Martin. 2003. "The Challenges of Implementing Decentralization: Recent Experiences in Uganda." *Public Administration and Development* 23(January): 105–13.

Ostrom, Elinor. 1990. *Governing the Commons: The Evolution of Institutions for Collective Action.* Cambridge: Cambridge University Press.

———. 2000. "Collective Action and the Evolution of Social Norms." *Journal of Economic Perspectives* 14(Summer): 137–58.

Page, Scott. 2007. *The Difference: How the Power of Diversity Creates Better Groups, Firms, Schools, and Societies.* Princeton, N.J.: Princeton University Press.

Petrie, Ragan. 2003. "Trusting Appearances and Reciprocating Looks: Experimental Evidence on Gender and Race Preferences." Unpublished paper, Georgia State University, Atlanta.

Platteau, Jean-Philippe. 1994. "Behind the Market Stage: Where Real Societies Exist: Parts I and II." *Journal of Development Studies* 30(April and July): 533–77 and 753–817.

Platteau, Jean-Philippe, and Tomasz Strzalecki. 2004. "Collective Action, Heterogeneous Loyalties, and Path Dependence: Micro-evidence from Senegal." *Journal of African Economies* 13(February): 417–45.

Popkin, Samuel. 1979. *The Rational Peasant: The Political Economy of Rural Society in Vietnam*. Berkeley: University of California Press.

Posen, Barry. 1993. "The Security Dilemma and Ethnic Conflict." In *Ethnic Conflict and International Security*, edited by Michael E. Brown. Princeton, N.J.: Princeton University Press.

Posner, Daniel N. 2004a. "The Political Salience of Cultural Difference: Why Chewas and Tumbukas Are Allies in Zambia and Adversaries in Malawi." *American Political Science Review* 98(4, November): 529–45.

———. 2004b. "Measuring Ethnic Fractionalization in Africa." *American Journal of Political Science* 48(October): 849–63.

Poterba, James. 1997. "Demographic Structure and the Political Economy of Public Education." *Journal of Fiscal Analysis and Management* 16(1): 48–66.

Putnam, Robert. 2007. "*E Pluribus Unum*: Diversity and Community in the Twenty-First Century." *Scandinavian Political Studies* 30(2, June): 137–74.

Rabin, Matthew. 1993. "Incorporating Fairness into Game Theory and Economics." *American Economic Review* 83(5): 1281–1302.

Reinikka, Ritva, and Jakob Svensson. 2004. "Local Capture: Evidence from a Central Government Transfer Program in Uganda." *Quarterly Journal of Economics* 119(May): 679–705.

———. 2005. "Fighting Corruption to Improve Schooling: Evidence from a Newspaper Campaign in Uganda." *Journal of the European Economic Association* 3(2–3): 259–67.

Richman, Barak. 2006. "How Community Institutions Create Economic Advantage: Jewish Diamond Merchants in New York." *Law and Social Inquiry* 31(Spring): 383–420.

Roth, Alvin E. 1995. *Handbook of Experimental Economics*. Princeton, N.J.: Princeton University Press.

Ruffle, Bradley, and Richard Sosis. 2006. "Cooperation and the In-Group–Out-Group Bias: A Field Test on Israeli Kibbutz Members and City Residents." *Journal of Economic Behavior and Organization* 60(2): 147–63.

Sally, David. 1995. "Conversation and Cooperation in Social Dilemmas: A Meta-analysis of Experiments from 1958 to 1992." *Rationality and Society* 7(1): 58–92.

Sampson, Robert J., Jeffrey D. Morenoff, and Thomas Gannon-Rowley. 2002. "Assessing Neighborhood Effects: Social Processes and New Directions in Research." *Annual Review of Sociology* 28(1): 443–78.

Sampson, Robert J., Stephen Raudenbush, and Felton Earls. 1997. "Neighborhoods and Violent Crime: A Multilevel Study of Collective Efficacy." *Science* 277(5328): 918–24.

Sears, David O. 1986. "College Sophomores in the Laboratory: Influence of a Narrow Data Base on Social Psychology's View of Human Nature." *Journal of Personality and Social Psychology* 51(3): 515–30.

Secord, Paul. 1959. "Stereotyping and Favorableness in the Perception of Negro Faces." *Journal of Abnormal Social Psychology* 59(3): 309–15.

Sekhon, Jasjeet. 2008. "Opiates for the Matches: Matching Methods for Causal Inference." Unpublished paper, University of California, Berkeley.

Shafir, Eldar, and Amos Tversky. 1992. "Thinking Through Uncertainty: Nonconsequential Reasoning and Choice." *Cognitive Psychology* 24(4): 449–74.

Smith, Natalie. 2000. "Ultimatum and Dictator Games Among the Chaldeans of

Detroit." Talk to MacArthur Foundation Anthropology Project. Cited in *Foundations of Human Sociality: Economic Experiments and Ethnographic Evidence from Fifteen Small-Scale Societies* by Joseph Henrich, Robert Boyd, Samuel Bowles, Colin Camerer, Ernst Fehr, and Herbert Gintis. New York: Oxford University Press, 2004.

Spolaore, Enrico, and Romain Wacziarg. 2009. "The Diffusion of Development." *Quarterly Journal of Economics* 124(May): 469–529.

Tajfel, Henri, Michael Billig, R. P. Bundy, and Claude Flament. 1971. "Social Categorization and Intergroup Behavior." *European Journal of Social Psychology* 1(40): 149–78.

Uganda Bureau of Statistics. 2002. Uganda Population and Housing Census 2002. Kampala, Uganda: Uganda Bureau of Statistics.

Videras, Julio, and Christopher Bordoni. 2006. "Ethnic Heterogeneity and the Enforcement of Environmental Regulation." *Review of Social Economy* 64(4): 539–62.

Vigdor, Jacob. 2004. "Community Composition and Collective Action: Analyzing Initial Mail Response to the 2000 Census." *Review of Economics and Statistics* 86(1): 303–12.

Wilson, Rick K., and Catherine C. Eckel. 2006. "Judging a Book by Its Cover: Beauty and Expectations in the Trust Game." *Political Research Quarterly* 59(2): 189–202.

Wit, Arjaan P., and Henk A. M. Wilke. 1992. "The Effect of Social Categorization on Cooperation in Three Types of Social Dilemmas." *Journal of Economic Psychology* 13(1): 135–51.

Wood, Elisabeth. 2003. *Insurgent Collective Action and Civil War in El Salvador*. New York: Cambridge University Press.

World Bank. 2004. *World Development Report 2004: Making Services Work for Poor People*. Washington: World Bank.

World Values Survey. 2001. European and World Values Surveys four-wave integrated data file, 1981–2004, v.20060423, 2006. Surveys designed and executed by the European Values Study Group and World Values Survey Association. File producers: Madrid, Spain, and Tilburg, Netherlands: ASEP/JDS and Tilburg University. File distributors: Cologne, Germany: ASEP/JDS and GESIS.

Yamagishi, Toshio, and Nobuhiro Mifune. 2008. "Does Shared Group Membership Promote Altruism?" *Rationality and Society* 20(February): 5–30.

Index

preferences mechanisms (*cont.*) other-regarding, 8, 74–78, 109; partner selection in the Lockbox game, 85; policy preferences across ethnic groups, variation in, **81–82, 186**; preferences in common, 8–9, 78–83; preferences over process, 9, 83–85; success rates in the Lockbox game, impact of partner choice on, **85**; the three types of, 7–9

Prisoner's Dilemma (PD): coethnic cooperation with enforcement, 124–29, **192–93**; coethnicity and cooperation in, 110–12, **113, 190**; collective action, as a problem of, 107–9; cooperation in by player type, **111, 189**; cooperative behavior outside the lab and while playing, 140–42; effects of defection on punishment behavior, **128, 193**; effects of ethnic composition on punishment behavior, **130, 194**; enforcement of sanctions in, 112–16; as experimental game in current study, 105–6; free rider problem, illustration of, 8; payoff matrix illustrating, **108**; players' interpretation of, 136–37, **138**; players' understanding of the rules for, 135; punishment behavior by type and player action, **190**; tit-for-tat strategy in, 15, 203*n*18

public goods: ethnic diversity and provision of (*see* ethnic diversity and collective action); in Kampala (*see* Kampala); as non-excludable and non-rival, 201*n*3; provision of, variability in, 1–3; responsibility for provision of, 28–30. *See also* collective action

Public Information Box (PIB), 69–71, 75, 110

Putnam, Robert, 5

Puzzle game, 88–89

racism, collective action and, 9

Ray, Debraj, 12

reachability mechanism, 10–11,

94–96, **97,** 156–57, 202*n*15; coethnicity and cooperation through, 120–24; correlates of, **191**; ethnic *vs.* universal norms sustaining cooperative behavior and, 116–18; logic underpinning, 108; offers in the Dictator game and, **123, 192**; reachability

readability mechanism, 10, 89–92, 154–55

reciprocity: across ethnic groups, sustainability of, 124–29; coethnicity in collective action and (*see* Prisoner's Dilemma); coethnicity of an individual's acquaintances and, 94; collective action in homogeneous communities and, 105–6; ethnic *vs.* universal norms sustaining, 116–29, 131, 157; as a "group heuristic," 203*n*17; in a single encounter, 203*n*18; solving collective action problems through, 109; as a strategy selection mechanism, 11–12, 97–101, 156–57; technologies facilitating, 12, 156–57

Reid, Nancy, 203*n*20

Reinikka, Ritva, 171, 204*n*6

Richman, Barak, 12

Ruffle, Bradley, 214*n*7

sanctions: effects of defection on, **128, 193**; effects of ethnic composition on punishment behavior, **130, 194**; effects of external on coethnic cooperation, **126–27, 192–93**; enforcement of in Prisoner's Dilemma, 112–16; ethnic *vs.* universal norms as pathways supporting, 104, 116–18; external to the game, impact of introducing concerns regarding, 97–102; punishment behavior by type and player action, **115, 190**; reciprocity norms across ethnic groups and, 124–29; technologies facilitating, 12

Schmidt, Klaus M., 73

Seki, Erika, 17

Senegal, 162